Person-Centred Therapy Today

Person-Centred Therapy Today

New Frontiers in Theory and Practice

Dave Mearns and Brian Thorne

With guest chapters by Elke Lambers and
Margaret Warner

SAGE Publications
London • Thousand Oaks • New Delhi

First published 2000
Reprinted 2002, 2002, 2003, 2005, 2006, 2007

SAGE Publications Ltd
1 Oliver's Yard, 55 City Road
London EC1Y 1SP

SAGE Publications Inc
2455 Teller Road
Thousand Oaks, California 91320

SAGE Publications India Pvt Ltd
B-42 Panchsheel Enclave
PO Box 4109
New Delhi – 100 017

British Library Cataloguing in Publication Data

A catalogue record for this book is available from the British Library

ISBN 978-0-7619-6560-2 (hbk)
ISBN 978-0-7619-6561-9 (pbk)

Library of Congress catalog record available

Typeset by Photoprint, Torquay, Devon
Printed and bound in Great Britain by Biddles Ltd, King's Lynn, Norfolk

Dedication

This book is dedicated to Elke, Kirsty and Tessa – dear wife and daughters for Dave and for Brian an unfailing source of friendship and welcoming acceptance.

Contents

Preface

Since we first co-authored *Person-Centred Counselling in Action* (Sage, 1988, 1999) the world of counselling and psychotherapy has seen many changes. Not least it has become altogether more 'professional' with increasing emphasis on standards, account-ability and ethical responsibility. In many ways we welcome these developments and have often been instrumental in their evolu-tion. Indeed, we care so profoundly about the work we do that we will go to inordinate lengths in order to ensure that our clients receive the best possible companionship in the often perilous journeys which they undertake. Our 'guest' contributors, Elke Lambers and Margaret Warner, further reinforce this commitment to companionship of the highest quality in their chapters on supervision (Chapter 10) and on fragile and dissociated processes (Chapter 8). We are most grateful to them for responding so readily to our invitation and for providing such powerful evi-dence of what it means to be working responsibly but coura-geously at the very frontiers of the approach.

This present book is in some ways a celebration of all that has been achieved in the last decade or so. While person-centred therapy is in sad decline in its country of origin, there has been an astonishing growth both in Britain and many other European countries (see Thorne and Lambers, 1998). The fact that our own previous book has sold more copies than any other counselling text in Britain is perhaps an indication of the development and the popularity of the approach and there are many occasions when we are both humbled and amazed by the sales figures. This new book, however, is not prompted primarily by feelings of celebra-tion and satisfaction. On the contrary, as the new millennium begins, we are apprehensive about the future and are baffled by the misconceptions which still abound about the theory and practice of person-centred therapy. We ask ourselves how it can be, for example, that despite the growing and impressive body of literature about the approach, despite the almost universal respect in which its originator, Carl Rogers, is held, despite the existence of countless person-centred therapists and their clients, there still exists the denigratory and scurrilous myth that person-centred therapists merely nod, reflect the last words of their client and can only be trusted with the most superficial concerns of middle-class clients. We have concluded that such misconceptions are not always the outcome of ignorance but in some cases, at least, have much deeper roots. It would seem that our approach has the strange capacity to threaten practitioners from other orientations so that they seek refuge in wilful ignorance or in condemnatory dismissiveness.

This book attempts to address this confusing state of affairs. By placing overriding emphasis on the person-centred therapist's capacity for relational depth (Chapter 5) and by exploring the implications of this for theory and practice as well as for the spiritual/existential discipline of the therapist (Chapter 3), we state clearly and unequivocally our belief in the power, profundity and subtle elegance of the approach. What is more, we place it in the context of a world which is struggling with unparalleled challenges brought about by ecological disaster, technological advances and cross-cultural conflict (Chapter 1). It seems to us that a therapeutic approach which does not take on board the reality of the knife-edge on which the world currently finds itself must inevitably warrant the accusation of fiddling while Rome burns. Both we and our clients are citizens of a global community which is poised between hope and despair and this is the back-drop against which the psychic dramas in the therapist's consulting room are played out. To evade or ignore that reality is to collude with the forces which resist awareness and refuse responsibility.

As its title conveys, this book marks 'new frontiers in theory and practice'. It updates theory on the therapeutic conditions (Chapter 5) and introduces the new person-centred theory of 'configurations' (Chapters 6 and 7). In Chapter 8, Margaret Warner offers a full statement of the theory and practice of working with 'fragile' and 'dissociated' process while, in Chapter 10, Elke Lambers takes the theory and practice of supervision forward by grounding it in the development of the counsellor's congruence. Arguably, the most important contribution to theory is presented in Chapter 9 where Rogers' theory of the Self is revised.

Person-centred therapy is not, we believe, set in tablets of stone either as a theoretical system or as an applied practice. We attempt in this book both to develop the theory and to refine the practice of an approach to human suffering and human potential which we believe has much to offer as we enter the new millennium. We are not, however, under any illusion that the task will be an easy one. In some ways the core of person-centred therapy can be summed up in the words 'it pays to be human in the therapy room'. And there lies the nub of the challenge which confronts us. Being fully human in any situation is not only an existential task of formidable proportions, it may be a costly one in terms of personal investment and personal risk (Chapters 1, 2 and 11).

The rewards, however, are incomparable because to take the risk of being fully human today brings with it the promise of a vibrant tomorrow. This book is written in the belief that real hope lies beyond despair and that this is the hope on which person-centred therapy is founded and by which it is sustained and nourished.

Professor Dave Mearns
Professor Brian Thorne

Guest Contributors

Elke Lambers is Co-Director of Person-Centred Therapy (Britain) and has been involved in the training of person-centred therapists since 1985.

Margaret Warner, PhD is Professor, Illinois School of Professional Psychology, Chicago Campus; Training Staff Member, Chicago Counseling and Psychotherapy Center.

Acknowledgement

This book was written principally in Scotland and East Anglia and its evolution and completion owe much to the dedicated efforts of secretarial staff in the Universities of Strathclyde and East Anglia. We wish to pay particular tribute to the tireless commitment of Heather Robertson of the Counselling Unit at Strathclyde without whose consummate skill and empathic tolerance of our demands, our task could have been infinitely more difficult.

Acknowledgement

1   Towards an inhuman society?

A costly commitment

This book begins in hope. Hope, it should be understood, is not to be confused with a facile optimism, for often we do not feel particularly optimistic about our profession or about the society of which we are members. Hope, as we understand it, finds its anchorage in the unquenchable yearning of the human person who has touched the core of his or her own nature and has glimpsed, if only for a moment, the glory of being fully alive. We have had many such glimpses and refuse to deny what we know from experience even when others would have us believe that we are deluded or, worse still, when we ourselves harbour massive doubts and are tempted to settle for a quiet life of academic indifference. Hope, thus conceived, makes it possible to envisage, with Theodore Zeldin, the end of 'the wasteful war between optimists and pessimists' (Zeldin, 1998: 79–80). We are, we believe, at a crucial point in the evolution of humankind and we need a vision which takes full account of the data and at the same time maintains the spirit of adventure while not being discouraged by inevitable failures.

Such a vision is buttressed by our daily experience as person-centred therapists and trainers of meeting with those who courageously refuse to accept the distortion of their identity by societal, cultural or familial forces. It would seem that such people are inspired and supported by an instinctive recognition that they are part of a worldwide company of those who are no longer willing to submit meekly to the power of others but rather affirm their right to a full humanity and to a quality of interpersonal living which does justice to the human person's capacity for intimacy and mutuality. What is more, the opening up of communication networks throughout the globe is enabling individuals to find like-minded spirits beyond their own limited spheres and to discover reference points outside their own environment. There can be no doubt, too, that the courageous struggles of women and many minority groups during the final decades of the twentieth century have brought into the mainstream consciousness of Western democracies the vision of gender and racial equality. There are fresh winds blowing through our culture which seem to herald a new dispensation where the individual is honoured and relationships between people can attain a vibrancy and a depth which were previously reserved for the exceptional few.

Notwithstanding the potency of this vision, however, we also experience sadness because this same society which has within it the seeds of a new order seems in other ways to be increasingly bent on creating an environment which is conducive to the destruction of persons rather than to their fulfilment, to the fracturing of community rather than to its enhancement. Many of our clients have fallen victim to the uncontrollable pressures of a society in transition where change is often so rapid and bewildering that the individual can no longer find a sure reference point and where the escalating demands for enhanced performance both at work and in the home engender feelings of inadequacy and worthlessness or induce degrees of mental, emotional and physical exhaustion which ultimately become insupportable. What is more, among the ranks of the therapists there are those – and we count ourselves among them – who view with deep misgiving signs of the apparent capitulation of the emerging profession of counselling and psychotherapy itself to the darker side of the current zeitgeist (Gladstone, 1997; House, 1996; House and Totton, 1997; Mearns, 1999; Mowbray, 1995; Smail, 1997; Thorne, 1997). The legitimate but often obsessional concern for higher standards, public accountability and cost-effective results is increasingly forcing many therapists to adopt attitudes or to pursue objectives which are radically at variance with their core values and beliefs. Such 'contamination' can be seen in the life of the professional associations which seem at times to be more concerned to win the approval of Government, or to mollify an accusatory press, than to serve the best interests of clients and remain true to the priceless repository of knowledge and practice which decades of therapeutic endeavour have created. This book is written in the belief that surrender to contemporary obsessions can be halted and that a recovery of nerve is vital to the future of counselling and psychotherapy in our country. We are also bold enough to believe that the person-centred tradition has a significant contribution to make at a time when sterile surveillance and a preoccupation with risk limitation are threatening to undermine the liberating transformation which therapy at its best can engender in the lives of both individuals and communities. We are not so naive, however, as to imagine that this will be an easy task. On the contrary, it seems increasingly possible that alignment with the theory and practice of person-centred therapy may be costly in terms of personal commitment and professional credibility.

A ravaged world

The appalling genocidal conflicts which have been played out in the closing years of the twentieth century make the writing of books seem oddly futile and yet therapists claim to respond to the deepest pain of human experience. If, in the face of the horrors of Rwanda, Somalia, Bosnia, Kosovo and Chechnya, we have nothing to say, it would suggest that the faith of counsellors is shallow indeed and that we are perhaps no more than psychological technicians who tinker away with occasional success at the neuroses of the affluent. Perhaps, however, in a grim way, the seemingly endless tide of refugees in so many parts of the world prompts us to take stock of the human condition and to wake up to the forces which threaten humanity as the new millennium begins. For Europeans particularly, that awakening is encouraged by media coverage which depicts not only the emaciated bodies of African men, women and children, but also the humiliation and degradation of people dressed like ourselves who were once earning their livings as teachers, lawyers, engineers, journalists, waiters or factory workers. In our hearts we know that with a different twist of fate, we, too, could be in the ranks of the dispossessed, stripped of our identities and belonging nowhere. The refugee becomes a sinister symbol of what can quickly happen once personhood is denied and people are transformed into disposable units or contemptible impediments to the greed or power-mongering of others.

Threats to identity

It may seem melodramatic to perceive the genocidal violence of the last decade as in some way symbolic of a more general sickness which permeates the global community. Indeed, many commentators have been tempted to see these nightmarish conflicts as a kind of throw-back to a previous era, an anachronistic aberration which is somehow contrary to the flow of history. Such a perception is hard to sustain. The ideologies of, for example, Adolf Hitler and the Serbian leader, Slobodan Milosevic, may appear very different but they have in common a denial of the right to personhood of millions of people. The removal of documentation, personal belongings, money, car number plates and so on communicates to desperate people that they have no right to identity, that they are henceforth non-persons with no place to call their own and no distinguishing mark to register their uniqueness. The experience for the luckless victims of such psychological viciousness – that is, if they escape with their lives – is one of complete depersonalisation. In an extreme form, however, they suffer what is increasingly the fate of many who eventually find their way to the therapist's door as the new century begins. For the person-centred practitioner there is the frequent encounter nowadays with those who have all but lost their hold on personhood and who experience themselves not as persons but as powerless pawns in a macabre game whose rules they cannot grasp or as refugees from a society which is 'cleansing' itself.

The 'new capitalism'

The work environment is notoriously the place where such loss of identity is seemingly endemic. It would appear that the new capitalism, with its brave new world of risk, flexibility, short-term project work and relentless competitiveness, is depriving many workers of any fixed reference points for stabilising their sense of who they are. It can be instructive to travel these days on an inter-city train in Britain. Whole carriages are sometimes taken up by men and women in suits who are glued to their laptops or mobile phones. The endless tapping and the raised, anxious voices typify a world where everything is on the move, where millions of pounds can be lost or gained in minutes and where the individual is rootless and caught up in a perpetual state of transition. Richard Sennett, the sociologist, describes in his book *The Corrosion of Character* (1998) the world of the multi-nationals where workers are continually being asked to re-invent themselves in the service of economic forces over which they have no control. In the preface to his book, Sennett poses questions which have so far found no answers and yet they are fundamental to any enduring sense of identity:

> How do we decide what is of lasting value in ourselves in a society which is impatient, which focuses on the immediate moment? How can long-term goals be pursued in an economy devoted to the short term? How can mutual loyalties and commitments be sustained in institutions which are constantly breaking apart or continually being redesigned? (Sennett, 1998: 10)

This dramatic shift in working patterns and the predominance of short term objectives presents new challenges to often vulnerable and insecure people whose sense of identity is sometimes fragile in the extreme. Counsellors in the workplace are daily confronted by exhausted employees who only too readily blame themselves for their lack of resilience or their inability to survive in a context which seems to ignore their needs as human beings and treats them instead as machines devoid of feelings. The acknowledgement of vulnerability in such an environment can be difficult, for it brings with it the risk of being deemed weak, inadequate or dispensable. Authenticity (a prerequisite for mental health) becomes dangerous, and to trust others to be responsive, let alone empathic, can seem at best foolhardy and at worst psychologically lethal. The final tragedy occurs when the man or woman who has attempted at great personal cost to portray the all-coping behaviour of the infinitely flexible worker is peremptorily declared redundant because the bottom has fallen out of the market or a systems driven administration sees enhanced profits as dependent on the euphemistically termed process of 'downsizing'.

There can be no doubt that there are those who thrive in an environment whose very challenges contribute the material from which identity can be forged. For others, however, the personal sacrifices can be great. Expense account living may serve to mask the quiet desperation of highly paid 'leaders of industry' who inwardly mourn the loss of intimacy and bear the guilt of being the absent spouse or parent. Counsellors not infrequently share the pain of those whose work situations have led to a breakdown of family relationships and to a loss of emotional connectedness which leads to intolerable loneliness. Perhaps, however, such suffering is to be preferred to the limited vision of the dedicated worker who is apparently content to put career advancement and material gain above everything else or sees loss of spouse and family disintegration as a regrettable but inevitable price to be paid. It is now almost possible to conceive of an individual who on his or her deathbed could truly regret that more hours had not been spent in the office. If it is accepted that the workplace for millions of people has changed irrevocably, the challenge becomes increasingly stark. How can human beings ensure that they do not lose their humanity in acquiescence to the profit-making demands of the rapacious multi-nationals which employ them?

The educational environment

The conflict between remaining recognisably human and meeting performance standards begins early now in many schools, for we are told that Britain's very survival as a strong competitor in the world's markets depends on her citizens attaining an ever higher level of educational achievement. Testing and constant surveillance seem increasingly to be the central planks of educational practice even at the primary stage, while the rigorously enforced national curriculum can threaten creativity, spontaneity and the relaxed social discourse between adult and child on which the developing person depends for affirmation and a sense of relatedness. There is little time for play and not infrequently the performing arts struggle to retain a foothold in the school curriculum against the pressing claims of literacy, numeracy, science and information technology. Academic achievement becomes the single measure of a school's effectiveness and league tables record the winners and the losers. It is now regarded as acceptable that such policies as 'naming and shaming' and 'zero tolerance' become part of the educational standard and that performance related pay should be seen as an appropriate reward for 'successful' teachers. The Office for Standards in Education (OFSTED) in England strikes fear in the hearts of teachers and it is no exaggeration to suggest that in some areas the trampling of the inspectors' feet conveys the same sense of impending doom as the sound of the sergeant major's boots mounting the barrack room steps (cf Thorne, 1998b: 29). It is fear which now often reigns in the staff rooms of our schools and in such a situation the irony of putting 'spirituality' on the agenda and attempting to evaluate it along with everything else can almost pass unnoticed.

Once again it is the counsellors who are 'privileged' to accompany those whose lives have been blighted by the implementation of policies which seem to focus on performance to the detriment of persons. Teachers and pupils alike succumb to incapacitating stress and in the safety of the therapist's office they pour out their misery and not infrequently talk of suicide. It is an open secret that many teachers in recent years have left the profession in Britain with their physical and mental health impaired and often crippled by anxiety, a viral illness or a depressive state which makes their return to the classroom impossible. In the universities, too, counsellors attempt to stem a relentless tide of student clients, many of whom live permanently with the fear of failure – meaning for some anything less than a first class degree. For many of their teachers the situation is no better and there are university staff whose love of learning and teaching has been all but extinguished by the permanent need to attract research money, or by the threat of research or teaching quality assessment exercises. The surveillance mania is corrosive and now that students are no longer simply students, but part of a commercial empire, there is the additional threat of dissatisfied customers who are not slow to consult their lawyers. The educational world can become little more than a contractual jungle where blaming and shaming are activities which accurately reflect an ethos which is essentially punitive, judgemental, unforgiving and soulless. Many university vice-chancellors will privately acknowledge that universities are now in effect business enterprises and as with any other business 'the bottom line' is financial solvency. Downsizing, audit trails, customer satisfaction and cost-effective products are now the management-speak of the senior common-room – that is, where such a facility still exists.

There is, of course, another side to this story. It can be argued, with justification, that in the past some university academics have been content to rest on their laurels and have neither advanced the development of their discipline, nor attended conscientiously to the needs of their students. What is more, there are those who believe that a largely unaccountable university sector has consumed large sums of public money for the education of an intellectual and social elite. Clearly, as in so many other areas, change was inevitable and probably long overdue. Sadly, however, the opportunities which change should offer seem at the moment to be obscured by the devastating outcomes of a transition process. This process often runs out of control and leads to persons being forgotten in the interests of economy or in the frenzy to achieve so-called results. It need not be so.

Anxiety and technology

It is often observed that the rooms of isolated and alienated adolescents are full of the latest wonders of technology. Clearly we are in the midst of a period of transition as far as technology is concerned. Geoff Mulgan, Director of Demos, has suggested that we can now find an invisible line cutting through the middle of most western societies. 'On one side of this new line are the people brought up before computers became part of everyday life. On the other side are the generations for whom computers are becoming unexceptionable' (Mulgan, 1997: 14). As in all transitions, the experience of fear and anxiety typifies much of the response to the new world of 'cybernetics', a term coined originally by the American scientist, Norbert Wiener, to define a systematic science which could be applied to almost everything from household devices to the management of schools, factories or battle campaigns. The fears and anxieties are so multifarious that they are impossible to codify. Underlying many of them is the wholly justifiable terror that what promises to offer human beings more control over their lives, more freedom, more options will, in fact, end up by exerting a new form of dictatorship. Far from *offering* more control, unfettered technology will increasingly *take* control of our lives, so that in the end we shall become more impotent, more a prey to forces which we are powerless to resist.

The consulting rooms of many therapists would suggest that the futuristic nightmare which some doom-mongers predict is not altogether impossible. There, the casualties of technological advance proliferate. Alongside those who have been made redundant in the wake of computerised systems, there are those whose lives are run by the insistent urgency of merciless machines which demand immediate action or provide such a mass of data that the human brain collapses under the weight of overload. There are those, too, who dread the e-mail which 'flames' them with little chance of redress, or those whose partners have 'fallen in love' on the internet and are amorously engaged with a screen in the study. Perhaps most sadly of all, there are the parents who lament that they have 'lost' their children to video games, television screens and 'surfing the net'. This new addiction can induce a psychological incarceration which cuts the victim off from normal human communication. Such gloom in the face of technological advance may seem a very 'modernist' reaction and unworthy of intelligent thinkers in a postmodernist era which almost rejoices in the death of metanarratives and welcomes alternative, even contradictory, perspectives. For our part, we do not relish the prospect of being labelled as grumpy old curmudgeons who fret about the internet in the same way that our parents condemned television, or our grandparents fumed about the telephone or our great-grandparents ranted about the steam railway. Nor would such a labelling be justified, for we are fully aware that, as so often, there is another side to this story. Technological advance offers opportunities and provides new challenges. Nothing is achieved by saying 'no' to what is clearly here to stay and there can be little or no prospect of relating to the alienated adolescent if we simply condemn as 'wrong' the technological miracles by which he or she is enraptured.

We are not at all sure whether as person-centred therapists we have a stake in the question of whether we live in a postmodern time, for it could justifiably be claimed that we still remain faithful to a metanarrative even if that narrative insists on the uniqueness of subjective truth. For us, the debate about modernist or post-modernist perspectives can be as vapid and time-wasting as the diversionary conflict between optimists and pessimists. What is clear is that we cannot possibly know at this stage whether information technology will ultimately enhance our freedom or engender new forms of oppression. If, however, we value – as we do – the power of relationship to facilitate human development and if we believe – as we do – that much misery in the world is the result of the abuse of power, then there is much to be welcomed in the steady advance of computer technology. The challenge, as Theodore Zeldin has elegantly expressed it, is 'to develop a new tone' which at one and the same time is 'both hopeful and aware of the likelihood of failure' (Zeldin, 1998: 78). Such a tone will be strengthened and inspired by the fact that information technology makes life very difficult for totalitarian governments and gives infinitely more freedom to the handicapped and the geographically isolated. It also offers new possibilities for preserving affectionate relationships through e-mail's creation of an entirely new kind of letter-writing culture. But it might all end in disastrous failure and we need to be able to cope with that possibility if we are to remain hopeful. To be blindly optimistic will simply lead to the kind of impotence which we experience currently in the face of the increasingly polluted, traffic-jammed cities of the world which have resulted from the time-saving, freedom-enhancing motorcar. As person-centred therapists we set much store on remaining open to experience. Such openness demands a willingness to respond to new challenges while acknowledging and accepting that failure is often as likely as success. If that sounds like a philosophy of risk-taking we would not wish to refute such an interpretation.

Gender and race

If, as we suggest, it is progressively difficult to hold on to a sense of identity while belonging to a society which demands constant change, much will depend on locating firm reference points. In the past, gender and race offered such rallying points and we see many examples still of those who attempt to fall back on their sexual or national identity as a means of shoring up their fragile sense of self. Sadly, in an increasingly multicultural world, the resort to nationality as a means of affirming identity runs the likely risk of creating conflict rather than creating community. National groups can only offer solid anchorage if they not only tolerate but celebrate other national groups. Sadly, this is rarely the case and as a result, nationality frequently offers not so much identity, as a means of identifying the enemy.

Finding identity in sexuality is also no easy solution in many western societies at the present time. Indeed, there has probably never been a period when establishing sexual identity has been more complex. The powerful impact of feminism and the enormous influx of women into the workplace have turned previous role stereotypes upside down and, among highly educated women especially, there is often an agonising conflict between career and family aspirations. For men, the situation is no better, for they no longer have by birthright the 'bread-winner' ticket on which to pin their identity and often have the added task of developing caring and empathic skills to fulfil new family roles and to respond to women who increasingly demand a higher level of 'emotional intelligence'. If we add to this the gay and lesbian revolution, the questioning of the marriage contract, the escalation of divorce rates, the perplexing range of sexual behaviours observable in our society and the reactionary opposition to all of these, it is scarcely surprising that, again, the consulting rooms of therapists are besieged by those who struggle with issues of gender and sexuality of almost boundless complexity.

As well as the confusion around issues of sexual identity and behaviour this is also an area in which many are prone to leap to condemnatory judgement. This is typical of a culture where there is, as there has been throughout history, a need to find a scapegoat (Girard, 1996). Perhaps more than in the past, however, guilt and self-denigration have a field day because they are constantly reinforced by media attention and there is apparently no means of reversing the process. Despite the withering of the 'meta-narratives' of religious and philosophical moral systems it would seem that we still yearn for ourselves and others to be perfect and when manifestly we or they are not, there is nowhere we can take our wretchedness or our rage and have them understood and alleviated. We are left to stew in our own juice and often sink beneath the weight of self-recrimination or a lack of self-forgiveness.

Responding to the challenge: counselling in the workplace

One of us (Thorne) currently spends much of his professional life as the counsellor to the employees of one of the country's largest finance houses. There are few industries which have experienced such tumultuous change or upheaval in recent times. What is now one of the most competitive and pressurised work arenas was only a few years ago a haven for those who wanted a safe job where they could legitimately expect to stay until retirement age with little to disturb the generally placid tempo of life.

Keith was one such person who joined the company straight from school and had progressed up the career ladder satisfactorily enough until, to quote his own words 'the gale began to blow in 1992'. Since then, Keith had been struggling to retain his equilibrium in a world of growing unpredictability where everything can change within a week and where new technology or new legislation required that he acquire new skills and new knowledge on the hoof. When he first came to the company's counselling service, Keith was on the verge of collapse and about to resign. He was depressed and ashamed that he could no longer cope. He deemed himself a failure and could find no consolation in the fact that for thirty years he had been a perfectly satisfactory employee. He had all but lost the sense of his own worth and identity. Now, over a year later, Keith feels very differently about himself. Within the counselling relationship he gradually regained his self respect, allowed himself to have a period of sick leave which his general practitioner was only too willing to endorse and began to take stock of his life calmly and reflectively. He no longer works for the company but left with his honour intact and with a handsome severance package. He now works part-time for a charitable organisation, has revitalised the relationships with his wife and family and, at 55, declares himself to be happier – and more self-aware – than at any time in his life. The gale of change which had all but destroyed him had, in the end, engendered a process of transformation which had given him back control over his life. Fate had given way to destiny.

Stephen was a very different kind of client. He is one of the company's 'high-fliers'. An Oxbridge graduate with a first-class degree and a Harvard MBA, he has had a meteoric career and at 32 holds a senior management position in a crucial area of the company's marketing division. When he first presented himself he had been working non-stop, fourteen hours a day for fifty consecutive days without a break even at weekends. Not surprisingly, he had hit the buffers, collapsed in his office, and was plunged into deep depression exacerbated by complete exhaustion. Eighteen months later, Stephen is still with the company but he, too, is a changed person. He has not lost his intellectual sharpness and he has regained his motivational energy. During the period of his four-month spell of sick leave he was able to access with his counsellor a deep sense of ambivalence about his own self-worth and become aware of a punitive behavioural pattern which resulted in his driving both himself and those under him with almost merciless fervour. He also discovered that his wife was in despair because she felt she had not met him for five years. From his own painful and almost annihilating experience, Stephen now sees with almost blinding clarity that his potential fate symbolised the dire path of destruction on which the whole company could be launched. His keen intelligence combined with his undoubted ability, informed now by his suffering and growing self-awareness, makes him an invaluable asset to a company which is progressively facing the human implications of its changed place and function in the financial marketplace. There is a growing realisation throughout this massive organisation that unless its employees are encouraged to value themselves and each other their working lives will deteriorate into a living hell and the company itself will eventually end on the same scrapheap to which many of its employees will have been condemned. Stephen is now powerfully allied to those forces within the organisation which recognise that the company's ultimate and long-term success will depend on the creation of a climate of human responsiveness which fully takes into account the needs of those who are for the most part involved in the achievement of short-term objectives and who face the challenges of an almost permanent state of transition. With many of his more far-sighted and self-aware colleagues Stephen is, in fact, helping to forge an answer to Richard Sennett's fundamental questions (1998: 6) about the pursuit of long-term goals in an economy devoted to the short-term. Such goals have to be conceptualised in terms of human identity and human relationships. They start from the basic assumption that work is for the enhancement of men and women and not for their immolation.

A recent tragedy provided a glimpse into a workplace environment which offers to individuals the opportunity to scale the highest peaks of their human potential. A small sector of the financial company described above suffered an appalling blow when two of the most popular members of their team were killed in a road accident during the weekend. Counselling staff who were asked to come alongside a group traumatised by shock discovered a remarkable situation. It was apparent that the thirty-strong sector was not simply a workforce. Facilitated largely by the example and love of life of the two young men who had been so tragically killed, these thirty persons, mostly young men and women, were deeply bonded to each other and shared much of their social life together. Now, in their corporate grief, they were able to weep together, to acknowledge openly their vulnerability and despair and to welcome a counsellor, not as someone who would take away their pain, but as a companion who would not be afraid of their desolation. This was, in short, a deeply loving 'family' which had lost two of its most precious members – and they happened to be work colleagues in a vast public limited company which is beginning to wrestle with the challenge of what it might mean to create a truly human environment for its employees. The suffering and the stature of these young people were awesome and it was their shared pain which revealed their greatness. It is such revelations which sustain the hope of which we spoke earlier and point again to the 'wasteful war between optimists and pessimists'.

Person-centred therapy in an inhuman world

The society we have portrayed is one where on many fronts it becomes progressively more difficult for individuals to develop a firm sense of their own identity and then to hold on to it in the face of multifarious forces which seem to require almost constant readjustment both literally and psychologically. For many young people, particularly, the sense of helplessness and powerlessness which this constant process of change induces can be further heightened by profound anxieties about the ecological future of the planet. The ostrich-like attitudes which all-pervasive materialism reinforces towards ecological concerns exacerbate the experience of a world out of control where human beings seem bent both on denying the core of their own natures and on destroying their homeland. The anxieties about genetically modified crops are further evidence of the grave mistrust felt by increasing numbers, not only of the motivations of international companies, but also of the scientific community which so often seems both arrogant and divided. In an environment where trust has broken down in so many spheres of human endeavour, it is perhaps foolishly naive to expect the psychotherapeutic and counselling community to provide a haven of stability and unified sanity. After all, counsellors are themselves part of the society in which they operate and it would be surprising if they were not themselves subject to its uncertainties and prevailing trends.

Having said this, it is nonetheless disturbing for many person-centred therapists – ourselves included – to witness much of what seems to be happening within the British counselling scene at the present time. In the next chapter we explore in detail the dangers and the possible opportunities of the accelerating movement towards professionalisation and for the moment we confine ourselves to the main thrust of our anxieties. The tension inherent in any profession is how to create a regulated environment which ensures a high quality of practice in the service and protection of the client and offers to the practitioner a creative milieu for the development of his or her capacities. Our perception is that at the present time, a legitimate concern to achieve the former is resulting in the creation of a movement towards statutory registration for all therapists which threatens to become a punitive straitjacket rather than being a healthy evolution. The prevailing mistrust which permeates society, the obsessional concern for empirically validated methodologies and the 'bottom-line' insistence on the achievement of cost-effective results are all engendering a climate where a narrow judgementalism becomes the dominating force and the fear of making mistakes governs the counsellor's behaviour rather than a deep and demanding commitment to the client and to the therapeutic process.

The underpinning beliefs and the resultant practices of person-centred therapists stand in stark contrast to the darker aspects of the world we have described. Essentially we continue to have confidence in the resourcefulness of the human being and in his or her ability to lead a constructive, positive, life-affirming and socially creative existence. We believe that human beings flourish best when they can experience acceptance and understanding rather than adverse judgement and a lack of informed responsiveness from others. We are profoundly committed to offering ourselves to our clients without simulation and to moving into relational depth with them when they invite and welcome us there. We know that this is risky work and that there will be times when we shall be taxed to the uttermost. We also know that we shall be open to misunderstanding and that there are those who will be only too ready to accuse us of exceeding the boundaries of responsible professional involvement in those cases where things do not turn out well.

Mercifully, we are aware that the hope which we strive to embody, despite our own doubts and inadequacies, is shared by others both within the world of psychotherapy and counselling and outside of it. There are now many voices raised in our society in protest against the threats to our humanity, not least those that attempt to articulate the primacy of the spiritual in the conduct of human affairs. In this respect we are also encouraged by the knowledge that, towards the end of his life, Carl Rogers, the originator of our approach, was urgently concerned for the peace and preservation of the world and believed that when he could be fully present to another person, simply his presence was a healing force and gave access to resources which, almost despite himself, he described as 'spiritual', 'mystical', 'transcendental' (Rogers, 1986). This is the inheritance to which we wish to remain faithful even if the thought of the cost we may have to pay for such fidelity sometimes makes us tremble. The young novelist, Bidisha

Bandyopadhyay, was 21 in the year 2000. While not denying the pervasive pessimism which sweeps through her generation and which has led to politics 'being considered more of a national pantomime, part-comedy and part-tragedy, than a tool of the people' she has written:

> The next century can only be regarded as one more opportunity for us to try and effect some good. We as Thomas Hardy put it in 'Tess of the d'Urbervilles' over a hundred years ago, are full of 'unexpended youth' bringing with it hope, and the invincible instinct towards self-delight. (Bandyopadhyay, 1997: 199)

As person-centred therapists we would wish, with her, to keep alive such hope and not to capitulate to despair or to seek refuge in a sterilised and risk-free form of therapeutic activity which harms and benefits nobody.

2 Is therapy losing its humanity?

My friend Joe

Reconstructing how Joe had come to be a long-term hospital patient is not easy. It is like attempting a jigsaw puzzle with most of the pieces missing. Perhaps people get into psychiatric hospital more by accidents of social circumstances than anything else. Joe might still have been playing his part in his secluded rural community if he had not returned to the city. Cities do not tolerate deviance and are quick to pathologise the perpetrators.

From what could be reconstructed, Joe's childhood and adolescent life in the city found him initially doing well at school but later dropping out. His family life had offered a mixture of neglect and emotional abuse by an absent father and a mother who had her own problems. After a spell in an adolescent unit Joe had gone to the country, initially living rough but gradually finding a place in the community.

No-one knew why Joe had returned to the city – maybe he had found some strength and wanted to have another go – maybe he had wanted to try again with his mother. In any event, he had spent much of his last two years as a hospitalised patient interspersed with periods 'on the outside' where he had difficulty in looking after himself.

Ironically, it was only when Joe got to the point of moving out of the hospital into a supported house that he encountered the local mental health project and for the first time over the years of his distress was offered professional therapeutic support from an experienced person-centred therapist. His therapist offers the following general view of Joe:

> He is a 'lost soul'. I never really understood that term until I met Joe. Literally, he has 'lost his soul' some time back in his adolescence. The result is that he is more 'empty' than people usually are. He rarely uses the word 'I' – to him there isn't much of an 'I'. If you don't have an 'I' all you can do is to

'wander' in your life – you can't have 'purpose'. Also, he gets really anxious – the slightest pressure on him raises his anxiety – he gets wildly distressed, incredibly frightened – he might be dangerous to himself in those times because his fear is bigger than his need to live.

The therapist and Joe were 'in contact' for one and a half years – she takes up the story of that work:

Joe and I had 106 contacts during that 18 months. About a third of those were formal 'sessions' with him sitting down, facing me, in a room, like private practitioners do. Another third of our contacts were telephone calls from him, sometimes about practical things to do with our meetings and other times when he was anxious. Far from discouraging his calls to me at home I saw these as important examples of his 'reaching out' to another in relationship – for Joe it would have been normal to neglect relationships and to roll up in a ball when he was anxious. The remainder of our time together was informal meetings – not sitting down facing each other in a therapy room, but going shopping with him, waiting for him outside the Job Centre, visiting the area in which he had lived as a child, and many more things. In this kind of work you are intentionally *expanding* the contexts for 'contact' because there is a 'contact-deficit' in this kind of client and 'contact' is the basis for person-centred therapy.

Throughout our 18 months the possibility of Joe's suicide was always with us. At times the possibility expanded to a probability and once it felt like an inevitability. His life was like a leaf floating upon a pond, so delicately balanced that I dare not push it lest I cause it to sink.

Yet, all the time we were together Joe was 'in relationship' with a person – me. Also, he was gradually piecing together understandings of his past and tentatively experimenting with himself in the present. In so far as I could create a relationship without fear, I was offering him a context where he could edge out of his inner world.

Some of our sessions were intense. I remember sitting in his room, with him on the floor staring silently at the carpet for three hours as he faced his emptiness.

I never offered Joe more than I could sustain and I tried not to offer him less. With this kind of client it is the quality and intensity of your *commitment* which is crucial to the work.

Near the end of our time together a remarkable thing happened. We were walking to the local café when a bike mounted the pavement and knocked me over. The bike rider offered profuse and inadequate apologies but he was waved away by Joe saying 'it's alright – *I'll* help her!'. I doubt whether Joe had ever asserted himself so strongly – he surprised both of us.

We stopped working together when Joe returned to the country. He had found that he could survive in the city but returned to the country where he felt there was 'more of a place for me'. My fantasy is that one day I will be having lunch at a quiet village pub and the door will open and the locals around me will say 'Hello Joe!'.

There is a quiet humanity to this therapist's account of her work with Joe. Within her working context she was functioning fully as a person-centred practitioner. She was working not only with past material of the client but with the present relating between the client and herself, using all of life's contexts to establish the necessary 'psychological contact' – Rogers' (1957a) first 'condition' for therapy.

Perhaps most important is her statement: 'I never offered him more than I could sustain . . .' Here was a therapist who was aware of her own limits and was able to assess these quickly and consistently across the range of experiences in which she met her client. This is not a picture of an idealistic but inexperienced therapist who felt that she should offer her client everything, ignoring her own needs in the process. Offering a committed and extensive relationship is powerful only if it comes from a secure place. Inexperienced therapists need to attend to the warning offered towards the end of this chapter – working with the therapeutic context as an active variable in the process is dangerous if it is fed by the therapist's needs.

Equally important is the second half of her sentence: '. . . and I tried not to offer him less'. If we have the audacity to enter into the world of a troubled person then we had better be sure that whatever we have to offer we can offer it consistently (see Chapters 3 and 8).

Some private practitioners could not do this work – they are grounded by the security of their physical office and other tight boundaries. In the therapy profession we need to respect such individual difference but we must also take care that the definition of 'boundaries' is not made by such practitioners as a means of idealising their own inadequacy. Work is not made more 'professional' by restricting it to a physical office and regular time slot.

Nor should the professionalism of the work be judged solely by the outcome for the individual client. This is well illustrated by Joe. Although we might surmise that the support he received from his therapist was an important event in his life and perhaps one of the first offers of real, consistent engagement made by another person to him, it was still only one event in Joe's life and probably a very small one compared to those in his history and the torment which he continued to experience. In that circumstance it would be dangerous for the therapist and the profession to judge the therapist and the therapy offered in terms of whether Joe, day after day, continued not to make the choice to end his life. On any one day the balance might feel tipped towards death – the therapist cannot make that choice and she cannot stop that choice. Indeed, the therapist seemed aware of that when she said: 'His life was like a leaf floating in a pond – so delicately balanced that I dare not push it, lest I cause it to sink'.

In this chapter we will be looking at the professionalisation of counselling/therapy (using the terms interchangeably), outlining the challenges which this sets for person-centred therapy but also retaining as our touchstone the humanity of the endeavour.

The professionalisation of counselling/therapy

During the past 20 years in Britain, therapy has developed beyond its beginnings in the voluntary settings. When viewed comparatively, voluntary sector counselling is a most unusual phenomenon. Indeed, in some European countries it is very difficult even to explain the concept of counselling in the voluntary sector because there is no concept of voluntary work. Yet, within Britain, the early growth of counselling happened within large voluntary organisations. However, that area of growth has not continued during the past 20 years and counselling, instead, has developed in an increasing number of settings where it leads to professional appointments with practitioners being paid for their services. An early location for paid work was within private practice, but other contexts soon developed such as student counselling and school counselling, followed by the work of counsellors employed by social work agencies and projects, and, in more recent times, larger scale developments such as counselling within health settings, particularly primary health care and counselling in work settings.

As this evolution from voluntary to paid practice has taken place there have been understandable moves to professionalise counselling. Indeed, the voluntary sector has also followed that drift towards professionalisation to an extent where the distinction between 'voluntary' and 'professional' is objected to on the grounds that the voluntary sector wishes to be seen as offering a professional service.

Within Britain the most influential agency for the professionalisation of counselling has been the British Association for Counselling (BAC). The work done by the Association, principally through the unpaid work of its members, has made huge strides in developing professionalisation with respect to training, supervision, accreditation/registration and ethics/complaints.

In the early days of counselling, the voluntary sector offered guidance on the amount of training appropriate to voluntary work. It would have been unthinkable to consider a one-year full-time training as a meaningful demand for those who were asked to offer their services freely. Also, in the early days of the development of counselling as a paid activity, much happened within other professions such as nursing and social work. Here, even less attention was paid to specific counselling training. Instead, it was judged that basic training for social work also constituted a qualification for the person to engage in the activity of counselling. Within nursing, the position was even more presumptuous – that the stereotypical qualities of a nurse were all that was necessary to offer counselling support. Typically, appointments to counselling-related posts required social work training rather than counselling training and early primary care counsellors could only be paid as nurses, while school counsellors had, of course, to be qualified as teachers. In those early days counselling was not a profession in its own right but something which people did, with little or no training, as a part of another profession. Within Britain it was the growth of BAC and its attention to professionalisation which led to the expansion of dedicated counselling training courses and, indeed, to the accreditation of training courses from 1988. BAC's work on the accreditation of courses represents an astounding achievement on the part of its early designers. They isolated nine central 'elements' which might be required of all training courses, regardless of the therapeutic model that grounded the training. Every training course was expected to have an admissions policy, to attend to theory, skills, personal development, professional development, therapeutic practice and supervision, as well as having coherent assessment and evaluation systems (BAC, 1988, 1991, 1996a; Dryden et al., 1995). Not only was this structure fair to all therapeutic approaches but the guidelines were drawn in such a way as to be only minimally prescriptive of structures like the basic length of an accredited course and, instead, to challenge individual courses to put forward and justify their best practice with respect to the nine elements of training. This approach honoured the fact that a number of training courses had already been in existence for 15 years and had developed coherent yet different ways of offering professional training. Another distinctive feature of the course accreditation scheme was its *developmental* nature. Courses were actively helped, through the accreditation process, to develop their training to a point where their accreditation application could be successful. Sometimes this resulted in courses being involved in the application process for two or three years while they developed and tested new ways of meeting the objectives.

Within Britain there is a norm of lifelong counselling supervision for therapists. This contrasts with other parts of the world, including the USA, where supervision is seen to be essential only during training and probationary service – the assumption being that a fully trained professional does not require continuing supervision. The thinking within Britain, as exemplified by BAC, is that although a practitioner may be fully trained, therapy is an activity which is inextricably connected with the practitioner's emotional wellbeing and the ebb and flow of their life circumstances. Therefore, it is deemed appropriate that therapists maintain a regular supervisory contact in which they can continue to monitor their functioning in relation to clients.

The approach taken by BAC to supervision is truly *radical*. 'Supervision' in every other helping profession is little more than thinly disguised management monitoring. To its credit, BAC has managed to retain a strong empowering and developmental dimension to supervision, emphasising the creation of a supervisory relationship in which the therapist feels sufficiently safe to explore the most difficult and potentially threatening dimensions of her work. The job of the supervisor is not to judge, nor to sanction, but to act as facilitator to the therapist's exploration and development. This developmental approach to supervision is well

stated in the report of the working group into supervision commissioned by the Professional Committee of BAC:

> Supervision works best in the relationship of trust where there may be
> a measure of accountability. That relationship can be severely hindered
> by the presence of a strong dynamic of power and accountability.
> Maintaining an ethos in which supervision is about the oversight or
> control of the counsellor can lead to the development of a climate of
> fear. This can lead to counsellors being unprepared to make or to admit
> to making mistakes and learning from these and may additionally lead
> to counsellors avoiding taking responsibility for their practice. (BAC,
> 1998a: Para 3.6)

The counselling approach to supervision contrasts, for example,
with 'supervision' in the profession of social work – an activity
conducted by the line manager and only rarely experienced as
'empowering'. Indeed, it is interesting to note the number of
practising social workers employing counselling supervisors to
support their own development (Mearns, 1995).

As with training, the approach taken by BAC in relation to
supervision is respectful of all the varied mainstream therapeutic
approaches. Some of the more cognitively or behaviourally oriented approaches might argue that the lesser degree of emotional
involvement of their practitioners in the process would obviate
the requirement for continuing supervision post-training. However, that argument has not been seriously presented.

There comes a point in the development of every profession
when the question of accreditation/registration for practice must
be faced. It is difficult but not impossible to conceive of a
profession existing without criteria for the registration of practitioners. For example, Mowbray recommends 'non-credentialled
registration'. This conception allows freer access to the profession
and switches the emphasis to de-registration on the basis of
upheld complaints (Mowbray, 1997). The problem with this is that
the bulk of bad practice in any profession goes without complaint.
Indeed, a particularly bad practitioner may disempower a client to
such an extent that it is the client who identifies himself as the
guilty or inadequate agent. While the difficulties of establishing a
meaningful registration system are considerable, switching the
monitoring to a complaints procedure is not an improvement.

Failing alternatives, the assumption is made that installing an
accreditation or registration scheme which makes demands upon
the training, practice, supervision and personal therapy of the
practitioner will result in more reliable practice. As is repeatedly
pointed out in the excellent and critical text, *Implausible Professions,*

edited by House and Totton (1997), there is no research evidence which offers support to the assumptions made by the advocates of accreditation/registration within therapy. Some good research could be useful here, as in many other areas of the developing professionalisation of therapeutic work.

Undeterred by the lack of an evidential base and the doubts there are about the whole notion of accreditation/registration of practitioners, BAC constructed its individual accreditation scheme in 1983 and it has evolved to the present day. Despite considerable criticism the scheme has continued and expanded unlike parallel attempts to accredit counselling supervisors and trainers which have not found such a dramatic uptake. Part of this vigour will be related to the fact that selection criteria for a number of jobs increasingly refer to 'BAC Accreditation' though it is rare for that not to be followed by the caveat 'or equivalent'. This caution reflects the fact that still only 14 per cent of BAC members have gained accreditation. For many years BAC held firm in refusing to weaken its training or practice criteria simply in order to improve this statistic. However, the AGM in 1999 produced the first significant dilution of standards when members set the NVQ (SVQ) criterion at level 3 – an academic level considerably below that offered by graduate and postgraduate courses.

A Code of Ethics and Practice is not a particularly contentious dimension of the development of a profession until that code is enacted by means of a Complaints Process. Numerous associations within the profession, for example, the United Kingdom Council for Psychotherapy (UKCP) and the Confederation of Scottish Counselling Agencies (COSCA) developed their specific and fairly brief Codes of Ethics and Practice. The Code produced by BAC was more ambitious in the detail it offered and in how it expanded to reflect learning from cases examined by its complaints process. Not only did the Code for counsellors expand but other codes were developed to cover supervision, training and work using counselling skills. Work had even begun to develop a code of ethics and practice for counselling organisations before the Professional Committee of BAC called a halt to review the process and question the effects of developing a plethora of ever more detailed codes.

While some of the problems of becoming over-specific in Codes of Ethics and Practice and in the complaints process which must rest upon those codes will be critically examined later in this chapter, it must be acknowledged that the BAC contribution in this regard was huge. The complaints process was praised by politicians in high office (Jamieson, 1998) and BAC cut no financial corners to make this process as open to complainants as possible. A particularly important figure in relation to counselling ethics is Tim Bond, a former Chair of BAC and 'state of the art' author on the subject (Bond, 1993, 2000).

The opportunities of professionalisation for person-centred therapy

In the USA, person-centred therapy has never fully engaged with the institutional dimensions of therapeutic practice. Although the early foundation was strong, centred within the University sector, linked with the developing discipline of psychology and dialoguing with the research community, Carl Rogers himself became disillusioned with the functioning of institutions and the approach did not, in any substantial way, engage the challenges and conflicts of professionalisation. Of course, this was in the 1960s, when the spirit of the time was to challenge and even reject institutions for their dehumanising impact. The approach 'sold' itself not in terms of its integration into institutional practice but for the quality of its ideas and its emotional appeal to practitioners and particularly to the public. The immediate boom which the approach experienced reinforced the choices made and silenced any voices of antidisestablishmentarianism.

In those early times it was presumed that professionalisation would carry only dangers for person-centred therapy. Inevitably, there will be conflicts between an approach which is 'person-centred' and the workings of institutions which, logically, should be 'institution-centred' and we shall explore these later in this chapter. However, it is interesting in the present day to find the person-centred approach firmly established within the professional and institutional therapy domains in Holland, Belgium, Germany and Britain, as well as many other countries of the world.

Examining the situation in Britain in more detail provides what could be a useful case study for those in other countries. There is no doubt that person-centred therapy in Britain has been strengthened by its engagement with the professionalisation process. In the 1970s and early 1980s the approach suffered greatly from the 'superficiality myth'. There had been no person-centred training courses run by people who themselves had been trained to depth in the approach and the result was that practitioners from other approaches and even those who called themselves 'person-centred' had an incredibly superficial view of the approach, seeing it as comprising only the three therapeutic conditions of empathy, unconditional positive regard and congruence. Carl Rogers' efforts to specify and delineate the therapeutic conditions had led only to an over-simplification in the minds of others. There are still those in other approaches who prefer to think of person-centred work in simplistic terms, but a major impact of engaging with the professionalising dimensions of therapeutic practice and dialoguing with workers from other disciplines has been a deepening awareness of and regard for the approach. One thing which has contributed greatly to that dialogue has been the expansive rather than defensive attitude taken by person-centred practitioners who have actively sought to articulate the approach's thinking (Barrett-Lennard, 1998; Bozarth, 1998a; Mearns, 1994, 1997a; Mearns and Thorne, 1988, 1999; Merry, 1995, 1999; O'Leary, 1999; Rennie, 1998; Thorne, 1991, 1992, 1998a; Thorne and Lambers, 1998).

Within Britain, person-centred therapy tended to associate itself with the professionalising work of BAC rather than the United Kingdom Council for Psychotherapy (UKCP). Indeed, although the person-centred approach is one of the largest therapeutic approaches in Britain it has never been represented within UKCP. At the time when UKCP (previously UKSCP) and BAC were developing there were no national organisations for the person-centred approach. The Association for Person-Centred Therapy: Scotland (PCT Scotland) was founded in 1986 and the British Association for the Person-Centred Approach (BAPCA) in 1989. The absence of these organisations earlier in the 1980s meant that there were no formal bodies which might be consulted by UKSCP and BAC and no institutional process by which the approach could be involved with the developing professionalisation of psychotherapy/counselling. The result was that the work of engaging with professional organisations was left very much up to individuals in the approach. This work was considerable and person-centred specialists made the pragmatic choice of investing their time in BAC. It was only small matters of difference which inspired this choice. From the outset UKSCP had a personal therapy requirement for training and the person-centred approach is clinically unsuited to the 'prescription' of therapy (this is discussed later in this chapter). Another reason for not choosing UKSCP was that the approach would have been included among the group of 'humanistic' therapies. Although person-centred therapy is always positioned thus, it does not in fact have much in common with the other established humanistic therapies. The governing feature of person-centred therapy (PCT) is not its 'humanistic' orientation but its forsaking of mystique and other 'powerful' behaviours of therapists. In this regard many humanistic therapies are as different from PCT as psychoanalysis. A third and more minor consideration was the discomfort which person-centred therapists felt at the inclusion of hypnotherapists in UKSCP.

Engagement between person-centred therapy and the professionalisation process had greatest impact in relation to training. The professionalisation of counselling encouraged the approach to articulate its principles and practices of training and to consider the whole issue of curriculum. Even the very first training consideration, that of selection of course members, presented a useful challenge to the person-centred approach. Early person-centred courses believed that 'self-selection' was consistent with the person-centred philosophy. Unfortunately, some people are attracted to counselling training as a dimension of their own difficulties and the results of their self-selection can be both time-consuming and sad for everyone concerned (for a full discussion of this issue, see Mearns, 1997a: Chapter 5). The person-centred approach soon realised that it was not sufficient simply to leave the matter of selection entirely to the applicant. This closer examination of selection for person-centred therapy training courses revealed some trends which came to be addressed by course providers. For example, some applicants saw the training experience as important chiefly for the personal growth opportunities which it offered. In the early days of training this issue had not been addressed – it seemed perfectly appropriate for people to enter training for this reason. Later, the morality of charging large training fees for growth experiences came to be challenged. Another difficult issue surrounded applications which came from people whose self-esteem was fairly low – the person-centred approach was seen as a good way of working for those who had a fear of having impact in relation to the client. Of course, the person-centred approach is probably more impactful in relational terms than any other if the notion of 'relational depth' is integrated. The training experience also tends to be uniquely challenging in personal terms, thus creating difficulties for students who did not have sufficient confidence in their own integrity. Courses which were not alive to this issue tended to recruit a high proportion of people whose fear was so large that it inhibited the training process. Awareness of the responsibility of courses in relation to selection pushed them to face this problem.

The question of curriculum soon raised questions on how 'student-centred' or 'tutor-centred' courses should be. It was consistent with the approach to make courses highly student-centred yet how could we also ensure that students became aware of the whole field from which they were making their choices? This led to even more interesting questioning about person-centred group process. For example, it was commonly assumed that it was 'person-centred' to throw decision-making open to the community of those attending. In fact, this is not a 'person-centred' approach but a 'community-centred' approach, which does not necessarily pay more attention to the needs of the individuals concerned unless they are able to voice those needs amid the strong voices of others. In similar vein, the thinking behind the use of the large group had to be explored. Since the California period of Rogers' work it had become an unquestioned assumption that person-centred gatherings of any kind should start from the format of a large unstructured group without much regard to contextual variables and aims for the process (see Mearns, 1997a: Chapter 10).

The question of student assessment posed obvious problems for person-centred training and was a good example of the integrative dialogue which took place between the approach and the chosen professional body (BAC). It was important for the approach to delineate and justify the rationale for self-assessment so that the trainee could be kept at the centre of the evaluation process, thereby maintaining an essential plank of the 'responsibility dynamic' within the approach (Mearns, 1997a, 1997b). Although the whole ethic of student self-assessment runs precisely counter to the 'deficiency model' which permeates the British education system and most of its professions, the principle of self-assessment was accepted by BAC. Indeed, there arose an interesting example of a course which professed itself to be person-centred and yet operated only on tutor-assessment – the BAC panel assessing the course challenged the trainers on this inconsistency!

This integrative dialogue between the approach and the professionalising process not only allowed PCT to remain 'included' but because person-centred practitioners played a full, active and constructive role in dialogue with colleagues from other approaches, the approach gained a measure of respect for its values and differences. Furthermore, engaging with the professionalising process helped PCT courses to face important challenges and to clarify their working methods. In this section we have only briefly summarised a few of the critical issues where person-centred therapy training benefited from its dialogue with the agents of professionalisation – much more detail is given on these and other critical training issues in the only book thus far to be written on person-centred training (Mearns, 1997a).

When considering the opportunities of professionalisation for person-centred *supervision* a first conclusion might be that there would be no impact because the 'developmental' approach to supervision taken by an organisation such as BAC was perfectly synchronous with the person-centred approach. Yet, the focus provided by the professionalisation process helped the approach to sharpen its distinction between supervision and therapy. In person-centred supervision the principal focus is the *therapist* and not the client. The view is taken that nothing can meaningfully be done to understand the client because he is not present in the supervision room. Hence, in person-centred supervision, the attention is devoted to the behaviour, experience and development of the therapist in relation to her clients. As Elke Lambers outlines in Chapter 10, a major objective of the supervisor is to facilitate the therapist's development of her congruence. Within this orientation it is inevitable that the boundary between 'supervision' and 'therapy' is more challenged than would be the case in approaches to supervision which favour the client more as the unit of study. Furthermore, with the emphasis of the approach on following the needs and directions of the supervisee it was common, in early person-centred supervision, to find that individual supervision sessions, or a whole series of sessions, became indistinguishable from therapy. Where the supervisee could determine the agenda without limits being imposed they tended to put their need for therapy before their need for supervision. This was something of a problem because ethical guidelines within the profession demanded that therapy and supervision be clearly distinguished from each other. The challenge, then, was for the approach to stop doing therapy when the label was supervision but not to swing too wildly to the other extreme and lose the very distinctive nature of person-centred supervision in attending to the person who is the therapist. Person-centred supervision aims to raise and consider the dimensions of the therapist that are involved in the therapy process and to consider the development of the therapist in regard to these dimensions. There then comes a line between the raising and consideration of those dimensions and their further exploration which is properly within the domain of personal therapy.

When one of the authors (Mearns) was Visiting Fellow to the Center for Studies of the Person in La Jolla, California, during 1972/73 he found that it was easy to elicit the services of Carl Rogers as supervisor because none of the graduate students could use him in that role. The reason for this was that Carl Rogers was not certificated to practise as a therapist in the state of California. Of course, it was easier for Carl Rogers to stay clear of external accreditation/registration than it would be for a new therapist with no reputation. There is absolutely no doubt that Carl was correct in his claim that external accreditation/registration was antithetical to an approach which emphasised the internalising of the locus of evaluation not only for clients but also for therapists. It is not consistent with the approach to wave accreditation as a symbol at prospective clients because our adequacy can only be shown properly through our interaction with each individual client. Interestingly, the accreditation process within the profession takes a similar view and sees itself not as testimony to the good practice of the therapist but simply as a statement that the practitioner has undertaken the processes of training, supervision, practice and personal therapy embodied in the accreditation criteria. Presented in this fashion, it has been possible for the majority of suitably experienced person-centred therapists to engage with the accreditation process, but there is no denying the intrinsic incongruity.

Engaging with the Codes of Ethics and Complaints Process within the profession has largely been a distressing experience for those person-centred therapists who have been most involved and this will be explored later in the chapter. However, there have also been positive results from the set of challenges which comprises a Code of Ethics. Although a code can come to look like a 'rule book' when it evolves into ever more detailed paragraphs, essentially it is merely a set of 'challenges' for the counsellor. Indeed, Tim Bond is diligent in pointing out that most problems we have with ethics arise from conflicts between opposing ethical principles (Bond, 2000). Such conflicts have helped the person-centred approach to consider a number of its practices and presumptions. For example, the person-centred approach does not take the same line on *boundaries* as do most psychodynamic approaches (from which the notion originates). In person-centred therapy we expect a more fluid, less structurally 'boundaried', relationship between therapist and client but it is useful for us to question ourselves in this regard – there will be times, for example, when this fluidity is actually presenting a problem for the client – a problem which is difficult for him to voice and therefore difficult for us to appreciate.

The person-centred approach will always have problems with those parts of a Code of Ethics which expect the therapist to take a degree of responsibility *for* the client. However, most of the responsibilities which are delineated in the BAC Code of Ethics and Practice for Counsellors (BAC, 1997) are actually responsibilities which counsellors should hold *towards* the client and there is absolutely no reason to expect a person-centred therapist to be any less stringent in regard to these responsibilities than practitioners of other approaches. The delineation of responsibilities expressed within Codes of Ethics and Practice sharpen consideration of the whole area of responsibility for person-centred practitioners.

One of the major and continuing conflicts which ethical codes and complaints processes have drawn to the awareness of person-centred practitioners is the matter of the social and temporal construction of reality. Person-centred therapy exists in the here and now and between the two individuals in the room. If there is clarity on the relationship and the work being undertaken between the therapist and the client at this moment then the person-centred therapist feels she has attended to all the relevant variables. However, many complaints arise sometime after therapy has ended and often when the client is reviewing the therapy from a different social perspective, perhaps 'aided' by those who draw a different construction upon the therapy. Most other therapeutic approaches can, to a large extent, prepare for such changes in the client's reality, principally by making absolutely sure that the therapist's behaviour cannot be later interpreted in any problematic fashion. The person-centred therapist would find that difficult because such an impression can only be assured by the therapist maintaining an excessive detachment in relation to the client. If a client requested 'a hug' at the end of a session therapists of some other traditions would refuse, while the person-centred therapist would consider the request as something unique and not to be met with a policy response. At a later time, and in concert with other constructions of reality, the therapist who refused contact might be disliked and even maligned but there is no basis for complaint under present Codes of Ethics (though it would be useful to consider 'inappropriate distancing' as an ethical item). However, the person-centred therapist who responded positively *could* be ethically challenged if the client's reality later changed. It would be positively dreadful if person-centred therapists responded to this dilemma by retreating into conservative behaviour and this is a danger reflected particularly among trainees operating in fear of the Code of Ethics and Practice. However, as well as this apparent danger, the matter of the social and temporal construction of reality raises an important challenge to the person-centred practitioner. It is vitally important for the practitioner to remember that, although her work with a client appears to be imbued with considerable power, it is, in fact, only a tiny element in time and in the client's total social existence.

Person-centred therapy has clearly benefited from the opportunities created by the professionalisation of counselling. This was achieved because the approach decided to 'bite the bullet' and engage with professionals of other disciplines. In so doing, it achieved an integrative dialogue which resulted in learning for all parties. In this sense the approach helped its natural popularity to be professionally realised. Of course, there is always a down side to 'opportunities' – if one side of the coin says 'opportunity' then the other must say 'danger'. We shall look at those dangers for the approach in its engagement with professionalisation later in this chapter, but first we must turn over the coin which says 'professionalisation' to reveal its other side – 'institutionalisation'.

The institutionalisation of counselling

The greatest danger for an approach which aims to be 'person-centred' is to function within an environment which does not allow latitude for persons. The environment of professional counselling has not reached this point, but we should recognise that the processes of institutionalisation tend to accompany professionalisation and be aware of the drift in that direction. In monitoring that movement (Mearns, 1999) we might pay attention to: the slide from potentiality model to deficiency model, the drift from functionalism to structuralism, pressures towards manual- isation, the politics of appearance, and the loss of humanity.

The slide from 'potentiality model' to 'deficiency model'

The question of whether we focus on the potentialities or the deficiencies of the human being is an age-old philosophical dia- lectic. To explain the language further, within education a defi- ciency model perspective is that the learner's basic state is one of 'deficit' and that we must 'fill her up' with everything she will need. The potentiality model perspective is that, far from being 'deficient', the learner has a huge array of potentialities man- ifested in embryonic skills and talents. Our educative task within this model is to create the environment where she can exercise these embryonic skills and develop her potentialities.

Generally speaking, within education, 'deficiency rules!' though we find from time to time the odd 'out-cropping' of the potenti- ality model. It is both fascinating and horrifying to read the recent Glasgow report on the mental health of young people, quoting statistics such as 25 per cent of 15-year-olds are depressed (Glasgow City Council, 1998). The report goes on to conclude that mental health services for young people have failed. It would be fascinating to develop mental health services for young people based more on the potentiality model, but that does not earn the development grants – only if things are phrased in deficiency language like 'keeping young people off drugs' does it fit the moral and political spirit of our time.

Deficiency model language is easy and suits simple minds. Educators in any sector are continually badgered to ensure that their students are 'filled-up' with appropriate elements from the moral and political curriculum. Historically, much of that was religious – now the messages are differently sourced but reflect a similar conservative moral philosophy.

Interestingly, most approaches to therapy are oriented towards the potentiality model – they aim to help the person become more flexible and confident to practise and develop his potentialities. It is not only the person-centred approach, with its notion of the 'actualising tendency', which is oriented to the potentiality model. Even Rational Emotive Behaviour Therapy, as evidenced in the writing of Windy Dryden (1998), emphasises notions very close to the actualising tendency. Instead of being so aware of the differences between approaches and becoming dismissive of each other, we would do better to be excited by our similarities.

Appreciation of the potentiality model shared by most approaches also distinguishes counselling from our mainstream culture and partly explains the frequent prejudice against it. It is *not* fashionable to regard the disturbed client as having potentialities, currently blocked. It is much more in line with our culture to regard him as deficient and to seek to 'correct' him.

It is extremely difficult to obtain public funding for projects underpinned by the potentiality model – projects are better framed in deficiency language, telling the purchaser exactly what specific changes of behaviour or attitude can be bought for their donation. Drug projects, social services projects and mental health projects have a much better chance of funding if they can take on the deficiency outlook. It may be theoretically logical to design projects in such a way that they do not seek to invade and redirect the client, but to engage and help to liberate him or her, but that is not a deficiency oriented aim. It is possible, indeed likely, that a person who is helped to realise more of his potentialities will play a fuller part in our mainstream society but potentiality aims are not oriented towards such morally directed objectives. Funding is generally hooked into the conservative norm, whether the finance derives from government, industry, commerce or charitable trusts. These are all mainstream agencies within society and will themselves be judged in deficiency terms, so it is not surprising that they pass on the same requirements to those who benefit from their funding.

Any 'institution' within our society tends to become contaminated by society's preference for the deficiency model – this is an intrinsic part of what we call 'institutionalisation'. Counselling, then, can expect to feel both an external and an internal pressure to shift from potentiality model to deficiency model. Of course, where *any* measure of professionalisation is taking place some degree of deficiency model policies will have been introduced. For example, the presumption that a professional counsellor should have been trained is a deficiency model assumption. So, it is not that we should hold exclusively to a potentiality model and deny any drift towards a deficiency model but, rather, that we should

monitor the drift and, as a profession, exercise some consciousness and choice over our destination.

There are three general principles which tend to come together
in the establishment of deficiency model policies:

1) The policy has been inspired by the 'rare exceptional case'.
2) There is no research evidence for the policy.
3) The policy makes 'good moral sense'.

Here follow some examples of deficiency model policies introduced either at a national or organisational level within counselling.

- There should be no physical contact between counsellor and
  client.
- 'Contracting' should be achieved in the first session.
- Counsellors can't work with abused clients until they have
  done the 'abuse' course.
- Counsellors need personal therapy.
- Trainees need to be grounded in the Code of Ethics early in the
  training.
- Trainee counsellors must display non-prejudiced attitudes.
- Clients who exhibit prejudiced attitudes should be confronted
  on these by the counsellor.

All these policies exhibit the three aspects mentioned earlier. They
are inspired by exceptional cases, they are unsupported by
research evidence, and each of them makes 'good moral sense'.
Because of their 'good sense', it is difficult to argue against any of
the policies, except perhaps the last one which appeared in NVQ
draft competencies for counselling. The problem is not with one
particular item, but with the total accumulative weight of such
policies. Working with new trainee counsellors gives a poignant
insight into this problem. A set of policies like these continually
emphasises to the trainee what they do not yet know. They inspire
a sense of deficiency and even desperation, as one trainee inti-
mated:

> Every time I am with a new client I am scared that they are going to
> bring up something that I haven't yet been taught or that I will do
> something that I don't yet know is wrong.

This trainee is not approaching the training as a context which
will help her to release and develop her potentialities – the
accumulation of deficiency model policies breeds deficiency
model thinking.

The drift from functionalism to structuralism

Another related symptom of creeping institutionalisation, and a special case of the slide to a deficiency model, is the gradual replacement of functionally expressed criteria with structural definitions. 'Guidelines' accompany all dimensions of professionalisation. In counselling we have guidelines for accreditation/registration; guidelines for supervision; guidelines on counselling workloads; guidelines on ethical practice; guidelines for training courses and many, many more. If we take guidelines for training courses as an example, a 'functional' expression of a guideline states the objective that needs to be met and requires the course to articulate how that is to be achieved within its core theoretical model, whereas a 'structural' framing of a guideline dictates a *prescribed* solution. Put another way, a 'functional' expression of a problem allows for a divergence of solutions while a 'structural' expression requires a convergence to a stated solution. Inevitably, the institutionalisation of any profession tends to result in the gradual slippage from functionalism to structuralism. Below are three examples of functional and structural expressions of training guidelines taken from the person-centred training text, Mearns (1997a: 208).

FUNCTIONAL	STRUCTURAL
How does the course address the problems of trainees working with 'difficult' clients?	Courses should build-in a system of client 'assessment' to protect trainees from difficult clients.
Does the course effectively address the issue of the trainee's personal maintenance and development during training?	The course should require trainees to be in personal therapy during the training.
Is the course's assessment system sufficiently robust to protect the profession?	The course must be tutor-assessed.

The drift from functionalism to structuralism is an inevitable consequence of providing *clarification*. For example, the 'supervision criterion' in the BAC Individual Accreditation Scheme originally required the counsellor to be under 'regular and sufficient' supervision. Inevitably questions arose as to what constitutes 'sufficient', and in the absence of a specific guideline individual applicants made ridiculous proposals, like the counsellor who felt that his two hours supervision per year was 'sufficient'! Soon a statement of 'sufficiency' was introduced which, in effect, became a *rule* to which applicants must adhere.

BAC became aware of its excessive drift towards structuralism in its early drafting of the information sheet 'How Much Supervision Should I Have?' (BAC, 1998b). Faced with hundreds of demands for clarification on this matter, BAC actually tried to answer the question before those involved realised the impossibility of that endeavour. Initial drafts of the paper contained complex equations by which a member might compute precisely the hours and minutes of supervision they would be expected to have under multivariate conditions. The realisation then dawned that not only could this question not be answered in a way which would cover all situations, but the Association would be doing its members a great disservice by failing to encourage individual enquirers to consider the various factors involved in making a judgement about the sufficiency of supervision. The final guideline outlined the variables and encouraged the counsellor to consider how these factors applied to their specific situation and to assess supervision needs in consultation with their supervisor (BAC, 1998b). A similar, functional expression was constructed for the guideline on 'counselling workloads' (BAC, 1999), but in other areas we still tend to find a surfeit of structural expressions in guidelines. For example, the *quality* of counselling practice during training is not measured in a course accreditation assessment, but it is essential that trainees achieve the minimum 100 hours of client work. Again, it is easy to see how the structural definition became necessary: the 'rare exceptional case'. There was, for example, the training course which felt that 10 hours of practice was sufficient for their students. Even now, it would be useful to have a functional discussion of the *quality* of counselling practice, raising issues that would be discussed not only among trainers but between trainers and trainees.

As guidelines drift from functional to structural expression, practice within the profession becomes *narrowed*. It is no longer possible to work in a slightly different way and be prepared to justify that difference – now it is forbidden to come to a different solution, whatever the rationale. In a journal article, Mearns (1997c) introduced the notion of *training therapy* and *training group therapy* as structures which might be very effective in feeding personal development during training. However, innovations such as these, which involve regular meetings between trainer, therapist and trainee, cannot be researched because of the structural boundaries which are required between personal therapy and training. Structural guidelines may help to answer questions of clarification but the definition they provide constrains the profession from exploring and expanding its edges.

This argument is not to suggest that we must always fight the drift towards structuralism, but it is important that we are aware of the creeping nature of such institutionalisation so that we have the opportunity to build in some further structures by which such a drift may be monitored and which enable challenges to structural guidelines to be formulated. For example, such an anti-institutionalisation structure might be a 'boundaries commission' to which those involved in the profession could propose specific and considered deviations from structural guidelines. The expectation would be that the appellant would be prepared to monitor and evaluate the alternative policy, feeding their research findings back to the profession. Certainly, this is an unusual suggestion but it is unusual simply because institutions generally do not attend to the ever advancing process of institutionalisation. Within the profession of therapy we place great value on diversity and on the 'reflective practitioner' – perhaps in this professional arena more than any other we can find creative ways to maintain and enhance our conscious awareness.

Pressures towards manualisation

As a profession grows and attracts more public funding it increasingly faces questions as to its nature and definition. The political and economic climate demands that public resources should only be invested in activities which have a proven effectiveness. In this way the ineffective, the unreliable and the potentially dangerous extremes within a discipline become trimmed to leave a safer and more reliable core. This process defines, ever more clearly, the core activities, competencies and standards appropriate to the profession thus enabling training to be more precisely targeted and assessment more reliable.

The approach outlined in the previous paragraph sounds very 'professional' and responsible. It certainly makes sense that the public should be assured its investments are resulting in appropriate outcomes. Precisely the same process has been developed in the USA by medical insurance companies eager to define, and it must be said also to restrict, their expenditure. 'Treatments' must be able to be validated and specified precisely both in qualitative and quantitative terms. This is part of what is called 'managed care' whereby providers must stipulate the amount of treatment which will be required for a specific problem. The treatment itself must be precisely specified in a form which ensures that different treatment providers are offering exactly the same service. This results in the *manualisation* of treatment. The concept is the same as that found in a car maintenance manual where the quality of defining the precise sequence of steps which must be taken to a prescribed standard is measured by the extent to which different mechanics can use the manual effectively. Currently, in most parts of the USA and also in Germany, therapeutic approaches are only accepted by insurance companies if they can be provided in a manualised form. Other therapeutic approaches which insist on being more open-ended, or which have not proved themselves able to be presented in manualised form, are not eligible for funding.

Although it is not yet as fully established, the same kind of movement exists in Britain, where the current judgement made by the Health Service is that the case for counselling is 'not proven'. The way to obtain 'proven' status is through *efficacy* studies, which demand that the treatment is manualised (so that researchers can be sure that a standard treatment is being applied). Within the medical field in Britain, counselling will stay 'unproven', until or unless it meets the 'gold standard' criteria of efficacy studies, including manualisation (see Seligman, 1995 for a critique of the criteria for efficacy studies).

Approaches which are highly directed and focused upon specific behavioural operations can more easily meet the criterion of manualisation. Therefore, it is not surprising that the bulk of the positive research findings on therapy in the health sector pertains to cognitive behavioural approaches. This is not to say that these approaches are any more effective than others – it simply reflects the fact that they are the only approaches which can adequately be investigated under the manualisation criterion of efficacy studies. Counselling approaches which have a high 'relational' component cannot meet the criteria for efficacy studies (Hemmings, 2000; Seligman, 1995) and will never be 'proven' within this framework, which is both lamentable and ridiculous because there is considerable research evidence to suggest that it is precisely the relational dimension which is most closely associated with effectiveness (Bozarth, 1998b).

One of the significant steps which counselling bodies have been taking, perhaps unwittingly, towards manualisation is the wealth of resources we have been pouring into work on National Vocational Qualifications (NVQs) and Scottish Vocational Qualifications (SVQs). In defining, in measurable ways, the competencies required for counselling, this initiative is undoubtedly working in the direction of manualisation. Unfortunately, the effect of all competency driven schemes is to end up with 'lowest common denominator' competencies – competencies which are reduced to a level that can be operationally defined and reliably assessed. It is often possible to *define* higher level skills, but the problem comes in their reliable *assessment*. For example, within the person-centred domain there is the concept of 'meeting the client at relational depth' (Mearns, 1996, 1997a). This is a high level skill requiring considerable degrees of the therapeutic conditions in integrated form. While it is possible to define the skill, it is not feasible to break it down into competencies because it is the very integration of the activity which manifests its power. Higher level skills such as this represent the fabric of person-centred therapy and other approaches have their equivalents. A competency driven scheme or a treatment which required manualisation could not handle such higher level skills and would have to consider much simpler events, called elsewhere 'surface relational competencies' such as 'clarifying', 'not interrupting', 'listening', 'summarising', and 'asking open-ended questions' (Mearns, 1997a: 20). Hence, if we can reduce our counselling work to surface relational competencies, we will be able to meet the criteria of competency driven schemes like NVQs/SVQs and in turn the requirements of manualisation. For a strident critique of the folly of the NVQ/SVQ initiative in counselling, the reader is referred to Gladstone (1997).

It is important at this early juncture to resist vigorously this tendency towards manualisation. Therapy in the USA has found itself driven down this route, partly because it is grounded firmly within the profession of psychology which is generally sympathetic to the requirement of behavioural specification. However, therapeutic practice within Britain is by no means restricted to psychology and draws from a wide range of disciplines, many of which would be anything but sanguine about the drift towards manualisation. Once again, we have an opportunity to observe the early stages of the drift and to make conscious decisions about the development of our profession.

The 'politics of appearance'

In the later stages of the institutionalisation of a profession, as with any degenerative disease, we find a slippage into dysfunctionality. One marked symptom of this degeneration is a loss of contact with reality and an excessive attention to illusion. When the 'politics of appearance' takes hold we find that the institution becomes less concerned with what it *actually* achieves and more attentive to its public *appearance*. This can go to the extreme where what the institution is achieving becomes absolutely unimportant. Whenever helping services become institutionalised they find themselves losing sight of their earlier helping aims and becoming more and more embroiled with the political dimension of their existence. Increasingly, finances are drawn away from actual client care and pressure is put upon workers to cover more with less. They will be colluding well with political masters if they can be *appearing* to cover 1,000 people ineffectively, rather than offering an adequate provision to 100. The term 'spreading the service thin enough to be ineffective' is more than a joke – it is a political reality.

In counselling, we need to be aware of this danger whenever time limitations are introduced. This is not to say that short-term counselling cannot be effective. Indeed, both the authors have been convinced in recent years that much can be achieved in a few sessions (Goss and Mearns, 1997b; Thorne, 1994, 1999). However, we need to investigate the circumstances which are amenable to a briefer intervention and those which are not. A simple policy decision to spread the service thinly to all clients is not using such clinical judgement.

Any counselling service can run into the problem of spreading its service too thinly, but this is particularly pronounced within health service contexts where there is considerable political pressure towards *equity* of provision. It is incumbent upon Health Care Trusts to show that they are offering an equal or equivalent service to all patients in their geographical area. Yet, there is rarely an even spread of primary care counsellors, so the constant danger is that the counsellors will be asked to cover four practices instead of two, and, as a result, lose the important practice involvement dimension of working with the primary care team. The counsellor then becomes little more than a visitor to the practice, coping with whatever referrals are thrown to her rather than engaging in a dialogue on the nature of these referrals.

Another dimension of the politics of appearance is defensive policy making where policies are drawn up in response to the individual exceptional case as a means of showing to the world that the profession eliminates its bad practice. As we discussed earlier in relation to the 'structural' framing of guidelines, deriving policies from the exceptional case inhibits majority practice and the development of the profession.

In the latter stages of degeneration into the politics of appearance, a counselling service might find that safe irrelevance is preferred to risky helping. We find many examples of this within community care. There is an enormous potential for a vibrant counselling and support service for people whose degree of distress is such that they previously would have been hospitalised. Workers in this field, particularly from a person-centred perspective, will know that there is a need to get fully involved with this kind of client in order to make even the necessary psychological contact. Certainly, there are some projects which support the worker in such a degree of involvement but, increasingly, the politics of the situation are discouraging. Recently, we found a manager of such a service saying to the counsellor 'perhaps you had better stop working with that client in case she commits suicide'. The manager was concerned that a suicide might reflect badly on the project. There is a fair chance that the counsellors in that service were pleased with the 'professionalism' of its work, but perhaps they were losing sight of what the work should really be about.

The loss of humanity

Perhaps one of the saddest consequences of growing institutionalisation is the consequent loss of humanity in the profession. In response to issues already mentioned, we can see how a trainee might become inhibited from the expression of her own humanity with clients as she struggles with fears about whether she is breaking any 'rules', written or otherwise. One example concerns 'touching'. Within the last 10 years we have seen the outlawing of even appropriate human physical contact between counsellor and client, and not just in counselling approaches which always held that rule, but even in those approaches, like person-centred, where human contact is of prime importance. In writing the second edition of Person-Centred Counselling in Action (1999), we found that we had to completely rewrite the pages on 'touching' because of the sea change in therapeutic discourse which had taken place in the 11 years since the first edition (1988).

Another example of the loss of humanity in relation to clients relates to the therapist's growing nervousness regarding the temporal and social construction of reality described earlier in this chapter. This can lead therapists to restrict their congruent human expression towards clients, in the knowledge that although the relationship is strong at this moment, this could change with time and the pressure of other influences and the therapist's behaviour might subsequently be symbolised differently by the client and even become the basis for complaint.

As well as withdrawing dimensions of practitioners' humanity from the client, an institutionalising profession may begin to lose a measure of humanity in its dealings with its own members. The area where this degeneration shows itself most clearly is in the handling of complaints. Mature professions will have struggled towards a balance where both the complainant, and the complained against, are treated with the humanity which they deserve and decisions are reached without regard for the public's perception. However, newer professions can go through a phase when the desperation to achieve a positive public image can cause a punitive imbalance. The profession of therapy is at this difficult stage, with trainees fearful of being pilloried for what they do not yet know, and experienced practitioners realising that a combination of circumstances rather than a malevolent act could lead to their demise.

The dangers of institutionalisation for person-centred therapy

The growing institutionalisation of the profession is more dangerous for person-centred therapy than for most other approaches because PCT is particularly grounded in the potentiality model which tends to be undermined by institutionalisation. Our view is that the pressure towards deficiency model thinking is not yet so strong that the person-centred approach has to subvert itself or remove itself from the mainstream (see Chapter 11), but there are dangers to which we will certainly have to attend if the trend continues.

One danger is that if there is growing prescription on how the counsellor should engage with the client, the basic 'person-centredness' of the work might be challenged. For example, both the present authors might be deemed to be somewhat sloppy with respect to contracting in the first session with clients. It is not our habit to begin each session with an array of contracting details unless that seems relevant for the client at that moment. When encountered by a distressed client in a first session we would prefer to respond to the person immediately and fully, perhaps only at the very end of the session coming to a few basic elements of contracting sufficient to meet the client a second time. In any retrospective complaints procedure which did not entertain the conflict of ethics involved in such situations, we would certainly be found guilty of erring in relation to 'initial contracting'.

Increasingly, prescriptiveness upon training courses could also create difficulties for person-centred training. For example, a deficiency model approach to the issue of prejudice and equal opportunities is to expect the trainee to be schooled in relation to all the main groups against which prejudices may be held. In this context, trainees can feel that they are not equipped to work with clients in a group unless they have been trained for work with that specific group. This conflicts dramatically with the potentiality model approach to prejudice, which is based on the clear finding from social psychology research that there is a considerable correlation in prejudice towards different minority groups reflective of a general dimension of ethnocentrism, which in turn has been linked to authoritarian personality formations. On this basis, person-centred training does not treat the various prejudiced groups separately, but endeavours to approach the issue of prejudice individually from within each trainee, creating situations where elements of prejudice can come to light and be examined in a climate reflective of the potentiality model rather than the deficiency model. However, in taking this generic approach to prejudice, person-centred trainers may find that they are not meeting requirements to address minority groups separately.

Precisely the same difficulty arises when we consider counselling provision for specific problems. If the prescriptiveness for training continues to increase we may well find that the expectation is to take a more 'problem-centred' approach to training. This would be undermining to person-centred training where the emphasis is on working with the person rather than the problem. Indeed, it would initiate quite contradictory thinking to presume that clients with the same problem should be worked with in the same way.

The personal therapy requirement for accreditation is an example of structural prescriptiveness which presents considerable conflict for the person-centred approach where there is strong opposition to the 'prescription' of therapy. In some other approaches, notably psychodynamic and gestalt, therapy is seen as an *educative* process which can be engaged for the illumination which it provides – in this context, the prescription of personal therapy allied to training makes perfect sense. However, therapy in the person-centred world is not principally an 'educative' process, though learning will result. It is a means of meshing the symbolised (or symbolising) incongruence of the client with the congruence of the therapist. It is *not* an appropriate process for people who are merely wishing to have an educative experience. This crucial dimension of the approach emerged in the major 'Wisconsin Project' research (Rogers et al., 1967) when attempts at establishing a control group of 'normal' persons could not be sustained (Coulson, 1987). In the absence of symbolised incongruence, clients did not feel the need to maintain the therapy. We should not be surprised by this fact – it was spelled out by Rogers as one of his six 'conditions of the therapeutic process': 'That the first person, whom we shall term the client, is in a state of *incongruence*, being *vulnerable* or *anxious*' (Rogers, 1959: 213). Person-centred therapy simply does not work with clients who are not experiencing incongruence in their living and wanting to change that incongruence. In theoretical language, that experience of incongruence reflects a disturbance in the balance between the promptings of the actualising tendency and the restraining forces of 'social mediation' (see Chapter 9). The experience may take the form of 'anxiety' where the incongruence is only subceived, or 'threat' where it is already symbolised (Rogers, 1959: 204). In either case, the person's internal system is indicating an important imbalance and urging action. In these circumstances the client, depending on his perception of the therapist's willingness and ability, may be open to engaging at relational depth. In the reverse circumstances, where there is no perceived or subceived problems of balance, there is no intrinsic motivation to open fully – indeed, that may be potentially threatening to the homeostasis. Any 'work' which was undertaken in these circumstances would have to be superficial and in dialogue with the person's defences – indeed such work might achieve little more than exercising the defences and even increasing their sophistication. The person-centred approach is an entirely different therapeutic system from the psychodynamic and gestalt models which operate at a more superficial relational level. The power of the approach is in the realness of the therapeutic relationship (see the notion of 'relational depth' illustrated in Chapters 3 and 5 and in Mearns, 1996, 1997a). That relationship is not only dependent upon the skill of the therapist, but upon the acute need experienced by the client.

Another potential danger for person-centred therapy in the institutionalising of the profession is that a greater 'parental' role will be expected of therapists and of trainers. The 'responsibility dynamic' (Mearns, 1997a) within the person-centred approach delineates the appropriateness of the person-centred therapist/trainer being responsible *to* her client or trainee and the inappropriateness of the therapist/trainer being responsible *for* her client/trainee. However, in other therapeutic traditions, a more parental role is accepted and even expected. Difficulties around this are already being experienced by person-centred therapists challenged by psychodynamic colleagues on the matter of 'boundaries'. The majority of person-centred therapists who run foul of the BAC Complaints Process do so in relation to clause B.5.1:

> Counsellors are responsible for setting and monitoring boundaries throughout the counselling sessions and will make explicit to clients that counselling is a formal and contracted relationship and nothing else. (BAC, 1997)

The psychodynamic world is, rightly, more scared about boundaries than person-centred practitioners. Certainly, person-centred therapists would avoid situations where they were being put into two incompatible roles in relation to the client, but they would not forbid feelings and expressions of friendship, either on their part, or from the client. Nor would they be overly concerned, depending on the work context, if the therapy was being restricted to specific 50-minute sessions, or was more flexibly packaged. As illustrated at the beginning of this chapter with Joe, some work contexts such as mental health projects, hospital therapy or therapy in other residential settings, may involve and gain from meetings outside the therapeutic hour. There is a greater gulf of understanding between the person-centred and psychodynamic orientations on this matter than any other. From a person-centred perspective, the *therapeutic context* is an important variable which will affect the therapeutic process. In working with a range of clients beyond that which is normally encountered within private practice, we find many people whose hurt, or fear, or abuse, or whose profound existential despair, makes a stereotyped therapeutic context of one hour a week in a west-end office a trivial pursuit. If they cannot be offered more it is not safe for them to engage. This is well illustrated in Margaret Warner's invited chapter on 'fragile' and 'dissociated' process where the client requires the therapist to take a flexible but consistent attitude to the therapeutic context and where it can be important for the client to have a say in the detail of its definition (see Chapter 8). An institutionalised system has a ready response for this population of potential clients – 'they are not suitable for therapy'. The reality is better reconfigured as, 'they may not be suitable for the therapeutic context we are prepared to offer'. However, if we view the therapeutic context as an active variable in the process, we may be able to create a boundaried system for work which offers something more. In an earlier book this position is described and a crucial caution pertaining to inexperienced therapists is emphasised:

> It is important that person-centred counsellors who are choosing to work with more demanding clientele and more involving therapeutic contracts are able to be flexible in the way they work while ensuring that they are in full control of the work. Structural aspects of the work like frequency of sessions, length of sessions, the possibility of crisis 'call-outs' and working in settings which are safe for the client rather than familiar for the counsellor, are all factors which may be varied by the experienced and well-supported counsellor. One of the problems with this suggestion of entering into wider contracts with clients is that it is sometimes the most inexperienced and inappropriate practitioners who are attracted to working in this way. Inexperienced workers should rigorously avoid engaging in such wider contracts because the danger is that these would be sustained by the needs rather than by the professionalisation of the counsellor. (Mearns, 1994: 10)

In even suggesting the therapeutic context as a variable which may be altered by the therapist in consultation with the client these authors have been accused by psychodynamic colleagues of condoning and encouraging 'unethical' practice. This issue is so divisive between the approaches that it is almost impossible to sustain dialogue upon it. From a classical psychodynamic perspective, it is critical that the humanity of the therapist is hidden from the client and from the person-centred orientation it is crucial that her humanity is seen. There is no resolution of these opposites and to date there has been little respect between them, which is a pity. Elsewhere, this issue is discussed through the notion of 'transference abuse' and 'institutionalised transference abuse' (Heron, 1997). Of course, the 'psychodynamic' approach is, in fact, an extremely diverse community and with some parts of it, particularly those which acknowledge and seek to work with the 'real' relationship, considerable resonance is found with person-centred therapy. The literature is well developed with important reference points represented within modern psychoanalysis by workers such as the Boston group (Stern et al., 1998) and psychoanalytic 'Self Psychology' with Heinz Kohut and colleagues (Kohut, 1971, 1977, 1982, 1984; Stolorow and Atwood, 1992; Stolorow et al., 1992, 1994). Particularly good entry points to this literature are the writings of Kahn (1985, 1996, forthcoming) and Tobin (1991) who offer expert articulation between 'Self Psychology' and person-centred therapy (as does Margaret Warner in Chapter 8 of this book). While this kind of dialogue offers hope for the future, the reality is that if the profession is to become institutionalised under present mainstream psychodynamic influence, their need for a narrowly and structurally boundaried context may require the person-centred approach to be defined as 'unethical'.

The danger for person-centred practitioners is that 'boundaries' come to be defined 'structurally' rather than 'functionally'. A functional analysis would require the therapist to consider, delineate and justify her actions and in that way to be accountable. On the other hand, a structural analysis would simply demand behaviours such as: not meeting the client outside the therapy room; not offering any support other than therapy to the client; not permitting the client power in determining the therapy contract; not modifying the terms of the therapy contract and not engaging with any other persons close to the life of the client. It will be a great pity if the psychodynamic need for a structural expression of boundaries causes a major schism within the profession.

In training there are similar difficulties with an emerging 'parental' role if the trainer is expected to take an increasing responsibility *for* the trainee. Already courses are expected to intervene between the trainee and the counselling practice agency to draw up 'contracts' of agreement, even if that agency is the trainee's place of paid work. This policy change certainly arose from specific difficulties and might or might not prevent these in the future, but as well as preventing difficulties in that tiny minority of cases, it is also constraining of everyone involved and puts the person-centred trainer into an inappropriate parental role in relation to the trainee's work in her place of employment.

It is possible that the growing practice of 'assessing' clients for work with trainees might also impinge on the trainer–trainee relationship. It is really about time that the profession demanded some empirical evaluation of the process of client 'assessment' which has been lifted unquestioningly from the medical model. We have our doubts as to its effectiveness in determining those clients who should not be referred to trainees. Equally, we are aware that this assessment process can be a dreadful experience for clients who have to tell their story to yet another person who will disappear at the end of the session. There are alternative ways of increasing the safety of the experience for both trainee and client. In the free public counselling clinic operated by the University of Strathclyde, client assessment is relinquished and the emphasis is put on the experience of the trainee. If the trainee is uncomfortable with the work or if difficulties become evident through supervision, then the trainee has the option of relinquishing the work *or* continuing with extra support provided by the service. Invariably, trainees opt to continue with extra support. Our experience with this strategy is wholly positive. It is extremely rare for the trainees to experience acute difficulty, or for that to become evident later in the work, but where it does, the extra support provided increases the safety of the endeavour and can also help the trainee to make striking advances in their work. Once again, there can be different ways of solving a problem and the profession needs to be wary of taking the structural approach by dictating only specific solutions such as, in this case, formal client 'assessment'.

It is also possible that a more 'parental' role will become expected of the supervisor. Earlier in this chapter we praised the counselling approach to supervision and compared it favourably with supervision in the other helping professions. However, perhaps we are naïve in our view on events. It is possible that the potentiality model approach to supervision within therapy is an accident of its early development and that *any* helping profession will gradually evolve its supervision into a deficiency orientation so that supervision will become a means of 'policing' the counsellor's behaviour. Even now there are voices in that direction and concerns about whether the supervisor could be seen as culpable in law for the actions of their supervisee, as has occurred in the USA (Austin et al., 1990; Mowbray, 1995). Interestingly, this fear is not upheld in a legal consultation commissioned by BAC (Jamieson, 1999). If there should come a time when the supervisor is deemed to be responsible *to* the client then the logic of that scenario is that the supervisor is therefore responsible *for* the supervisee and we are left with the same format for supervision found in social work and other helping professions. Perhaps this matter will prove to be an important 'tracking' issue for the institutionalisation of the profession.

As well as these challenges to basic 'client-centredness' and the greater encouragement of a 'parental' role, it is not inconceivable that the whole person-centred approach could be deemed unethical. It may seem bizarre to suggest that the largest approach within Britain (according to book sales) could be challenged on bringing the profession into disrepute, but, in so far as person-centred therapists are currently facing such charges for practice which is not wildly deviant from the norm, it is an argument which we must face. There are certainly psychodynamic practitioners who would have no difficulty in defining the person-centred attitude towards boundaries and the therapeutic relationship to be, de facto, unethical – indeed, this argument has already been put to one of the authors. The willingness of person-centred therapists to extend sessions, increase frequency of sessions, allow telephone contact, engage in home visits, and respond to client requests for mild physical contact like a hug, are all so manifestly inappropriate within other theoretical models that they are automatically taken as evidence of therapist inadequacy or, indeed, *over-involvement*. It is fascinating that ethical challenges are made on the basis of over-involvement, yet there are no codes which describe a pattern of systematic therapist *under-involvement*. It seems strange indeed that a profession which emphasises the power of relationship should not be prepared to challenge members who offer clients such a degree of detachment in the face of pain that the client experiences this as abusive (Allen, 1989).

In order to explore whether the profession has moved so far that the person-centred approach may now be deemed unethical, we might consider how Carl Rogers would fare if facing the charge that his practice was bringing therapy into disrepute. In

Chapter 7 of this book we note that Carl's functioning as a therapist changed quite markedly through his career. For example, it is fascinating to compare his work in the published *Case of Mary Jane Tilden* (1946) with the *Case of Jim Brown* (1962). Both of these cases are reproduced in part by Farber et al. (1996). The difference of 16 years between the cases finds Rogers moving from being quietly reflective, yet highly attentive, to being engagingly 'present', energetic and obviously committed even to a client (Jim Brown) who is extremely silent and labelled 'schizophrenic'. It is this later Carl Rogers who more closely reflects person-centred therapy in the present day, where the therapist is expected to be thoroughly committed, fully engaged and highly 'present'.

In considering the accusation that his work with Jim Brown might bring therapy into disrepute, we might drop charges that in working with this hospitalised schizophrenic patient, he was functioning beyond his competence despite the fact that many of his sessions were characterised by long silences and that, by his own admission, he did not know where things were going. However, we might be more worried about Dr Rogers' attention to 'boundaries' and even the possibility that he might be emotionally over-involved with this client. As evidence for this we would note the fact that, on his own admission:

> I had, on several occasions, given magazines and small amounts of money to Jim Brown, and I loaned him books. There was no special rationale behind this. The hospital environment was impoverished for a man of Jim Brown's sort, and I felt like giving him things that would relieve the monotony. (Farber et al., 1996: 235)

Here, we might be disturbed not only at the gifts, but about the fact that this practitioner had 'no special rationale behind this' – in other words, these gifts were not a systematic part of the therapy. We would also note that Dr Rogers was in the habit of giving this client cigarettes. We would have to take into account conventions of that time (1962) where it would be fairly common for one human being to offer his packet of cigarettes to another, a practice which has largely disappeared with the growing vilification of smokers and smoking. Yet, we would also note that this habit of Dr Rogers was not so simple because he was not in fact a smoker and actively would search the drawers of the meeting room for spare cigarettes to give to Brown.

When person-centred therapists face a Complaints Panel where the majority of the panel are psychodynamically oriented, the question of *encouraging client dependency* is almost always raised.

Generally speaking, psychodynamic practitioners are not familiar with the theoretical rationale of person-centred therapy, such as that which is detailed in relation to the 'difficult edge' of therapeutic work (Chapter 8). Furthermore, psychodynamic thinking in this area of 'dependency' is so perverse due to its sensitivity in regard to the ever present danger of 'transference abuse' (Heron, 1997), that virtually any act of human kindness would be deplored as potentially encouraging dependency. The reality is that pathological dependency is fostered by transference relationships and challenged by 'real' relationships. Even Carl Rogers' influential early colleague was aware of this dynamic when she wrote, in 1933:

> The patient does not need to be warded off, except as he demands response in kind or carries his impulses into unacceptable action. He will not cling forever unless he meets counter-resistance in the therapist. (Taft, 1933: 291)

Yet the understandable psychodynamic fear of encouraging dependency tends to focus not on the nature of the relationship, but simply upon the therapist's behaviour. In this regard Dr Rogers would be found to be naive at best. In relation to Jim Brown, and at a fairly critical point in Brown's despair, Dr Rogers not only reflects Brown's lack of care about himself but actively professes his own care for Brown:

> . . . that is why you want to go, because you really don't care about yourself. You just don't care what happens. And I guess I would just like to say – I care about you. And I care what happens. (Farber et al., 1996: 238)

At this moment of great vulnerability for his client it may well be judged that Dr Rogers' strong statement of caring might induce a dependency reaction. Indeed, the client bursts into tears and sobbing thereafter. The undisciplined nature of this intervention is further evidenced by Dr Rogers' commentary upon it:

> This was the spontaneous feeling that welled up in me, and that I expressed. It was certainly not planned, and I had no idea it would bring such an explosive response. (Farber et al., 1996: 238)

In making judgements about impropriety, the investigating panel would certainly take into account the fact that this intervention was not part of a considered strategy.

Perhaps the clinching evidence on Dr Rogers' irresponsible behaviour in creating conditions which could easily arouse dependency was the fact that in his concern that the client Brown might be suicidal, Rogers gave Brown a note which he could carry at all times. This note not only gave Dr Rogers' office telephone number but also his *home* number. Rogers told Brown that, *at any time*, he could give this note to a staff member and be allowed to contact Dr Rogers by telephone. The case for the prosecution rests.

3 The 'heart' of person-centred therapy: spiritual and existential?

The community of person-centred therapy houses an interesting mixture of the religious and the humanistic among its members. Indeed, it is striking to find a large number of people for whom faith is central to their being and who find orchestration for that faith in their work as person-centred therapists. Equally, a considerable number of person-centred therapists are atheist or agnostic yet find that the person-centred approach gives expression to the deepest parts of their existence.

Perhaps this mixture is reflective of Carl Rogers himself. He was raised in the Christian faith, and spent two years in Theological College, before rejecting religion unequivocally, yet, throughout his life his considerable 'faith' gave strength to his contribution. He was a humanist with a fervent valuing of the human being in all shapes and guises. The degree and quality of his 'prizing' of people might equally have characterised the mission of a dedicated Christian. Perhaps being raised within a religious faith is a good training ground for humanism at its strongest.

Our aim in this chapter is ambitious. We want to speak to those whose basis for existence lies in their spiritual faith *and* to those who may be agnostic or atheist but who place great import on the existential dimensions of the person. Our underlying question is whether these may be two languages for the same experience.

It is difficult to mix the language of the religious and the humanistic – the tendency is for fears to be raised and prejudices exercised. At best, in an effort to prevent the expression of fear and prejudice, there is a tendency for each to moderate their words to a degree which fails to express the power of their experiencing.

As co-authors we represent both the religious and humanistic positions. Brian is a man whose religious faith is at his core and Dave is atheist. We each have our languages of the spiritual and the existential by which we experience the power of relatedness within person-centred therapy. We also have the advantage of a 25-year history together. That has been a remarkable experience of closeness, though we do indeed make an 'odd couple'. It would be difficult to think of two more different people – one former student referred to us as 'the bishop and the poacher', though each of us might quiver slightly at his label!

At the risk of over-simplification, it could be said that our relationship as friends and colleagues is marked by a shared spirituality which enables us to offer different articulations and interpretations of the same phenomena. We both stand in awe of the infinite resourcefulness of the human person and we are both moved to the depth of our beings by the invisible dance of communication between therapist and client. This linking of inner subjective worlds, we know from experience, has within it the power to heal and sometimes results in such a quality of relationship that, in Rogers' words, it 'transcends itself and becomes part of something larger' (Rogers, 1980: 129). These are the phenomena which we experience and recognise in common. What is more, we have both written at length about the theories of personality development and of the therapeutic relationship to which these experiences give rise. We even once jointly embraced a person-centred therapist's 'creed' (Mearns and Thorne, 1988: 18) although we shrank from this later and substituted a more modest list of 'propositions' (Mearns and Thorne, 1999: 20). It is this commonality of experience and understanding which affords us the freedom to articulate more extensive descriptions of the spiritual terrain without entering into hostile disagreement. There are times indeed when we believe we offer a not altogether irrelevant model to those who all too often enter into mortal combat in defence of spiritual 'truth', rather than acknowledge that what is shared in common is infinitely more significant than what apparently divides.

In this chapter each of us, in his own language, is going to speak about what we consider to be the 'heart' of person-centred therapy. Our languages are very different and we want to preserve that difference in the hope that all readers might find resonance in one or the other, if not in both. When we address the question of the 'heart' of person-centred therapy we are both going into our own hearts and to do that we must write in our own ways. Brian will express himself in terms of his Christian faith while Dave's language is entirely secular. He even avoids use of the word 'spiritual' although this has taken on a wider meaning in modern parlance and does not now require to be associated with a religious dimension. His avoidance of the word 'spiritual' is actually as a mark of respect for those to whom the belief in something larger than ourselves is core to their being. Instead, he makes liberal use of the term 'existential' to denote material which is so important that it is part of the fabric of our existence as human beings.

We shall begin with Dave addressing what he terms the 'existential Self' and introducing us to one of his clients, Bobby, after which Brian will explore person-centred therapy and Christian mysticism before going on to consider the problem of evil. The chapter will close with a final visit to Dave's client, Bobby.

Person-centred therapy and the existential Self [Dave]

Organised into societies, human beings tend to lose touch with their humanity and the humanity of others, yet both of these are at the existential *core* of the person. I use the phrase 'meeting at relational depth' (Mearns, 1996, 1997a) as secular language to describe a powerful phenomenon. It is identical to Buber's notion of the 'I-Thou' relationship (1937) even though Buber himself could not imagine that possibility within a therapeutic relationship (Buber and Rogers, 1960). In entering into this depth of relating, the therapist lays aside the layers of self-preoccupation which generally maintain our detachment from others, and reaches right into the client's Self. For the client, to be offered a meeting in that manner is an equally powerful experience. More often, the client, particularly in clinical settings, will find himself playing the 'object' role in what Buber termed 'I-It' relating (1937). Furthermore, the client is offered that depth of meeting without precondition or expectation. He does not have to give anything up or make any promises. He can decline the offer of relating at depth and still be as fully accepted. It is tempting to attach 'spiritual' terms to such offers for they seem to be beyond normal human experience. In fact, they represent an intensifying of human experience, which is only remarkable because we rarely invite each other to meet at this depth of relating.

If we choose to accept the invitation, we can spend accompanied time 'walking around' *inside* our Self, considering all the

elements and dynamics which comprise our phenomenal existence. That is also a dramatic experience for which we might well
use 'spiritual' language. I respectfully decline that language but
make use of the term 'existential Self' to denote the Self which we
know (perceive) and sense (subceive) – the Self which comprises
our internal existence – a Self which may be quite different from
the public images we offer. The central paradox is that this is our
most private place, which we also yearn to share. I have grown
into the habit of capitalising 'Self' not to imbue it with divine
entity (Van Kalmthout, 1998), but simply to denote the person as
she considers her existence. The capitalisation is intended to
emphasise the sheer magnitude, complexity, uniqueness and
beauty of this concept. The 'Self' is a truly wondrous entity when
perceived from within or when given invited access. Inside the
Self we find a multiplicity of elements (of thoughts, feelings and
behaviours) laid down from throughout our history. Even more
wondrous is the fact that the Self is a living, growing entity. It
organises the elements in a fashion which seeks both to protect
and enhance itself. Dynamics develop to cope with problems of
inconsistency. These dynamics are beautifully sophisticated
because they do not simply reduce everything to a consistent
sameness, but create ways in which we may be safely inconsistent
across different life settings (see Chapters 7 and 9). The structures
and dynamics within the Self develop ways of surviving which
may or may not be 'approved' by our culture (see 'Bobby' to
follow). Yet, the reality for the person-centred therapist is that
when we properly enter the existential Self of another we find
ourselves simply admiring the tenacity and the beauty of the
human's survival. At this point we have stopped being a representative of even the subtle 'social control' forces within our
society. We have entered the territory where nihilism and divinity
meet. It is time to meet Bobby, an erstwhile Glasgow gangster.

Bobby's survival

People survive oppression in different ways. Some adopt the
victim role thrust upon them and within that definition they limit
their existence, yet may keep quiet flames of potential autonomy
hidden and guarded, even disguised as apparent inadequacies.
Others survive by keeping *distance* – working on the principle that
if you do not engage with others you may still be hurt by them,

but at least the hurt will not be so personal. Yet others survive by themselves becoming the *oppressor* – as Bobby said: 'They can't hurt me if I stick my knife in first'.

Earlier in his life this had not been a metaphor for Bobby. He had been a feared and violent criminal. He had discovered that indiscriminate violence invoked most fear, though he had called it 'respect'. He had ritually mutilated people in public and for little reason – it had been a safety for him to be regarded as 'evil'.

It was an accident that Bobby came into therapy. He had become a successful businessman after developing his criminal activities into legitimate interests. Bobby was no longer physically violent – now he used *trust* as his weapon. He would create commercial situations where people would misplace their trust in him only to find him reneging on verbal agreements or enforcing previously disregarded 'small print' at the most opportune moment. His business had grown to such an extent that even suspicious clients were drawn into his web by their own greed. Bobby came into therapy because he struck his wife, Mary.

He was not close to Mary – he could not be close to anyone. But his code said that he should *not* strike his wife. And this disturbed him – for Bobby, to himself, was not a 'bad' person. He had huge and diffuse *hate*, born of his own early oppression which he would not describe: 'If I get into that it might weaken my hate . . . and I'd be defenceless'.

Even without exploring that early material it was possible to meet the various parts of Bobby's Self which had maintained his early survival but which now were offering only a shaky structure. As he said:

> There is a 'mental' me who just tries to shock people to keep them in their place. That was what I was doing when I hit Mary. But that wasn't right. I *do* feel sad about that – I want to hurt myself for that. That's what I did to myself as a kid when I felt bad – I would use my knife on me. But that's not right either – I shouldn't need to do that now. So, a bit of me is trying to do it different – that's why I'm here. But it's scary – I don't even know if I trust myself doing this. My whole existence has been devoted to getting my retaliation in first – I've become so good at it that now I don't even know when I'm doing it . . . I guess I'm *warning* you. When I hit Mary that surprised me . . . I may be going to hurt you and not even know it . . . God, I don't even know what 'I' means any more!

Working with Bobby was a moving experience. It was a rare glimpse at the inner workings of a person who would generally be regarded as 'evil'. A secular definition of 'evil' is that it is a hypothetical construct used to describe someone whom we fear and whom we do not understand. Once our fear diminishes or our understanding increases, the person is no longer evil.

I continued to be a little apprehensive in relation to Bobby throughout my work with him. There was a degree of unpredictability about him which he had cultivated. But Bobby was not 'evil', because I understood bits of him. I understood that sometimes a way to survive is to *hate* and that it is demanding to keep proving our hate to others and to ourself. I also understood some of Bobby's *defences*. He had grown them in response to his brutalising father and diversified them in relation to his sodomising key worker when he had been taken 'into care'. He had not been able to let these defences down in adult life. He had a good brain and he knew he didn't *need* these defences now – but his whole life had been constructed upon them – did he *have* a life if he let his defences down? Most desperate for Bobby was the fact that his façade was beginning to crumble. He was no longer gratuitously violent but that violence could erupt where he did not want it.

As well as being apprehensive in relation to Bobby, I *loved* him. Even now, as I write many years later, I find a tear for him. He was a full person, striving as much, or was it *more*, than any of us. When, as trainers, we separate unconditional positive regard from the other therapeutic conditions (see Chapter 5) we find it difficult to capture its quality in relation to a client like Bobby. In an effort to be comprehended by a student who still needs to condemn 'evil' behaviour, we struggle to draw a distinction between the client and his behaviour. We say that it is possible to value the client as a person of worth while still not 'approving' his behaviour (Mearns and Thorne, 1999). This separation helps the trainee to hold the dissonance until he is ready to experience the reality, but it is a weak structure. Indeed, it is far too close to that horrific expression 'love the sinner – not the sin' used by loving people to protect them from experiencing their own prejudice. The reality is that my behaviour *is* an expression of me: if you are judging my behaviour, you *are* judging me.

In feeling Bobby's struggle I experienced no inclination to judge his behaviour. It is difficult to explain, but meeting a person at relational depth and understanding dimensions of their very existence undermines any lasting vestiges of potential judgementalism.

In his own way, and it was very different, Bobby 'loved' me. One day he fell into a long silence after which he said: 'I think I will be able to tell you if I have to kill you'. Within Bobby's existential Self I understood this sentence and regarded it as a loving statement.

Brian: on person-centred therapy and Christian mysticism

For me, there is no incompatibility between the message of the Christian mystics and the concepts of the actualising tendency and the internal locus of evaluation. The mystic affirms through the experiential knowledge of sustained meditation that at the core of our beings we find God because it is the divine nature which we share and which ultimately defines us. Such a revelation makes it impossible to entertain anything other than the highest possible regard for the human person because at the deepest level we are God. To denigrate the human person is thus to desecrate the divine. What is more, the evolution into greater consciousness leads to an in-touchness with the divine energy and an absence of disharmony and inner conflict. And so it is that to accompany distressed clients so that they 'gain trust' in their own natures (or establish contact with the actualising tendency) and find confidence in their own perceptions (or discover an internalised locus of evaluation) is to share in a spiritual journey where the end goal is the experience of lovingness and belovedness which characterises the divine nature. Again there is no discrepancy between the 'fully functioning person' and the God-man portrayed in the figure of Jesus in the Gospels of the Christian Church. Jesus is the embodiment of the person who is totally self-loving and is therefore free to extend himself in the love of others. For me, it is in no way ridiculous or blasphemous to see in Jesus Christ the perfect person-centred therapist: this man whose compassion never wavered, whose empathic responsiveness extended to all he encountered and whose congruence permitted him to weep in public and to give expression to a cleansing fury. It is not perhaps without significance that as a young man Carl Rogers was immensely attracted to the personality of Jesus once he had discovered the flesh and blood person behind the distorted version portrayed by the evangelical Christianity of his upbringing.

Jesus, it will be remembered, never lost the sense of connectedness to his Father, and the Gospels frequently give glimpses in other ways of an interconnected spiritual world inherited by angels and spirits, both good and evil. The doctrine of the Holy Trinity is, perhaps, one of the greatest gifts of the Christian Church to humankind. God, it would seem, is a relationship and cannot exist except as an interrelated unity. At the heart of divinity there is a mutual interdependency which sustains the separate persons of the Trinity. It follows therefore that if we are in essence divine, we, too, are *essentially* relational and this, it would seem, is a truth which again informs the person-centred understanding both of personhood and of therapy. We need each other for our completion and in therapy there must be a preparedness on the part of the therapist to be truly involved, to be vulnerable if necessary and not to don the protective armour of therapeutic knowledge or methodology. Relational beings require relationship for their healing. What is more, where an in-depth relationship is established so that, to quote Rogers again, 'inner spirit has reached out and touched the inner spirit of the other' then the relationship becomes 'a part of something larger' (Rogers, 1980: 129). This 'something larger' is again compatible with my understanding and experience of Christian cosmology. The 'altered state of consciousness' which Rogers describes, gives me access to a world populated by angels and by the spirits of those who have left this life and have taken their place in the world beyond death. Less welcome perhaps, it also gives access to a world where hostile or tormented spirits roam, and this, in turn, provides insight into the problem of evil which the person-centred approach is frequently accused of avoiding or trivialising.

The problem of evil

Rogers himself freely acknowledged that he was not satisfied with his own rationale for the existence of evil in the world. He was adamant, however, that in his own experience human beings, once they felt respected and understood, soon reveal an essentially positive and forward-moving core to their personalities. Destructive and hostile attitudes or behaviour are the result, he believed, of experiences which have engendered fear and a deep distrust of others. Societal influences, too, which encourage aggressive competitiveness and a materialistic selfishness, play their part in creating an environment which makes it unlikely that persons will realise their full potential as essentially creative, self-affirming and socially constructive beings (Rogers, 1956: 14, 1982: 85). There is, of course, a logical flaw in this somewhat circular argument, of which Rogers was only too aware. How can it be that essentially creative and life-affirming persons can produce a society which is in many respects, so destructive an environment for human flourishing? Or, to put it in the language of person-centred theoretical constructs, how does it come about that human beings inflict on each other such powerfully negative conditions of worth that self-denigration rather than self-affirmation results? Society, after all, is made up of individuals. How is it then possible to hold to an essentially positive view of the person if in their group life those same persons behave so negatively and destructively towards each other? The logical inconsistency of this position has led many critics of the person-centred point of view, including Rollo May, to conclude that person-centred practitioners are wilfully blind to the 'shadow' side of human nature and that their resultant naiveté leads to a failure to acknowledge, let alone confront, the dark and destructive side of their own and their clients' behaviour and personalities (May, 1982: 10–21).

An evolutionary response to the problem of evil

There are two compelling responses to this, at times, bitter and contemptuous critique of the person-centred position and both are firmly grounded in experience. The first is the evolutionary response and the second the eschatological. The meeting in relational depth of counsellor and client provides the raw material for both responses. When such a meeting takes place there is a sense in which both persons are changed. When 'inner spirit' meets 'inner spirit' the nature of the relationship takes on a quality which both banishes fear and opens up new possibilities. Existential terror has, as it were, a worthy opponent in the relationship itself, which at one and the same time dispels inner loneliness and confers meaning. It is as if human beings, thanks to the mystery of their relating, evolve to conquer the existential fear and the destructiveness which flows from it. Such experience creates an altogether new context for exploring the problem of evil. Human beings, because they are fearful, wounded and self-punitive, behave destructively towards themselves and towards each other; they are caught, it seems, in a vicious circle of negativity which persists from generation to generation, a state of affairs which Christian theologians have sought to illuminate by seeing it as an inevitable outcome of the granting of freedom to his creatures by a loving God. If we were not free to choose between good and evil there would be no problem but we would no longer be human: we would be puppets on a string. This somewhat gloomy analysis of the human predicament is transformed once we adopt an evolutionary perspective and it is precisely such a perspective to which person-centred therapy lends itself. All therapeutic approaches are based on the assumption that change is possible but for person-centred therapists the nature of the change is utterly transformational. It holds out the hope of a movement from self-rejection to self-acceptance, from condemnation to affirmation, from being ignored to being profoundly understood, from leading a life of inauthentic pretence to one of openness and honesty. What is more, person-centred therapy demands of the therapist the willingness and ability to accept the other irrespective of his or her 'worthiness' of such acceptance, to enter deeply into the other's world so that understanding can take place and be received, to risk being authentically and vulnerably accessible to the other as a real and undefended person. It is the experience that such a transformation *is* possible and that person-centred therapists *can* embody such attitudes and behaviour towards their clients which underpins and authenticates what is, in effect, an evolutionary view of humankind. What is more such an evolution takes place not by avoiding evil but by engaging with it and by disarming it through the power of a relationship where spirit meets spirit, thus rendering evil both unnecessary and irrelevant. Fully evolved human beings no longer need or desire to be destructive of self or of others. They have better things to be and to do. Evil exists because we are not yet able to recognise the essential wonder of our own natures and to live it out in the world. Person-centred therapy offers the means of expediting such recognition and of implementing the way of being which flows from it.

There is, again, no incompatibility between such an evolutionary concept of the human being and the Christian theological interpretation of human relating. It is perhaps the Downside monk, Dom Sebastian Moore, who has captured this profound insight most compellingly for men and women of the 'new age'.

He sees human nature as participating in the divine nature and, because of this, the path out of inner loneliness and fear is the path of relationship where God meets God in emulation of the eternal dance within the Holy Trinity. Moore writes:

> Each of us is an 'I am' and in a creative relationship my 'I am' arouses your 'I am'. But your 'I am' brings out my 'I am' through a quality, a vitality, a vibrancy that goes through you: your 'I am' does not *of its nature* awaken mine, is not of its nature the awakening of mine. This becomes plain when we consider that, in being someone for another, you *feel* more of a someone. Now this selfhood in you, that *increases* when you relate creatively to another, existed before you met that other, was already there *to* increase with meeting. (Moore, 1982: 33)

It is difficult to imagine a more striking description of a relationship where spirit meets spirit and instantly gains access to a greater fullness of being and to 'something larger' than itself for which it is inherently equipped, and, through its yearning, prepared. In addition, the description is offered by a monk of the Western Christian tradition whose life, spent in community, has been permeated by prayer, nourished by meditation and subjected to the rigorous intellectual discipline of academic scholarship as well as the monastic vows of poverty, chastity and obedience.

An eschatological response to the problem of evil

The beginnings of an eschatological response to the problem of evil have been hinted at in recent times by Campbell Purton and Gordon Lynch. Using as his starting point the concept of unconditional positive regard, Purton has argued that the concept is little more than an invitation to a sentimental impossibility unless the human being is perceived as essentially spiritual. To offer unconditional positive regard to someone who seems bent on destructiveness and malevolence makes no sense, Purton argues, unless we construe the human being as having an existence beyond his or her own present one (Purton, 1998: 23–37). Purton is a Buddhist but his challenge to a key concept in person-centred theory has immediate resonance with the Christian insistence that we, like God, are essentially spirit and must therefore be regarded 'sub specie aeternitatis'. The offering of the core conditions to a being who has a life beyond this one – and perhaps had an existence prior to this one – opens up a richness of resource which is infinite. The 'something larger' which is accessed in the moment of profound relationship includes for the Christian the communion of saints since the beginning of time and the angelic hosts in all their power and glory. It also includes those dark forces and spirits which roam the cosmos and sometimes take up residence in the human race. To ask for the help of the angels and saints in the therapeutic journey is for me a common-sense matter of capitalising on the resources available – resources which are sometimes indispensable in the face of apparently intractable evil. Praying for clients and remembering them at the Eucharist are equally common-sense measures and not to do so would be to lack both concern and congruence. It would also be a squandering of those same precious resources. Needless to say, it will be the rare client who has a conscious awareness that his or her therapist is tapping into such resources in a disciplined and systematic way.

Gordon Lynch, in a seminal article in 1998, throws into high relief the challenges to counselling and psychotherapy posed by the cultural and intellectual world which we now inhabit. The move from 'modernity' to 'postmodernity' has given rise to the growing belief within academia that 'the representation of reality through language is dislocated from reality itself' (Lynch, 1998: 525). Lynch argues that the postmodern view of language as inadequate to describe a pre-existing reality undermines most theories of counselling and psychotherapy which were formulated in an era where so-called nomenclaturism prevailed with its basic assumption that words name objects which exist prior to their labelling. The postmodernist rejection of nomenclaturism leaves the way open for conceptualising 'a reality that transcends any form of representation' (Lynch, 1998: 529). Lynch, wearing the hat of a pastoral theologian, immediately sees the connection with the apophatic tradition of spirituality to be found in both western and eastern religions which embraces the idea that what is central to our existence can only be engaged with by moving beyond language and representation into silence. Lynch is careful, however, not to reject the usefulness of language for encountering the transcendent. He pleads for a recognition of both the value and the limitations of language. We need to use language but at the same time to acknowledge that it cannot of itself fully 'depict the true nature of an existence' (Lynch, 1998: 531).

Lynch's thesis throws immense light on the 'quality of presence' which makes possible the transforming therapeutic relationship and the recognition of 'something larger'. Words such as 'life', 'death', 'love', 'evil', 'holiness' can only reveal their full significance in the silence of communion where counsellor, client and the 'something larger' are interconnected in a world where time stands still. This is the world beyond words, where there is an instinctive recognition that to be human requires an acceptance of the fullness of our physical, emotional and spiritual beings, and that our verbal being offers but one entrance into this world which is both immanent and transcendent. For the person-centred practitioner there is again a welcome liberation in this view of language as something in the service of a reality which is beyond itself. Such a view honours the unique reality of the individual's verbalised attempt to articulate his or her experience but at the same time perceives this as but a small and provisional part of an infinitely greater reality to which the therapeutic encounter, if all goes well, will give increasing access. Perhaps that is why there are times, especially in the late stages of therapy, when it is the silence between two human beings, or their non-verbal responsiveness to each other, that brings the healing and the inner peace which Carl Rogers saw as a defining quality of the 'Person of Tomorrow'. Certainly at such times, with Julian of Norwich, it is possible to say 'that sin is nothing' (Colledge and Walsh, 1978: 137). The problem of evil has become irrelevant in an eschatological landscape where human beings have attained their full stature as eternal beings even if only for a moment on a wet Friday evening in the consulting room of a jaded person-centred therapist who has discovered the freedom and the humility of being fully present in the service of another.

A greater resourcefulness

It is perhaps by now evident that for me there is no incompatibility between the spiritual and existential terrain to which person-centred therapy gives access and my knowledge of, and personal indebtedness to, the western Christian mystical tradition. On the contrary, the two modes of apprehending the visible and invisible worlds enrich and illuminate each other. What is more, their coexistence in the mind and heart of the therapist makes for a resourcefulness in the face of fear, evil, powerlessness and hostility, which engenders confidence without taking away humility. Even the tenable hypothesis of a demonic strand in human affairs can be entertained without terror. Perhaps if that had also been possible for Carl Rogers, he might not have felt that his answer to the problem of evil or the dark side of human nature was less than adequate.

Dave: on 'evil'

I do not believe in 'evil'. Earlier in this chapter I offered a 'secular' definition of 'evil': ' 'Evil' is a hypothetical construct used to describe someone whom we fear and whom we do not understand'.

This is a disparaging definition because I *feel* 'disparaging' to those who would attach this four-letter word to a human being. Perhaps it is necessary to have a concept of 'evil' if we have a concept of 'God'. In those terms I believe I could come to understand it. But, attached to another human being, I find it unacceptable.

I have come to regard 'evil' as a concept relevant only to the user. Faced with someone whom I do not understand and whose behaviour rails against everything I believe in, and where I imagine I have support within my belief system, I create the conditions for the attribution of 'evil' – just as Christ might have been understood as 'evil' by the dominant culture of his time.

In therapy we work with some people who have survived desperate conditions for growth. Deprivation and abuse cause us to use any strengths we have in order to survive, supported only by the actualising tendency. When the need is as basic as survival we do not weigh the niceties of our methods – we go with what works. In so far as that might include deception, manipulation and even violence, we make no moral choices. In these circumstances, if we must attribute the label 'evil' we had better place it on to the actualising tendency.

We cannot work therapeutically with a person who is embroiled in this struggle for survival because therapeutic needs are less basic in the hierarchy than survival. However, we will work with many clients who are 'surviving' their survival. They no longer need the strengths which helped them to survive, but can they let them go? Can they let go that which was their lifeline?

This was Bobby's struggle – Bobby who was 'evil'. Meeting Bobby at an 'existential' level was the only way to work with him. It was only in that world that we could see his survival and his continuing terror. His system had helped him to survive thus far, but it was not a useful system for the rest of his life – and it was breaking down. He had hit Mary, and that was not part of the system. Bobby was in crisis.

Bobby's crises

Earlier in this chapter we left Bobby at a critical point. He had just told me: 'I think I will be able to tell you if I have to kill you'.

I knew that this 'kill' was not literal but existential. Bobby's defences were such that someone who made a relational impact upon him had to be 'killed'. Bobby was telling me that he would be able to tell me if he had to stop our work together. That was an unusual commitment for Bobby. Clients like Bobby do not often seek therapy because intimacy is dangerous, but therapeutic work is perfectly possible if the therapist is prepared to be absolutely congruent and if the therapist is not scared. We rejoin the therapy with Bobby facing two crises: his protective system was not working in his present life *and* he was experiencing intimacy:

Bobby: Are you scared of me?

Dave: I've been asking myself that question over and over. I know the answer, but I don't understand it.

Bobby: What is it?

Dave: I am *not* scared of you, yet sometimes I feel fear. It rushes through me and out the other end. It is strong, yet it doesn't stick.

Bobby: Like, I can be 'scary' with you, but you don't stay scared.

Dave: Yes.

Bobby: Probably what I need most is someone I can be scary with and who isn't scared.

Dave: It's like you can be a really scary person – but, *knowing* you, I'm not scared. I don't really 'understand' it, but it makes sense somehow.

Bobby: Do you know that *I'm* scared of you?

Dave: I think I must be *terrifying* for you – *because* I'm not scared of you.

Bobby: Yes – you are what I *want* and what I'm *scared* of.

Dave: Give me more.

Bobby: There is a new bit of me. Maybe it's always been there but it's stronger now. It is the bit that wants you. It feels that you understand it. It knows that you can help it come out.

Dave: 'It'?

Bobby: I don't have a name for it . . . I'm scared of it.

Dave: It's new . . . or maybe it's not . . . but it's different . . . and it might change your life . . .

Bobby: There is a comfort in just being an 'Evil Bastard'.

Dave: You were good at that.

Bobby: You've changed my present tense to a past tense.

Dave: Yes . . . I didn't realise I had done that . . . am I wrong?

Bobby: Don't be cocky with me Dave – I'm still dangerous.

Dave: I hear you.

[*Silence*]

Dave: How do you feel about that?

Bobby: How do I feel about the fact that I'm still dangerous?

Dave: Yes.

Bobby: [*pause*] . . . Sad . . . I feel really sad, Dave . . . [*pause*] . . . I'm so confused.

Dave: See if I can help. For my part I'm feeling two quite different things. One thing I'm feeling is a 'tension' – ok . . . a 'fear' . . . I *know* you can be dangerous. The other thing I feel . . . I'm a bit scared to say the word . . . I think it could be a bad word for you . . . But at times I feel a 'love' for you and I think you do for me too.

Bobby: It *is* a bad word for me Dave. When I feel that word I usually have to destroy it . . . whether it is in the other person or in me.

Dave: But where are you with it . . . *now*.

Bobby: Enough of me can hear it or I wouldn't be here.

Dave: That sounds big.

Bobby: It's frightening.

Dave: 'Enough of you can hear it' and it's 'frightening'.

Bobby: Yes, the 'new' me and the 'old' me.

Dave: The 'new me' can cope with that 'love' word and the 'old me' is frightened by it?

Bobby: And, of course, *both* bits have always been there – but one was buried – I always wanted it, but to risk it would mean my own destruction . . .

[*long pause*]

Bobby: Christ . . . God almighty . . . Why could I not have loved Mary?

Dave: Say more Bobby, I'm not following.

Bobby: Just at that moment I was really in touch with my 'love'. I've never used the word before. I felt so sad that I have not had that part of me in all the years I've been with Mary . . .

This session became even worse for Bobby as he realised that he had also not known his loving part in all the years of his life with his son, Robert. Bobby was now in crisis. His life, like anyone else's, was grounded in the Self he had had to be – the Self he needed to survive his own early abuse and neglect. But now he was 'a new person in an old life' (Mearns and Thorne, 1999). That is one of the saddest of existential events. You are ready to be different – you see how that difference could be enriching for you and those around you – but your relationships are grounded in who you have been in the past.

Bobby's coffin

'Despair', fully experienced, is life's most powerful emotion. In a later session, Bobby was in despair.

> *Bobby:* I've never known 'pain' before. 'Pain' is when you have no 'control'. As a kid I used to cut myself really bad and there was no pain . . . only 'punishment'. Now I feel 'pain'.
>
> *Dave:* You have no control.
>
> *Bobby:* I can *feel* my loss – I've lost Mary – and I've lost Robert. I tried to talk to Mary . . . to tell her about 'new' me . . . but it was ridiculous. After what I've put her through, even *I* wouldn't have believed me. I felt I was torturing her even more . . . So all I did in the end was to apologise to her. I don't know what to say to Robert. I know he hates me . . . and I don't feel I have the right to take that away from him.
>
> *Dave:* It's like . . . like you really understand that . . . you really understand 'hate'.
>
> *Bobby:* Yes . . . that's what my life has been about . . . and maybe it can never change.
>
> *Dave:* I feel cold and shivery.
>
> *Bobby:* That's because *I* feel cold and shivery.
>
> *Dave:* I'm scared.
>
> *Bobby:* I'm *not*.
>
> *Dave:* That's right, isn't it? This place for *me* is scary, but not for you – you've been here before. This is 'familiar'. It's horrible – but it's familiar.
>
> [*pause*]

Dave: Actually, maybe I *have* been somewhere similar before. It's like me, in my present, 'soft' life would find it 'scary' – but I could also see how it could be . . . 'comfortable'.

Bobby: It's the kind of 'comfortable' which no one else can share.

Dave: It sounds like a coffin.

Bobby: Yes.

Bobby the 'country hero'

[*A few sessions later*]

Bobby: I can let go of Mary, but I can't let go of Robert.

Dave: What does that mean?

Bobby: It's like I have the 'experience' to let go of Mary, but nothing in my experience helps me to let go of Robert.

Dave: Like, this is something *new* – the old ways won't work.

Bobby: Yes . . . the 'sad' me can let go of Mary although I don't want her to go. I can play the 'country hero' who genuinely acknowledges that what he did was wrong and he accepts the loss. But there is no part of me which can let Robert go.

Dave: So you can't 'orchestrate' an ending like in the 'country' songs?

Bobby: Ugh! That feels hard.

Dave: Yes – I think it came from a 'hard' place inside me. It's like I can see your 'country hero' – and I can even *like* him – but he's a pretty tragic character.

Bobby: Sure, but where else is there to go?

Dave: Like, there's nothing you can do about losing Mary – so you might as well play the country hero. I suppose you're right.

Bobby: Dave, it may sound pathetic, but believe me this is an improvement.

Dave: Like before, you might have played the 'country villain'.

Bobby: That's a good way to put it.

Dave: I got you side-tracked on Mary, but you were mainly talking about Robert – that there was 'no part of you which could let Robert go'. When we talked about this before you were using your understanding of 'hate' to let him go.

Bobby: And somehow that's not working. It's like in seeing you I've been trying to find new ways of being, but what is happening is that I'm losing the old ways.

> Dave: So you might have *no* ways to handle this . . . no control at all . . .
>
> Bobby: That scares the shit out of me . . . no control at all.
>
> Dave: It scares me a bit too . . .

Bobby the 'man'

[*next session*]

> Bobby: I've thought about Tuesday's session. You know, I played the 'Country Hero' throughout that whole hour.
>
> Dave: Tell me.
>
> Bobby: I was 'John Wayne' – hard as nails, bitter as shit and dumb as a door post. I wasn't far away from being the 'villain' either – when I realised I didn't have any control.
>
> Dave: Maybe that's why we were both scared.
>
> Bobby: Well, maybe I'm just going to have to survive without *having* 'control'. Maybe I'm going to have to cry and be desperate like everyone else. I've kept myself away from pain since I was a kid – maybe I just have to face it.
>
> Dave: . . . like a 'man' . . .?!
>
> Bobby: Dave, sometimes your humour is really twisted!

4 Person-centred therapy: anti-intellectual, unmanly and westernised?

Person-centred therapy is anti-intellectual?

The perception of person-centred therapy as essentially anti-intellectual is widespread. This perception is difficult to sustain in the light of the personal and professional contribution of the approach's originator, Carl Rogers. Not only was he the first therapist to subject the therapeutic encounter to the rigours of empirical investigation at a time when logical positivism ruled supreme and quantitative research methodology was the only model available, but throughout his professional career he also remained open to philosophical enquiry. The persistence of the widely held view of anti-intellectualism has its origins, it would seem, in a failure to accept the approach's conviction about the nature of the phenomena with which counselling and psychotherapy are concerned. Person-centred therapists are in no doubt that what matters is the *subjective* experience of client and therapist. Rogers himself in his cogently argued theoretical treatise of 1959 was quite clear that any evaluation of his theories must have as its starting point his belief in the 'fundamental predominance of the subjective' (Rogers, 1959: 191). Such a belief, then and now, runs counter to the culture which has emerged from a false scientism where obsession with so-called 'objective' data and empty statistical 'proof' often determines diagnoses, treatment plans and outcomes criteria. On a broader canvas, it is also a falsely reverential attitude towards the results of 'objective, scientific studies' which can determine government funding of psychotherapeutic activities or, even more ominously, the emergence of 'empirically validated therapies', much loved in recent times by American insurance companies (American Psychological Association, 1995). The respect for 'hard-nosed' science which permeates secularised Western society often results in a perception of reality which has scant regard for the uniqueness of personal experience and sacrifices the individual on the altar of the statistical average. This outlook can also result in a diagnostic formulation which omits the subjective data in favour of observable behaviour or change measured by pre-determined and prejudicially slanted criteria. Such a culture clashes violently with Rogers' 1959 observation that: 'Man lives essentially in his own personal and subjective world, and even his most objective functioning, in science, mathematics, and the like, is the result of subjective purpose and subjective choice.' He goes on in the same section of his theoretical statement to issue what is, in fact, an overt challenge to what still remains the prevailing wisdom in many areas of psychotherapeutic practice and research endeavour:

> it appears to me that though there may be such a thing as objective truth, I can never know it; all I can know is that some statements appear to me subjectively to have the qualifications of objective truth. Thus there is no such thing as Scientific Knowledge; there are only individual perceptions of what appears to each person to be such knowledge. (Rogers, 1959:192)

There is nothing, we would claim, about the person-centred therapist's commitment to subjective knowledge which is anti-intellectual. On the contrary, some of the world's finest minds have taken up a similar stance and Rogers himself towards the end of his life was both heartened and excited by what he saw as the emergence of new paradigms for scientific enquiry. Indeed, the current proliferation of heuristic and qualitative research studies in the realm of psychotherapeutic enquiry point to the growing intellectual respectability of such a stance. Sadly, however, such studies continue to fall on deaf ears when they seem to challenge the accepted wisdom established by so-called objective criteria which so often provide both administrative and clinical frameworks which are neat, apparently efficient and, most importantly, seemingly cost-effective. In no area is this more apparent than in the maintenance of what Jerold Bozarth has labeled the 'specificity myth' (Bozarth, 1998a: 163–4). Bozarth believes that the prevalent emphasis on the need for specific treatments, for specific dysfunctions, applied by specifically trained personnel, is based on a sham. There is what is no more than a pretence of objective scientific support for the effectiveness of technique-oriented treatments. In brief, so-called objective studies are used to perpetuate the belief that therapy should be *problem* centred, whereas a thorough review of psychotherapy research over the past 30 years or more points overwhelmingly to the conclusion that effective therapy results from the resources of the client and from the person-to-person relationship of the therapist and client – in other words, that it is *person*-centred. Bozarth in his book *Person-centred Therapy: a Revolutionary Paradigm* (1998a) quotes approvingly from Maureen O'Hara:

> It isn't the technique, it isn't the therapist, it isn't the lack of training. It isn't the new wonder drug, it isn't the diagnosis. It is our clients' own inborn capacities for self-healing, and it is the meeting – the relationship in which two or more sovereign or sacred 'I's' meet as a 'we' to engage with significant questions of existence. (O'Hara, 1995: 30)

We can justifiably conclude that person-centred therapy's emphasis on subjective knowledge is not sufficient evidence to label the approach 'anti-intellectual' and that there are even indications that such an emphasis is becoming increasingly respectable and influential among philosophers and researchers alike (Schmid, 1998). And yet the accusation that person-centred therapists are 'soft-headed' or 'woolly-minded' does not go away. Perhaps, as so often, the real source of discomfort for many of the approach's detractors lies in the famous core conditions, and, more particularly, in the concepts of empathy and unconditional positive regard and their application. The concentrated effort required to understand and accept another person leaves little room for debate, argument, analysis, evaluative judgement and other behaviours commonly associated with intellectual discourse and rational processes. On the contrary, empathy and unconditional positive regard invite a willingness to be bold in the world of feelings and a commitment to the withholding of judgement in the service of a cherishing compassion. Such words ring oddly in the context of a world where verbal warfare or, at least, verbal fencing are the common currency, not only in the day-to-day transactions of politics and business, but also in the private spheres of family and social life. It is hard not to conclude that person-centred therapy is often seen as anti-intellectual because it opens wide the doors to the expression of feelings and the experience of intimacy engendered by acceptance and understanding. Perhaps it is by definition anti-intellectual to reveal vulnerability and the need for validating relationships.

Rogers himself would certainly have refuted such a narrow definition of intellectual activity. On the contrary, his struggles to define the nature of consciousness and to follow the fluctuations of the self-concept were passionately informed by the desire to 'think rigorously'. Indeed, it is not altogether fanciful to see Rogers as a passionate thinker who, because he was committed to the exploration of subjective experience, inevitably became the intrepid adventurer in the world of feelings and relationships. For him, person-centred therapy was anything but anti-intellectual: it required the application of the mind to those areas of human experience where mind was so often at sea because it could not grapple with phenomena for which it was ill-prepared, and which it tended therefore to reject as unworthy of its attention. How often has it been said in committee meetings or at important moments of decision-making: 'Let's leave feelings out of this', as if feelings were irrelevant or inaccessible to rational discourse instead of being, perhaps, the crucial factor in achieving a creative outcome? Far from being anti-intellectual, Rogers struggled throughout his life to be faithful to empirical scientific enquiry, to the data of his own experience and to the promptings of the actualising tendency, as he sensed it in himself and in others. The 'rigorous thinker' informed the empathic and acceptant therapist who, in turn, allowed his therapeutic experience to feed back into his theoretical formulations. For Rogers, experience and meaning needed to converse as friends, and the language which they employed he termed 'symbolisation', an expression first used by Angyal in 1941.

In his 1959 statement, Rogers attempts to elucidate what he understands by the process of symbolisation which he sees as synonymous with awareness or consciousness. He distinguishes between accurate symbolisation where hypotheses implicit in awareness are borne out if they are acted upon and false symbolisation where they are not (as is the case with paranoid delusions, for example). But he goes further when he suggests that symbolisation does not necessarily result in verbal symbols but can be dimly experienced without full conscious recognition. With the concept of subception he postulates a form of symbolisation which 'permits the individual to discriminate an experience as threatening, without symbolization *in awareness* of this threat' (Rogers, 1959: 200, our emphasis). The importance of this central discussion of symbolisation is a powerful example of Rogers' determination not to drive a wedge between thinking and experience. For him, the human person was a unity where thinking, feeling and willing demanded parity of esteem. To see person-centred therapy as anti-intellectual is to deny the very heart of the approach and to accuse it of the very fragmentation which Rogers single-mindedly sought to prevent. To be accused of being anti-intellectual is for us a similar affront to our integrity and to what we believe about the essential unity of the human personality, however much it may appear disjointed and conflicted. Boy and Pine express this rather well:

> . . . it is equally important that the counselor attend to the client's cognitions. In viewing the client holistically, the counselor recognizes that cognitions and emotions are intertwined. With few exceptions, one does not appear without the other. Exclusive focus on either cognitions or emotions fractionate the client's expression of being in the counseling relationship. (1999: 39)

Person-centred therapy – unmanly and sentimental?

The accusation of anti-intellectualism, when it is linked to a distaste for the overt expression of feelings, not infrequently conceals a deeper discomfort with the approach. The person-centred therapist's trust in his or her client and the refusal to assume the role of expert, diagnostician or treatment prescriber removes many – if not all – of the arenas for exercising power. It also takes away from the therapeutic encounter the notion of a leader or director who will guide the client towards health or the resolution of difficulties. Instead, person-centred therapy proposes for the therapist the role of listener, empathiser and authentic companion, who positively 'prizes' all dimensions of her client and who is prepared to be open and vulnerable in his service. Such a role, when it is spelt out in this way, seems far removed from the male stereotype of the clear-thinking, decision-making activist who leads his team (or his family) along the road to achievement, success and material security. Not to put too fine a point on it, the person-centred therapist's work lacks the attributes of male dominance and seems to require the qualities more commonly associated with maternal warmth and female sensitivity. It is undoubtedly the experience of many male person-centred therapists that their female clients frequently tell them that they have never before experienced such empathic responsiveness from a man and contrast this unfavourably with the behaviour of their sexual partners or other male family members. On the other hand, this does not seem to detract from the therapist's maleness but on the contrary, in many cases, seems in the eyes of female clients to enhance it! An empathic, accepting male, it would seem, is an unusual but welcome exception to the norm.

There is something about person-centred therapy, we would suggest, which offers a radical challenge to the sexual stereotypes that are still prevalent in our society despite the challenge offered by feminism and the conscious attempts to eradicate sexism and gender discrimination. Empathic, acceptant men still seem a rare breed and there are still many women who find it difficult to express themselves confidently and congruently. What is more, we know from our own experience that there are times when as male person-centred therapists we are at pains to point out to male friends and acquaintances who are not part of the professional club that we still go to the pub, follow the football or in Mearns' case, at least, constitute a formidable presence at that ultimate male preserve: the car auction. At one level we are glad, even proud, that we can access our feelings most of the time, that we can weep when it is appropriate, that we can use language with emotional precision, that we can be tender and intimate with those who trust us. At another level, however, we can become acutely uncomfortable if we believe that we are perceived as lacking virility and unable to hold our own in a male environment. We know that if we are to be fully effective as person-centred therapists we need to be fully ourselves and that this will mean a capacity and a willingness to integrate all our attributes whatever labels conventional society may stick on them and however 'male' or 'female' we may appear to those who cannot see beyond the stereotypes.

The accusation of sentimentality usually comes from men (and sometimes women) who use the word 'sentimental' to describe feelings of which they themselves happen not to approve. There is often a moral undertone to such an accusation which may conceal a value system that attaches great importance to the suppression or eradication of feelings considered weak, unhealthy or even perverse. The person-centred therapist, by accompanying clients who are facing pain and feelings which are disturbing or even devastating, is caricatured as a sentimentalist who encourages others to wallow in self-pity to their detriment, when they could be getting on with their lives, burying their feelings and forgetting about the past. Essentially, the accusation of unmanliness and sentimentality is about the exercise of power. An approach which consciously goes about divesting the therapist of power and instead puts the control in the hands of the client is a monumental threat to all those therapists, whether men or women, who believe and want the power to help or to cure to be in their own hands and to be the result of their knowledge and expertise. What better invective to cast at the person-centred therapist than to suggest that he (or she for that matter) is behaving like a sexless hermaphrodite wallowing in a pool of inchoate emotion?

Person-centred therapy: westernised and limited?

It is somewhat puzzling that an approach which is criticised for lacking intellectual rigour and for apparently failing to honour the sacred cows of western science and the stereotypical western role models, is at the same time castigated for being *too* western and thereby limited in its applicability. Indeed, it is still common to hear the person-centred approach derided as too American, too middle-class and too focused on the articulate worried well. Such criticisms are breathtakingly obtuse when we consider that the revolutionary crux of Rogers' theory is such that it leaves room for an almost limitless extension of its application. By postulating the actualizing tendency as the *sole* motivating force for human development, and by placing absolute trust in the client's actualizing tendency if he or she can experience a relationship which provides a facilitative psychological climate, Rogers in one move refutes the accusation of being culture-limited, client-restricted or of condemning therapists to a boringly repetitive therapeutic repertoire. What is more, the remarkable work in recent years with institutionalised patients of such people as Gary Prouty and Dion Van Werde (Prouty, 1994; Van Werde, 1998) and the dedicated commitment of Ute and Johannes Binder to severely disturbed persons within the community (Binder, 1998) provide evidence enough of the culpable ignorance of those who state privately that person-centred therapy is suitable only for the neurotic American middle-class. The distressed and hospitalised citizens of Chicago, Ghent and Frankfurt-am-Main would, we suspect, have a rather different tale to tell.

The transferability of the approach across cultures raises perhaps more complex issues. Ghent and Frankfurt-am-Main are, after all, European cities and there is an acceptance even by most Americans that American roots are often in Europe. Certainly, this is the case with person-centred therapy and recent work by European practitioners has argued convincingly that Rogers' ideas, far from being alien to the European spirit, owe much to European philosophies and religious streams of thought (Schmid, 1998; Thorne, 1992, 1998a). One of us (Thorne) is even on record as suggesting that 'the person-centred approach has "come home" and that it may now be Europe's task to ensure that its revolutionary legacy is not lost to the world' (Thorne and Lambers, 1998: x).

The fact, however, that almost all of Rogers' work and much of that of the present authors has been translated into Japanese raises more intriguing questions about the transferability of the approach into specifically Asian or, for that matter, African culture. The basic postulates of the approach would appear to make its extension non-problematical: in practice, however, there are those within the person-centred community and outside it, who have raised important objections which cannot be lightly dismissed. From within the camp it is probably Len Holdstock who has most passionately argued that person-centred therapy needs to broaden its understanding of the self if it is to offer a truly global approach to human suffering and development (Holdstock, 1993, 1996a and b). He sees the approach as essentially sharing the prevailing view in the west that the self is independent and autonomous. The western emphasis on individualism and on the freedom of the individual has led, according to Holdstock, to a view of the self which can appear to be at base an egocentric, egotistical model of the person. Rogers, however, maintained that the more a person was in touch with the actualising tendency, the more it was likely that a high level of social consciousness would develop. Also, his concept of the fully functioning person points to well-developed qualities of altruism and social responsiveness. In Chapter 9 we attempt to present the mechanism of the actualising tendency as inspiring its own dialectic with the person's social world as he perceives it. The imperative of the actualising tendency must articulate with the person's social existence in order to gain access to expansive contexts for actualisation – the 'non-social' dimensions of existence offer limited orchestration for actualisation beyond mystical or transpersonal experience. Notwithstanding these implicit rebuttals, however, Holdstock and others are not convinced that the approach can so easily escape the accusation of being inherently individualistic or apolitical. When, in his later years, Rogers became much concerned with world peace, societal change was still seen as most likely to be brought about by empowering the individual. According to

Holdstock, although it is true that Rogers fully acknowledged the significance of others to and for the individual, his point of departure 'always remained the actualisation of the self as an independent unit of the social system' (Holdstock, 1996b: 399). For Holdstock, this is essentially a westernised view of the self and stands in striking contrast to the interdependent model which is characteristic of many non-western cultures. Interestingly, however, Holdstock believes that the person-centred understanding of the therapeutic relationship implicitly contains a concept of the self which is actually at odds with the notion of empowering an individuated entity. In short, the therapeutic relationship, as conceptualised by Rogers, is based on the *interdependent* nature of the self. Since this has never been fully acknowledged in the theory, there is a conceptual confusion at the heart of the approach which has a profound bearing both on clinical practice and on the philosophical and ethical acceptability of the approach to cultures where the individual is seen and conceptualised only in relation to the group and to the wider community. In such contexts, the primary task for a person is the establishing of interdependence and interconnectedness and the expression of individual autonomy is of secondary concern and could indeed entirely jeopardise the primary goal.

Holdstock and others – including the present writers – see the resolution of this apparent confusion as lying in a re-definition of what is meant by empowerment of the individual. If the human person is seen as essentially relational, in the sense that without others we cannot be fully ourselves, it follows that any notion of empowerment of the individual must by definition mean empowerment *within relationship*. It is similar thinking which has led the Austrian practitioner, Peter Schmid, to conclude that because human beings are relational and incurably social (and he maintains that, in a very un-American way for a man of his time, this is what Rogers believed from the beginning), it may well be that person-centred therapy is most logically and fundamentally group therapy, where the group is the interface between the person and the wider society. Schmid argues – and we agree with him – that being a person 'means being substantial, independent, individual and created from within, *but it also means* being relational, in relationships, created by others' (Schmid, 1996: 611). Such a concept of personhood endows the approach with at least a limited cross-cultural transferability, for it means that it can sit equally comfortably with the western notion of the independent self and with the non-western notion of the interdependent self, seeing both as running the danger of imbalance through over-emphasis on one to the detriment of the other (see Chapter 9).

Such a positive even if cautious conclusion would cut little ice with Pittu Laungani who, in 1999, launched a fierce attack on client-centred counselling and concluded, with ringing certainty, that 'any attempt to impose the client-centred therapeutic model on people from non-western cultures, particularly those from the Indian subcontinent, is doomed to failure' (Laungani, 1999: 144). So resounding a rejection of the approach from 'outside the camp' could be dismissed as based on ignorance but this, we believe, would be both complacent on our part and disrespectful to Professor Laungani. What has led him to so dogmatic and neg-ative a judgement?

The first and most potent attack is levelled at the person-centred premise of equality between client and counsellor. Laungani first argues that such equality is impossible and then goes on to claim that in Asian cultures the very idea is without meaning. Commu-nities are usually based on extended family networks where 'relationships are maintained on a hierarchical basis' (Laungani, 1999: 143). Laungani maintains that it would be difficult and probably impossible for an Indian client to imagine, let alone accept, a counselling relationship which promised equality. What is more, such a client would be expecting to look up to a counsellor as a person imbued with a special wisdom and quasi magical powers. This again would operate strongly against the idea of relating on equal terms and would also run counter to the person-centred belief that an individual has within himself or herself the necessary resources for moving out of his or her difficulties. The idea of the therapist as a facilitator or companion to the client's own journey of self-discovery would have no meaning in a culture where the guru or spiritual master is the natural authority and source of healing. Laungani's final objection to person-centred counselling is that it operates essentially at a cognitive level and on a contractual basis where clients agree to work with a counsellor on their concerns. Asian cultures, Laun-gani argues, tend to be relation-centred and not work-centred and are essentially emotional rather than cognitive. Clients therefore will look for 'a greater emotional connectedness with their ther-apists, which would allow them to express their dependency needs' (1999: 144).

What Laungani fails to recognise in these criticisms is the power of the core conditions and the spiritual dimension inherent in person-centred therapy. Indeed, in his list of 'major features underlying client-centred counselling' he fails completely to mention empathy, which is central to the practice of the approach, and puts at the top of his list the word 'secular' (1999: 142). It would appear, then, that he does not understand that person-centred therapy stands or falls on the therapist's ability to experience empathy for, and acceptance of, the client. If the therapist cannot enter the client's framework and be at home there, there is no chance that therapy will be effective. Confronted by a client who lives in a hierarchical world and who desires to be dependent, the person-centred therapist will be at pains to understand these aspects of the client's framework and to accept them even if she cannot assume the role of the hoped-for guru. Certainly the person-centred therapist will have no difficulty in offering emotional connectedness to the client – unlike practitioners of other approaches which are by definition cognitive or analytically based. Indeed, it could be argued that the non-western client's familiarity with a relating self, rather than an individualistic self, and his or her 'at homeness' with mystical and 'magical' experience makes the person-centred approach particularly appropriate. Laungani, it would seem, has little knowledge of the altered states of consciousness which characterise person-centred therapy when client and counsellor enter deeply into relationship and, in Rogers' words, simply the presence of the therapist is 'full of healing' (Rogers, 1986: 198). He has, like many other critics, bought into the notion that person-centred therapy is secular, dismissive of the spiritual and wedded to a value system which cannot tolerate dependency, hierarchy or the yearning for enlightenment. But the person-centred therapist's task is to have trust in the client's actualising tendency and to offer a relationship where the core conditions enable the client to feel understood, accepted and related to, as a real person, by a real person. There is nothing about that task which precludes cross-cultural communication and relationship. On the contrary, the emphasis on meeting the client on his or her own psychological terrain and on remaining open to the ensuing process offers, we would suggest, the possibility of a richness of encounter which can transcend cultures and provide a glimpse of a mode of relating which the world badly needs if it is to move with confidence into the new millennium.

Person-centred therapy: essentially seditious?

Carl Rogers described himself as a 'quiet revolutionary' and we find it difficult to avoid the conclusion that, as his successors, we have put on the mantle of revolutionaries without quite realising what we have done. It is difficult to acknowledge that by many we are regarded as dangerous, and that we incite fear, for like most people we crave acceptance and want to be regarded as good people. And yet the truth appears to be that we are not so regarded in many quarters. Accused of being naive, lacking depth, culturally limited, sentimental, unscientific, contemptuous of religion, egocentric and even narcissistic, we sometimes hold on with difficulty to a sense of our own worth. Yet we know from our work and from the dedicated endeavours of colleagues throughout the world that these accusations are false. We begin to recognise the legacy and the burden of following in the footsteps of an empirical scientist, a brilliant therapist and a lover of humankind who could write:

> A vast and mysterious universe – perhaps an inner reality, or perhaps a spirit world of which we are all unknowingly a part – seems to exist. Such a universe delivers a final crushing blow to our comfortable belief that we all know what the real world is. (Rogers, 1978: 8)

For the intrepid, such words engender excitement, but for the fearful they are best ignored, derided or forgotten. It is perhaps the good fortune or the unavoidable fate of person-centred therapists that the openness to experience to which they are committed makes such fearful responses impossible. And in the meantime the attacks will continue.

5 Revisiting the core conditions

Why bother to revisit?

Can there really be anything new to say about the famous 'core conditions' which characterise the effective relationship between the person-centred therapist and her client? It could well be argued that both Rogers himself and others have explored these concepts and their implementation with such thoroughness and in such detail that there is little left to discover. Recent books by Barrett-Lennard (1998) and Merry (1999) have in any case reviewed the terrain with elegant lucidity and freshness so that yet another foray could be seen as even more superfluous. Unconditional positive regard, empathy and congruence have come to be regarded as the taken-for-granted cornerstones of person-centred therapeutic practice, so well established that they can be re-polished, re-presented, illustrated with new examples but not essentially developed, deepened or challenged. Despite this unpropitious survey, we feel compelled to undertake the task for a number of different reasons. The first is undoubtedly a mounting irritation with the hi-jacking of the concepts into the mainstream of therapeutic practice, without, it would appear, any real understanding of their implications. We are increasingly weary of being told that all good therapists, whatever their tradition, offer their clients the core conditions before embarking on the *real* business of the therapeutic enterprise. Such statements clearly indicate a failure to understand the conditions as the attitudinal expression of a belief system about human nature and development, and about the healing qualities of relationship. They also fail to recognise that the relationship *is* the therapy and not a preparation for it. Another attempt to scotch such trivialising and erroneous representations of the core conditions is therefore appropriate.

A further reason for revisiting the conditions is our growing awareness that other colleagues in the British person-centred community are beginning to raise questions which merit attention. Purton has questioned the philosophical and clinical validity of unconditional positive regard as a concept outside a spiritual framework (Purton, 1998); Ellingham has suggested that congruence is a concept fashioned essentially from a Freudian perspective and therefore out of harmony with a process-oriented view of therapy (Ellingham, 1999) and Wilkins has made an impassioned plea for a more sustained and affirmative exploration of unconditional positive regard which he sees as the *essential* core condition (Wilkins, 2000). These sorties into discrete parts of the conceptual terrain again suggest that a more searching exploration of the total landscape might be justified.

The clinching motivation for revisitation, however, lies in our uneasy feeling that the core conditions have taken on separate identities which have detracted from a focused exploration of their essential connectedness. It is in their dance, their intricate interweaving, that the core conditions reveal their vitality and their potency as a healing force. There are moments when we fear that, despite our best intentions, we may ourselves have colluded with the tendency to separate them out in a devitalising way by affording each condition a separate chapter in *Person-Centred Counselling in Action* (Mearns and Thorne, 1988, 1999). As we say in that text:

> Just as empathy perfectly integrates with congruence, unconditional positive regard also takes its place as inseparable from the other two – inseparable, that is, except by writers who divide books into chapters! (1999: 63)

The therapeutic 'conditions' were originally separated out of the therapeutic 'relationship' simply to make them easier to investigate within the constraints of the dominant, 'reductionistic' research parameter of the time. The emphasis of 1950s psychology was to strive to be accepted as a 'science'. In order to achieve that status it had to emulate the accepted 'scientific' methodologies which required the separation and specification of 'variables' in such a way that their action could be followed and their effects measured. At the time, just as today within medical research, there was no tolerance for multivariate 'relational processes' such as is epitomised within the therapeutic relationship. Hence, the therapeutic relationship was broken up into 'empathy', 'unconditional positive regard' and 'congruence' and the context for the therapeutic relationship was defined by the other three 'conditions'. This division, for the purposes of research efficacy, prefaced a continuing narrowing process where, for example, the relational, process nature of empathy was lost and it came to be defined operationally in terms of empathic responses. It is the therapeutic relationship as epitomised by these denuded, reduced concepts to which practitioners of other approaches are referring when they equate the person-centred approach with their own forming of the 'therapeutic alliance' before they embark on more expansive therapeutic ventures.

In revisiting the core conditions we want to put them back together again. Only when they are all present in high degree do they unite into their mutually enhancing integration and offer the client something really special. They offer a relationship of incredible safety and vitality in which even the most feared dimensions of existence can be faced. This is what is meant by offering the client a meeting at 'relational depth' (Mearns, 1996, 1997a). Here, we are not interested in a 'partial' representation of the therapeutic relationship where the counsellor is fairly empathic, quite accepting and moderately congruent – that is offering nothing more than a tolerable 'therapeutic alliance'. Such a relationship is not going to be sufficient to encourage our client to enter the most feared closets of his Self. In reuniting the core conditions and meeting at 'relational depth', we are going back to Carl Rogers' own roots. Consider the following statement by Rogers' mentor, Jessie Taft, as she describes her *relationship therapy*:

> The reason why these experiences in relationship which I have called therapeutic, work healingly for the individual, is that there is present always in every human being underneath the fear, a powerful, more or less denied, unsatisfied impulse to abandon the ego defences and let the too solid organization of the self break up and melt away in a sense of organic union with a personality strong enough to bear it and willing to play the part of supporting whole. The therapist, who agrees to live for this limited time in the interest of the patient, who gives up temporarily the projection of personal needs and impulses in order to allow the patient to work through his own unmolested, provides an opportunity which is unique and irresistible in that it permits a realization of wholeness and security as part of a protecting supporting medium like nothing in human experience . . . (1933: 289–90)

Becoming ready to meet the other

To be with a person who is unconditionally accepting, empathically attuned and in touch with his or her own flow of experience is the gift received by the client of a person-centred therapist. But how does the therapist become a person capable of offering such a gift which has the power to comfort, to heal, to confer worth, to banish fear, to bring about transformation? The caricature of the person-centred therapist who spends most of her time nodding and repeating the last words of the client can convey nothing of the power of offering a relationship with such potentially far-reaching effects. What is more, the therapist who merely *simulates* the offering of the gift has no ultimate potency and after a while the client will find a way of escaping from a relationship which promised much but foundered on the rock of a scarcely veiled inauthenticity. For the person-centred therapist who does not embody the core conditions there can be no refuge in the exercise of skills or in the mouthing of fine feelings. It is a humiliating experience to be a person-centred therapist who cannot truly offer the core conditions but instead goes through the motions of doing so, while for the client it is an exercise in fraudulence which can deepen despair. Sadly, those who falsely conceptualise the core conditions as techniques to be deployed are perhaps the most culpable deceivers, for their shallowness leads to a prostitution of a life-enhancing gift.

It is worth remembering (as Bozarth, 1998a and Tudor and Worrall, 1999 have reminded us), that when Rogers first formulated his famous 'necessary and sufficient conditions' as applied to all helping relationships (1957a), and to client-centred therapy in particular (1959), the so-called core conditions were accompanied by three others – namely the need for psychological contact between therapist and client, the incongruence or anxiety of the client, and the experience of at least a minimal level of the therapist's acceptance and empathy by the client. The almost universal tendency of researchers to ignore the importance of the presence of all six conditions in order to be 'necessary and sufficient' has bedevilled much research and has left Rogers' hypothesis as yet not fully explored (Watson, 1984). Indeed, there is much that we need to research in relation to the therapeutic context. For example, it may be meaningful to consider the *sufficiency* of the therapeutic context (See Chapter 2 and Mearns, 1994: 9–11) as a relevant variable. The therapeutic relationship may be offering full potential, but is the *context* sufficient to encourage the client's engagement with the process? In the Wisconsin Study (Rogers et al., 1967) there is some concern that even a strong therapeutic relationship may not have been enough, because the context was not sufficient (Coulson,

1987 and see Chapter 9). Also, in Mearns' work with profoundly traumatised war veterans (1997d), the full offering of the therapeutic working was contextualised in daily therapeutic sessions within a regime which recognised that the client had to be offered a context large enough to house his fear.

This contextualisation becomes a complicating factor when we return to the question of how a therapist can become the kind of person who is capable of offering the core conditions. Clearly, to speak of 'a kind of person' is to refer to a way of being, which is not confined to a person's behaviour or philosophical stance within a particular role. In short, we are not talking about 'doing' person-centred therapy, but about what is involved in becoming the kind of person capable of undertaking the work of a person-centred therapist. This distinction is fundamental to any consideration of how a person-centred therapist becomes capable of offering the core conditions, for it extends the range of discourse, to quote Will Stillwell, to the 'broader spectrum' of the therapist's whole life (Stillwell, 1998). Stillwell has produced an interesting publication in which he provides transcripts of interviews with three seasoned practitioners from the generation following Carl Rogers, all of whom had been profoundly influenced by him. Stillwell's preconceived plan was to interview Ernest Meadows on congruence, Maria Bowen on empathy and Bob Lee on unconditional positive regard, because he viewed each of his interviewees as especially strong in the particular core condition. He carried out his intention but, revealingly, he writes in his introduction:

> It is true, in our meetings we discovered something about those core conditions. But little did I anticipate how each person had integrated Rogers' influence into the broader spectrum of his or her own life. I met them discovering themselves and the world. I met them finding wholeness in their own unique ways. I met them making sense of their own experiences, articulating a quality of separations overcome. (Stillwell, 1998: 3)

At some points in this book, notably in Chapter 9, we will suggest that Rogers' development of theory was not advanced during his 'California' period, but it is worth emphasising that the approach genuinely found its 'heart' during that time. Here we find writers, such as Stillwell and Bowen, able to describe the *quality* of relating offered by the person-centred therapist. Another writer and therapist from that period, André Auw, describes notions such as 'heart listening' in his beautiful book, *Gentle Roads to Survival* (Auw, 1991).

All these writers, as well as ourselves, contend that being capable of offering the core conditions is not a matter of how to do therapy but of how we are as a human being. This is profoundly unwelcome news for those who would prefer to practise a craft within the circumscribed hours and the fixed location of the therapeutic enterprise. The thought of 'switching on and off' the core conditions during specific hours is to make a travesty of what is essentially a response of the heart and head to human relating. The therapeutic conditions constitute a dimension of the person who is the therapist – this is the only way in which congruence can be fully achieved. The therapist is literally using her Self, which embodies the propensity to offer the therapeutic conditions. Only in the light of such an understanding does it make sense to consider the question of the person-centred therapist's formation and development. If I am to become this kind of person-centred therapist my empathy, unconditional positive regard and congruence need to come from within *me* – this way of being needs to become an integral part of *me*, not something which is contingent upon my client and a happy fit between us. It does not matter who my client is – I am always able to offer the therapeutic conditions. To become ready to meet the other, whoever they may be, means that I must become able to meet myself, whoever I am. Our question about the therapist's development is now reformulated: what enables (and what hinders) a person-centred therapist's quest for an ever deeper self-acceptance, an increasingly accurate empathic responsiveness to self and an in-touchness with the flow of experience which is uncontaminated by anxiety and defensiveness?

The struggle for self-acceptance

Those who seek the help of therapists have often been badly damaged by their experience of life. They may be acutely anxious or depressed and, almost certainly, their trust in other people will have been shaken and perhaps profoundly undermined. They are unlikely to be easy to relate to and they will not readily respond to an invitation to closeness. For the therapist there is every likelihood that the path to intimacy will be strewn with obstacles and hedged around with suspicion. The prospect of failure looms large and the therapist who is hooked into the need for success is on perilous ground. It can justifiably be argued, indeed, that the therapist requires a level of self-acceptance which will continue to sustain her at those times when a client attacks her – perhaps viciously – or abandons the relationship in anger or despair. What is more, the person-centred therapist can have little recourse to theoretical constructs or elaborate explanations of unconscious processes in order to maintain a sense of self-worth by pathologising or otherwise objectifying the client. It is of the essence of person-centred therapy that person meets person and there can be no protection from the rawness of encounter. It is because of this that the therapist's level of self-acceptance needs to be sufficiently robust to withstand the pain of relating to those who may prove to be aggressive, demeaning or even contemptuous and hostile.

Person-centred therapists may have a variety of ways of fostering and nurturing their self-acceptance. Mearns (1997a) provides an exploration of the ways in which a training course may create opportunities for the offering of 'support' and 'challenge' within open structures that can be used flexibly by the participants. That flexibility is important because the personal 'agenda' of each participant will be different. Of course, the participant on a training course soon discovers that the self-acceptance curriculum extends to his Self outside the course – it is not possible to compartmentalise self-acceptance. Inevitably, the person begins to challenge herself in other life settings and relationships and in that way takes ever more responsibility for his Self – a major step in the struggle for self-acceptance.

Having begun to culture their self-acceptance, therapists will attend to its maintenance in different ways such as those which are presented in the 'Being open to myself' illustrations at the end of this chapter. But, before that, we must consider one of the most difficult barriers both to the development of self-acceptance and also to the offering of the core conditions – guilt.

Guilt

The therapist who is burdened with guilt feelings cannot offer the core conditions because such feelings inevitably lead to self-preoccupation. There is a lack of self-acceptance, an inability to enter the other's world and a fear of the flow of experience because it may induce the intolerable pain of self-recrimination.

Guilt feelings are the arch-enemies of the core conditions and, as such, they warrant the most serious exploration and demand radical measures to ensure their domestication and, where appropriate, their elimination.

Inappropriate guilt feelings, while tiresome and the source of much pain, are conceptually a relatively easy target for the person-centred therapist. We are only too familiar with the havoc wrought by conditions of worth imposed by others so that we feel bad or inadequate because we have failed to come up to someone else's expectations. The tendency to run our lives in accordance with the need for positive regard from others is almost universal and is, indeed, a central postulate of the person-centred approach. But we know – if we are therapists with a modicum of self-awareness – when such a process is occurring. We know that we feel guilty because we have failed to satisfy the standards imposed by others whose approval we crave and, if we are determined enough, we can come to terms with a guilt which has its origin in a dread of rejection or condemnation. In this sense, such guilt feelings do not truly belong to us but spring from our fear of the judgement of others: they are literally inappropriate.

There is, however, another form of guilt which presents a much stiffer challenge and for the person-centred therapist it constitutes the major stumbling block to deep self-acceptance. There are those occasions when we are conscious not of having failed someone else or of having fallen short of externally imposed standards, but of *self-betrayal*, of having let ourselves down. This is a guilt which springs from the depth of our own being; it is appropriate because it belongs to us and we know that we have failed to be true to the meaning of our own lives. It is not a question of shaking ourselves free from the judgement of others but of coming to terms with shame, the sense of wretchedness at having so singularly failed to be the persons we have it within us to be.

The capacity to be *self-forgiving* in this profound sense represents a degree of self-acceptance which is of a different order from the resilience which can resist the adverse judgement of others; it comes from a conviction that, despite our imperfections and our inevitable self-betrayals, we remain a human being worthy of respect. This sense of enduring existential worth is not won overnight, nor is it usually so deeply internalised as to be invulnerable. For us, however, its centrality for the person-centred therapist cannot be over-emphasised and its development is a personal and professional imperative. Again, there will be many ways of developing and maintaining that sense of enduring existential worth and it is not our place to dictate the process and methods. As we characterised by means of our own differences in Chapter 3, for some this might mean a commitment to a spiritual path and for others it may be a thoroughly secular endeavour. For some it might be supported at every point by close, 'unconditional' relationships and for others it may be an experience characterised by solitude. There are many paths.

Empathic responsiveness

Empathy requires effort because it involves understanding and yet it is a natural response for the person who experiences the essential worth of his or her own being. Acceptance and empathy are partners. If I am of essential worth, then clearly I warrant understanding and the same must be true of the other. It is a logical and experiential impossibility to value someone deeply and then to withhold understanding and compassion. That is why it is often so difficult to differentiate between acceptant and empathic responses in the course of a therapeutic encounter; they come from the same source of essential valuing and as such are often indistinguishable. Maria Bowen, in her interview with Will Stillwell, goes even further and bears witness to the absolute centrality of the relationship with the Self to the therapist's response to the other.

> Empathy is something someone is – their presence – not what they do. Being in deep empathy requires a therapist to be committed to her own inner journey and experiential self-awareness. Because empathy emerges from our relationship with our own unwilling spirit. Entering the world of the other person, you're setting aside the boundaries, soul touching soul, being one with the other person. (Stillwell, 1998: 30)

An unwillingness to empathise is, we suggest, a lack of faith in the constancy of unconditional acceptance whether of the Self or of others. Defensiveness, which is usually manifested in a refusal to take on board new insights or new evidence, has its origin in the fear that something will be revealed which will prove insupportable. If I acknowledge this about myself or if I dare to face that in you, all will be lost because I shall no longer be able to love and accept myself or I shall lose my respect for you or I shall be unable to bear your self-denigration.

To be empathic is to take the risk that acceptance and compassion will remain constant and unshaken no matter how deep and revelatory the understanding. To refuse to empathise is to capitulate to the fear that understanding will lead to discomfort or, in the worse instances, to contempt or even hatred.

The therapist is nourished by her willingness to offer herself compassionate empathy, but this is not easy if she suspects that dark forces are lurking below the surface of awareness. The courage to be empathically disposed to Self springs from a preparedness to face the worst in the sure knowledge that the sense of worth will survive the process. The impediments to empathy whether for Self or others are formidable because they are fuelled by the terror of the unknown and by the nightmarish doubt about what lies at the heart of things. If, at the core of being, there is a creative, loving and positive force, then it makes absolute sense to pursue the path of empathic and compassionate responsiveness no matter what the cost. If, on the other hand, there is only cold indifference or, worse, a malign destructiveness, then empathic responsiveness is no more than impotent folly and unawareness a wise and stubborn refusal to face existential horror. There is, of course, a third and heroic possibility – that we ourselves have the power to co-create the cosmos and that at the heart of being there is a yearning and a longing for us to recognise the glory of our own natures and to accept the responsibility of co-creation. Whatever our existential stance, there is no doubt that intermittent empathy is of all responses the most confusing.

Confusion ·is perhaps the most seriously underrated of the states of mind by which we and our clients are regularly beset. 'I am confused', can sound anaemic, insignificant when compared with, 'I am anxious' or 'I am depressed' or 'I am in despair'. Yet confusion often points to a profound anguish about the nature of one's identity and the meaning of existence. When I am empathically and compassionately disposed towards myself, the mists of uncertainty begin to clear and I experience my worthwhileness and glimpse the joy of being alive, but when I withdraw from such tenderness towards myself, the darkness can quickly close in and I lose all sense of my value and place in the order of things. The same is true of our clients. To be understood and to feel accepted as one is is to experience the possibility of a world where it is possible to breathe without fear. Should such empathy be withdrawn, however – not through the therapist's clumsiness because the *desire* to empathise will suffice in the short-term, but because of the therapist's lack of will or failure to continue valuing the client – the impact can be devastating. To feel valued, understood and accompanied one week and to feel the empathy withdrawn the next, is to be plunged into confusion which will rapidly be augmented by memories of all manner of annihilating inconstancy in the past. Intermittent empathy is not only cruel but potentially lethal. That is why the person-centred therapist who can no longer be empathically disposed towards herself must quickly attend to her own lack of compassionate self-regard if she is to avoid engendering in her clients a confusion which may be the precursor of despair.

What does it mean to be congruent?

There is undoubtedly some unhappiness among the international community of person-centred theorists at the present time about the precise meaning of congruence. Barbara Brodley has concluded that in Rogers' own writings the meaning 'remains somewhat ambiguous' (Brodley, 1998: 83) and Len Holdstock, with his usual concern for cross-cultural compatibility, considers the concept to be 'in urgent need of attention' (Holdstock, 1996a: 48). In Britain, Ivan Ellingham draws attention to Brodley's and Holdstock's concerns and then goes on to launch a powerful attack on the concept as being dependent on a Freudian notion of the unconscious and therefore ill-suited to an 'organismic' view of the world. Ellingham argues that the Freudian unconscious belongs to the Cartesian-Newtonian paradigm and that the concept of congruence is therefore particularly in need of reconstruction or should perhaps be discarded altogether (Ellingham, 1999).

While appreciating the concerns of these writers, we are not convinced that, in practice, they present serious difficulties for the actual living out of what we term relational congruence. Rogers himself placed the emphasis on the therapist's openness to inner experiencing and on his or her willingness to be as aware as possible of that experiencing, to be the feelings and attitudes which are currently flowing within and to give expression to them when appropriate. It can, of course, be argued that awareness may be limited and that the therapist's congruence is therefore imperfect and, in this sense, lacks a meaningful authenticity. This, however, seems to us to miss the point. The Freudian paradigm, whatever else it implies, does not for one moment suggest that the unconscious can ever be made fully conscious. Even the most effectively analysed Freudian analyst still has to endure the fact that most of his or her psychic life remains hidden in the unconscious. What matters for the person-centred practitioner is the disciplined and dedicated intentionality to be as open as possible to inner experience, not to deny or distort it – in this sense to be as wholly present to the other as is consciously possible. There is then the further challenge of how to give expression to what is being thought, felt or physically experienced in such a way that the relationship is served and enhanced rather than obstructed or impaired. It goes without saying that such communication often demands the utmost sensitivity and exceptional skills of discrimination. Once we place the emphasis, however, on intentionality and on a resolute preparedness to face inner experiencing and to communicate it in the service of the relationship and not otherwise, it becomes quickly apparent that to be congruent requires a commitment of the therapist's will and a psychological fearlessness which exceed the determination and the courage implicit in the offering of the other two core conditions. For this reason alone we find ourselves in agreement with Watson who observed many years ago that 'congruence on the part of the therapist is a precondition for the therapist's experience of unconditional positive regard and empathy toward the client' (Watson, 1984: 19).

Being open to our self

The will and the fearlessness required in the quest to be open to inner experience are starkly revealed in solitude, for it is only too tempting to 'shut off' or to 'close down' when no other person is present to incite reflection or to provoke inner turbulence.

This is not to suggest that the person-centred therapist must be forever straining and striving to capture the flow of inner experience and can never relax into a novel, a TV 'soap' or the bliss of mental oblivion. Without such respites, the engagement with inner experience can quickly lead to cognitive and emotional overload or, in the worst instances, to breakdown or psychosis. Indeed, it could be argued that a commitment to congruence requires precisely such respites and that they should be jealously planned and protected. What is at issue is the therapist's commitment to ensuring that he or she does not run away from thoughts, feelings or physical sensations which arouse confusion, excitement, anxiety or the fear of stumbling on unwelcome discoveries about one's way of being in the world. For the person-centred therapist, it is not an option to push away inner experiences of this kind as if they had never occurred or to seek the 'quiet life'. On the contrary, it is the therapist's responsibility to explore such experiences and to bring them to the light of day. If this sounds like dragging something from the unconscious into consciousness, we would prefer a different conceptualisation. For us, it is trusting the process of self-discovery once the will and the intentionality to do so are fully established. Processes do not take place automatically, they need our connivance and co-operation. How we choose our mode of seeking must be our decision, but there is certainly no lack of possibilities. In solitude we may pray or meditate or write our personal journals, or engage with our dream life, or practise 'focusing', or go for long walks and breathe a more friendly air. Sometimes solitude provides no way forward and we need our supervisor, or therapist, or priest, or trusted friend or support group. What we cannot do, is pretend we have not glimpsed, heard or felt the promptings of the actualising tendency which sometimes provides such strange evidence of its essential benignity.

Each person will have different ways of being open to their Self. Our task as person-centred writers is not to pronounce on such ways – probably they need to be as varied as we are as people. Perhaps what we can offer is an insight into our own very different ways (see below)

Being open to my Self (Brian)

One morning, when I was feeling particularly unlovable because of other events in my life, I received a letter whose content was unexpectedly and powerfully hostile and critical. My first impulse was to push the letter and its contents away together with the incipient feelings which it engendered. There was too much going on to permit the experience of the letter and its reception to enter fully into awareness. I took the decision to close the door to the experience and its implications. In the days that followed, however, I began to be alarmingly aware of a dramatic loss of self-confidence and a creeping sense of incompetence and worthlessness. What is more, my day-to-day work with clients became increasingly difficult because empathic responsiveness was only achieved at the cost of immense effort and in the face of a desire to run away. And then the feelings and thoughts about the letter surged back into awareness and refused to go away. The letter had to be read and re-read and the thoughts and feelings which it engendered entered into and faced in their immensity. For a time it seemed as if I would drown in self-doubt which often tipped over into self-disgust and clients had to be judiciously rearranged to prevent complete dysfunction. Then, as if in response to some psychic call for help, friends who had in some cases not been in touch for years, phoned with loving messages or wrote to express gratitude for companionship in the past. A close friend listened generously to the bare outline of my anguish and my supervisor expressed unusual apprecia- tion and regard. Most importantly of all, I threw myself into the arms of God and spent many hours at the shrine of Lady Julian of Norwich. Gradually a sense of stability returned and it was possible once more to experience a resurgence of self- acceptance and to find empathic responsiveness no longer a task of almost insuperable difficulty. Openness to my Self in this instance had proved costly in the extreme but it was only when the turbulence and complexity of the inner experiencing had been faced and not denied that it became possible once more to offer the two core conditions to myself and subse- quently to others. This powerful and probably life-changing episode not only demonstrated the primacy of openness to Self for the person-centred therapist's way of being, but also provided further evidence – if such were needed – of the essential interconnectedness of the core conditions and how together they constitute a model of relating to the Self and to others whose apparent simplicity conceals inexhaustible riches.

Being open to my Self (Dave)

When I have difficulty in being open to my Self I am usually moving too *fast*. That speed can be highly productive but it also runs the risk of becoming detached from my experiencing of my Self. Generally, the first thing I lose is my feeling of connectedness with people and I am sure that comes across to them. I generally function better in therapy relationships because the pace is slow enough for me to catch up with my feelings. My Self becomes available to me as a 'touchstone' – one that willingly resonates with my client's experiencing, whatever that may be. In therapy I use my Self in all its aspects.

My metaphor for my Self is of a huge track of countryside with villages, hamlets, isolated cottages, forests, hills, hollows, roads, lanes, paths, wild parts, rivers, pools, heather, grass and of course some rather 'boggy' areas. I cannot always achieve it but, in principle, I am willing to enter any area if it will help me meet my client. My experience of the existence of my client at any moment can usually achieve at least a degree of resonance if I enter some part of my Self. I even have a dark forest I can go to when I need to feel the same lack of illumination as my client. And at times I need to put on my gum boots to enter one of my bogs.

This way of using my Self in work with others inevitably involves attending to the question of 'maintenance and repair'. Some places become worn through constant use and there is always the problem of vandalism. That vandalism is rarely wilful – it is generally a function of the client's need to abuse and my willingness to be abused. (I am perhaps unusual, or at least archaic, in that, as a person-centred therapist, I am willing to be abused by my client – and to work with the process.) But any area can suffer pain and I need to be aware of that lest the damage becomes malignant and areas begin to erect 'no entry' signs.

It is interesting to me that maintaining my access to all these parts of my Self is a largely solitary activity. I like spending time, even long periods of time, on my own, with different parts of my Self in various activities from writing to walking to living in the wilderness. (I relate this propensity for solitude to my experience as an 'only child'.) Yet, while this solitude can be good for touching depths, there are times when urgent remedial action is needed and it is here that I find resonance with Brian's reliance on the love of others – indeed I have used Brian in that way more than once.

Conclusion

The debate about the necessity and sufficiency of Rogers' six conditions will probably never be resolved because it is difficult to see how a convincing research design could ever be devised to test the complete package. Clearly, however, the conditions are not always *necessary* because there is ample evidence that 'therapeutic movement' can take place without them, a chance meeting with a far from empathic stranger in a train has been known to change a life in a positive direction as has the reading of a powerful novel. What does seem likely, however, is that the presence of the core conditions and their recognition at some level by the client is *sufficient* in most cases to provide a powerful context for positive development. This revisiting of the core conditions has perhaps supplied the key as to why this should be so, for it has demonstrated again not only the elegance of the conceptual map, but also the implications for the emergence of human personhood.

The therapist who is capable of deep self-acceptance, of a compassionate, empathic responsiveness to self and of a determined openness to inner experience is on the road, we believe, to becoming the kind of person we all have it within us to be. In the company of such a person those who are hurt and wounded, or have succumbed to annihilating self-contempt, may find it possible to access their Self more fully and find new hope. To revisit the core conditions is to discover again the power of the transformative dance which in harmony they present and to wonder at the mysterious but profound simplicity of their conceptualisation. It is sometimes difficult to avoid the suspicion that when in 1957, and again in 1959, Carl Rogers formulated his famous statement, he knew only too well that he was not only presenting a clinical hypothesis but throwing down a gauntlet with profound existential implications for the living of a human life. Either that or he had a mischievous and provocative sense of humour.

6 The nature of 'configurations' within self

Introducing 'configurations'

Jim's guardian

The client, Jim, starts his second therapy session with a statement about what had happened for him during and after the previous session:

> Jim: In the last session . . . you got behind the part of me that was meant to 'deal' with you. That part of me is my 'Guardian'. His job is not to let people *in*. I am very clever at not letting people in – I can even make people think that they *have* got in . . . like my wife.
>
> But last week, I let you in – I let you in to the inside of me. For a time you met the parts that make me up. I don't know if they were coherent to an outsider – they had never talked to anyone outside before. I mean, they are all involved, as parts of me, with other people, but only through the Guardian. One of them is my 'Bastard'. He is very angry and comes up with all sorts of denigrations of people. But the Guardian doesn't let them out – he instructs a warm smile instead. My Bastard was in there when you came in and he didn't want to kill you – he was happy you had come in, though he was scared. My 'sad and lonely part' was there too – maybe that was the part you touched . . . he still feels 'touched'. You met parts of me that only have life inside my head.
>
> I have been in turmoil all week – switching back and forward. I had to force myself not to cancel this session. My Guardian said 'cancel' but he was outvoted. I have been feeling and behaving like a little boy – excited and scared – the parts inside have been coming out more. My Guardian knows that this is dangerous.

Although Jim sounds at ease with talking about 'parts' of his Self, he had only named these parts in the week between the first and second therapy session. In that first session the therapist had met Jim, fully, at relational depth. In her notes she had written:

> Jim had a brusque exterior but he was also very vulnerable. I felt that I could meet his vulnerability very fully – the result was that we got to depth very quickly and stayed there for most of this first session.

Feeling met at considerable relational depth (Mearns, 1996, 1997a), Jim gave his therapist invited access into his existential Self. In that state, the client offers his innermost feelings and thoughts about his Self and his very existence. He is not giving a false picture layered with conscious defences and pretences – he is including the therapist in the inner-dialogue he has with himself. More than that, he is including the therapist in the moment to moment discoveries he is making about his Self while he is at the very 'edge of his awareness' (Gendlin, 1981, 1984, 1996).

When walking around inside their existential Self, clients some-times talk about different 'parts' of the Self. From this internal perspective the Self is not a diffuse conglomerate but a myriad structure of interacting components. If we were to view molecules of matter externally, they too would look like a conglomerate, but if we could examine the structure of the molecule from an inside perspective we would, similarly, see a myriad of interacting aspects.

While clients often use the simple word 'parts' to describe dimensions of their Self, for our own understanding we use the term 'configuration' instead of 'part' because each 'part' is itself made up of a number of elements which form a coherent pattern generally reflective of a dimension of existence within the Self. This leads us to an initial working definition for 'configuration':

> A 'configuration' is a hypothetical construct denoting a coherent pattern of feelings, thoughts and preferred behavioural responses symbolised or pre-symbolised by the person as reflective of a dimen-sion of existence within the Self.

Some people are easily familiar with configurations within their Self. These are parts which previously have been symbolised and their presentation in therapy, initially at least, takes on the appear-ance of what Carl Rogers called 'rehearsed material' (Rogers, 1977). Indeed, before the client has experienced meeting the therapist at relational depth, he may present particular 'parts' of himself which 'fit' that more superficial social exchange. This ability reflects our sophisticated skills of social exchange. However, as relational depth is established, such 'social portrayal' gives way and the client feels safer to explore the edges of his awareness of his Self. The therapist is offering a unique opportunity – a person who is willing and able to relate at depth with *all* the parts of the client.

Within the definition of 'configuration' we use the term 'symbolised or pre-symbolised by the person'. This position is distinctively person-centred. We are working, equally with the client, on material which is either already in his awareness or in the process of coming into awareness (see Chapter 7). We are making no pretence of working with so-called 'unconscious material'. An important discipline of the person-centred approach is to work at the level of the client's current symbolisation so that the client is at the centre of the endeavour. In any case, the notion of working with the client's 'unconscious material', while it carries great attraction for therapists who need to feel sophisticated, is somewhat illusory (see Chapter 9).

The term 'hypothetical construct' is properly used in the definition to remind us that these 'parts' of the Self cannot be directly observed as entities – they can only be *inferred* from the descriptions given by the person.

As clients become able to refine their symbolisation of configurations, they ascribe descriptive or metaphorical terms to denote them. Jim described his 'Guardian', his 'Bastard' and his 'sad and lonely part'. Sometimes the names which clients give to configurations are very common, like 'my little girl', 'my afraid part', or 'the wild me'. Person-centred therapists need to be careful to remember that although people may use the same or similar labels for configurations, each configuration of every person is unique. We cannot make any assumptions about our clients' configurations – we have to hear it from them, bit by bit, and work within their symbolisation rather than our own. Chapter 7 will say much more on 'staying close to the client's symbolisation'.

At other times the labels given by our client to configurations are unique, like 'my "Last Resort" me', 'my Don Quixote', ' "frightening her" inside', 'the Princess Bitch' and 'the convict'. It is often easier for person-centred therapists to work with idiosyncratic labels such as these because they have to listen carefully to the meaning the client gives to them rather than make assumptions based upon other clients.

The Self is a composite of its various configurations coexisting in a creative and self-protective conflict. Sometimes the combination of the configurations gives us a fairly simple gestalt, at least at that level of experiencing. For example, the client Jan described her Self:

> I am a . . . 'nothing'. I don't have views on anything; I can't sustain any relationship; I am neither happy nor sad about my life; I am neither strong nor weak . . . I am a nothing.

Jan was the kind of client who cancelled herself out. Sometimes the new therapist finds it difficult to work with this kind of client because there is nothing 'to hold on to'. The reality is that what can be held on to are the different parts of the client which are functionally cancelling each other out. As it transpired, one configuration within Jan tended to be positive and 'approaching' in relation to life events and the other was the opposite, negative and 'avoiding'. The task of the therapist was to hear the individual voices of the parts and not simply the zero sum message of the combination. It is interesting to analyse therapy tapes to find the times when the person-centred therapist has reflected the summative message and missed the separate parts. This is examined in Chapter 7.

At other times we are aware of the client's Self comprising a large number of configurations forming a highly complex gestalt. This is a proverbial 'army' of parts, or perhaps a better metaphor is that this is a complex 'family' of parts, as in the client Derek.

Derek was a successful business man and, in his own words, a 'disaster' in his social living. He eventually identified a number of different 'parts' of his Self including: 'clever me', 'bully me', 'lost little boy', 'me who knows what is right', 'me who has to destroy', and 'me who has to be protected'. In the various aspects of his life a different mix of the configurations would predominate with, for example, 'clever me' and also 'bully me' playing a big part in his working life while 'lost little boy' and 'me who has to destroy' were dominant in his life with his partner. In the therapy relationship, on the other hand, the three most obvious configurations early on were: 'lost little boy', 'me who knows what is right', and 'me who needs to be protected'. For some time the therapy appeared to proceed meaningfully but, not surprisingly, it impacted little upon his working life and only marginally upon his relationship with his partner. When that apparent paradox came to light in the therapy the door opened for the other, previously absent, configurations. The resulting work bore a strong resemblance to person-centred family therapy (O'Leary, 1999) with the therapist engaging fully with each configuration and assisting in the communication between and among the configurations.

While the term 'configurations' may be new, the phenomenon it describes is not. Workers from a wide array of therapeutic approaches have theorised on different 'parts' of the Self or of the personality. In object relations theory there is an emphasis on the introjection of significant others (Fairbairn, 1952); however, the object relations conceptualisation is reputed to be of more static and unchangeable images (Hermans et al., 1993). Probably the strongest parallel must be made with 'ego states' within Transactional Analysis (TA) (Berne, 1961), where the whole therapeutic approach is built on working with three parts of the Self and their subdivisions. Those who doubt the veracity of 'parts' within the Self would have difficulty with TA, which assumes that we *all* have the same major components. The notion of pluralism as a dimension of a normal person's adjustment to society has been argued by many philosophers and clinicians including Bearhrs (1982) and especially by Gergen (1972, 1988, 1991). Particularly important is the work on 'voices' reviewed by Hermans (1996) and advanced by Honos-Webb and Stiles (1998). 'Voices' are not just facets of the Self but are integrities of their own, within the Self. This is well described in the most important paper 'The dialogical self': '. . . we conceptualise the Self in terms of a dynamic multiplicity of relatively autonomous "I" positions in an imaginal landscape' (Hermans et al., 1992: 28). And, further:

> The 'I' has the possibility to move, as in a space, from one position to the other in accordance with changes in situation and time. The *I* fluctuates among different and even opposed positions. The *I* has the capacity to imaginatively endow each position with a voice so that dialogical relations between positions can be established. The voices function like interacting characters in a story. (1992: 28)

At first sight, Jung's complexes may seem similar to the notion of configurations: 'the complex forms, so to speak, a miniature self-contained psyche which, as experience shows, develops a peculiar fantasy life of its own' (Jung, 1970: 56). But closer examination reveals Jung's concept more as a hypothetical construct describing presumed unconscious processes, with much less conscious access and a lesser degree of personification than configurations. 'As a rule there is a marked unconsciousness of any complexes . . .'

(Jung, 1960: 98). Indeed, Jung's complex bears closer resemblance to elemental 'parts' within 'dissociated process' (Warner, 1998 and Chapter 8). Jung acknowledges that similarity and regards the aetiology of a complex as associated with trauma: 'The aetiology of their origin is frequently a so-called trauma, an emotional shock or some such thing, that splits off a bit of the psyche' (Jung, 1960: 98). We would not suppose any particular link between trauma and the formation of configurations, which we see as a 'normal' process of housing different and even dissonant dimensions of Self. Yet, perhaps Jung's 'complex' is not so far away, because he goes on to say, 'Certainly one of the commonest causes [of the formation of a complex] is a moral conflict, which ultimately derives from the apparent impossibility of affirming the whole of one's nature' (1960: 98).

John Rowan uses the term 'subpersonalities' to denote parts or configurations, and similarly emphasises that each subpersonality is itself a constellation of elements and dynamics (Rowan, 1990; Rowan and Cooper, 1999). John Rowan's 'subpersonality' may be more fully formed and autonomous than our notion of 'configuration' but we, like other therapists (Brown, 1979; Keil, 1996; Schwartz, 1987, 1997; Schwartz and Goulding, 1995) are clearly working with similar phenomena, albeit from very different therapeutic approaches. Relevant work has been done by Schwartz (1997) who came from the other direction in applying his concepts as a family therapist to work with individuals. However, a major difference is that Schwartz has, in recent years, come to emphasise a 'core' or 'real' Self among the 'parts'. In our current work on 'configurations' we have not yet found the need to hypothesise a 'governing' configuration, though that will certainly be the experience of some clients. This issue of governance within the family of configurations may prove to be an artefact of social or cultural influence. In Chapter 7, we emphasise the considerable vulnerability of clients to the therapist's influence while they are in the process of initially symbolising configurations. If the therapist has particular expectations as to the nature and dynamics of configurations it is likely that the vulnerable client will accommodate his symbolisation to that frame. In that way, practitioners who expect to find a 'governing' configuration may create it by their suggestive working. Perhaps the source of social influence is wider than simply the therapist – the values and philosophy within the client's social milieu may be the formative influence. Hence, a client living within a 'modernist' context might well symbolise a 'governing' configuration while our 'postmodern' client might not (see Rappoport et al., 1999, for an interesting discussion of pluralism and postmodern culture).

A key contribution has been offered by Mick Cooper (1999), who articulates the possibility of linking a plurality of selves with person-centred thinking. For example, he cites Rogers' observation of 'violent fluctuations in the concept of the self' (Rogers, 1959: 201) and offers a pluralist analysis:

> Such 'violent fluctuations' in the concept of self suggests that the theory of a single self-concept which filters out aspects of the experiencing-organism's lived-world propounded by Rogers (1951, 1959) would appear to be somewhat unidimensional. Rather, what these experiences seem to suggest is that the individual may have the possibility of accessing – and switching between – a *plurality* of qualitatively distinctive self-concepts, each of which may filter out aspects of the individual's lived world in qualitatively distinctive ways. (Cooper, 1999: 58–9)

Cooper also suggests that a pluralist conception of Self fits neatly with Rogers' theory of development where the child's paramount need for positive regard is recognised. As a means of maximising the receipt of positive regard from different sources, Cooper suggests:

> . . . the individual may then go on to develop a plurality of self-concepts: that is, a different self to maximise positive self-regard in relation to each social grouping – self-sacrificial in intimate relationships, self-assertive in the classroom, etc. (1999: 64)

Cooper offers a combination of acute observation and coherent academic analysis in his interweaving of plurality with person-centred theory. We fully embrace his contribution when we offer an integration of 'configurations' into Rogers' theory of personality later in this chapter.

As well as finding a convergence with the thinking of Cooper we have been excited by the dovetailing of our own work with that of Margaret Warner of the Chicago Counseling Center. Coming from different directions, we find a resonance both in our observations and in the ways of working which we have derived. In discussing 'dissociated process', Margaret describes the 'parts' within the client's Self. In her work she is relating with clients who may have experienced traumatic childhood abuse. In that circumstance the creation of 'parts' within the Self serves the same adaptive function as outlined in our own theory, but the 'protective' function can lead to some of the 'parts' becoming dissociated from each other to the extent that there is a loss of awareness between parts. Margaret describes her work more fully in her guest contribution to this book (Chapter 8).

It is important to note that while the notion of 'configurations' within the Self may bear some similarities with dissociated process, it is not on a continuum with dissociative identity disorder (DID), formerly known as multiple personality disorder. In considering Self in regard to 'configurations', we are embracing 'normal' dimensions of personality integration. In this we are in agreement with Ross (1999) in his view that pluralism within the Self is not on a 'dissociative continuum' with DID. Even in extreme cases of pluralism there are qualitative as well as quantitative differences with DID. In DID there is a qualitative difference in the *personification* of the parts – the parts may even have 'people' names rather than descriptive titles which is more common in configurations. Also, there is a much more profound *separateness* between the parts – as Ross says, there is a 'literal' separateness in DID, as though they are really different people. In 'normal' pluralism within the Self the owner knows that the parts are merely different dimensions of his Self. Another difference is in the degree of 'information blockage' (Ross, 1999: 193) in the system – as Margaret Warner illustrates in Chapter 8, some 'parts' in DID may even be unaware of others.

Perhaps one of the difficulties in exploring pluralism within the Self is the fear that it might be associated with DID, as one client observed, 'I have a proverbial "family" of different parts to myself. But I was always scared to talk about them in case I was thought of as crazy.'

Configurations which are established around introjects

The notion of 'introjection' began in psychoanalytic theory and has been received as common wisdom by every therapeutic discipline, particularly the person-centred approach. Within person-centred theory, an introject is an evaluation taken in from the outside and symbolised as defining a dimension of the Self. Perhaps because they are not borne of our own experiences in the world, but appear mysteriously in our psyche, introjects carry considerable power. They not only help to define the Self or a part of the Self but they serve to protect that part within its definition. Although the introject did not begin its life with the same amount of substance as those configurations which are derived from the person's actual experience of himself in the world, it will have accumulated its own supporting evidence through the 'self-fulfilling prophecy' effect, as described by one client: 'because I had swallowed the view that I was *unattractive* I behaved as *unattractive* – I even dressed as *unattractive* – in fact, I did an honours degree in *unattractive* by the time I was 20'.

In most cases, introjects will depict a positive, socialised image of the person. For example:

- I try hard at things.
- I am a warm, friendly person.
- I am pretty able.
- I am good at sports.
- I am my 'own boss'.

We may be happy for the support of such introjects in our life although there may be times when their experience is constraining. It can be a hard 'cross' to bear to have to 'try hard at things' or to be 'a warm, friendly person'.

Sometimes introjects are 'positive' but force the individual into an extreme and somewhat unreal position. For example:

- I am the best.
- Failure is not a possibility.
- I am a 'princess'.

Configurations built around introjects such as these carry an unreal quality – they resemble 'fairy tales'. The person has a part of their Self which carries a fairy-tale image and message: the 'princess' who must always be perfect, 'Cinderella' who could be wonderful if only she could find her 'prince', or the boy who could be the 'comic strip hero' if only he could do better than he can. The 'fairy-tale' configuration is prominent for some clients as they enter therapy. Indeed, they may enter therapy in search of perfection – as a means to achieve the narrative promised in the fairy tale: 'I *should* be a person who can carry it all – I *should* be able to be the "perfect" wife, mother and professional person'. Unfortunately, or is it fortunately, a successful therapeutic process more often results in a loss of the fairy tale and a colder reality: 'I *can't* be perfect and the more I try to be perfect the more I push others away from me'.

Other introjects are unequivocally negative in the message they carry about Self. They define and protect a negative, abused, or otherwise damaged self-concept from change or even the threat of change:

- I am a failure.
- I am worthless.
- I am dangerous to others.
- I am evil.

One of the coldest ironies of human existence is that the human being may choose continued negativity over the instability of possible change. This can only be properly understood phenomenologically. Perhaps the client, Jane, can offer one such phenomenological perspective.

'Cheating to fail'

> Jane: I can't remember a time before I was a 'failure' but I have come to recall the repeated messages to the effect that I was expected to fail at anything which was important. At school I didn't dare to succeed and even when I did it was a 'flash in the pan'. I actually remember 'cheating' in an exam in order to fail. It seems incredible to look back on it – now it makes me cry with anger. I was romping through the multiple-choice exam at a merry pace – I had quite forgotten that I was a 'failure'. When I realised that I was nearly finished and had found it easy I came out in a cold sweat of fear. I began to 'hear' the announcement of my good performance, the acclaim, the sarcastic comments of my father, the pressure to repeat the success and the inevitable later failure – so I changed a lot of my 'right' answers.

Although the damage created by such negative introjects can be considerable and enduring, they do not necessarily contaminate the whole Self. Other parts, predating the introject, may survive to reflect a different narrative. Indeed, new parts may be laid down even though they are inconsistent with the negative message. A degree of 'compartmentalisation' may become established in order to house the dissonant imperatives and minimise what might have been described as 'inconsistent' or even 'psychotic' functioning. The dissonance among the parts obtains space for expression in contexts such as therapy, where the person who defined himself as 'evil' might find himself 'becoming aware of parts of me which aren't evil' or the person who saw himself as 'powerless' 'finding that I can feel my own power'. The 'figure-ground' relationship between the parts may oscillate to a degree that the person even begins to experience what it feels like *not* to be 'ruled' by the negative introject. Of course, this process of dissonance enhancement initially may bring its own pain as well as joy.

Some introjects are particularly sophisticated in their restorative self-protective function. They are embodied in configurations which do not put in an appearance until, or unless, they are really needed to protect the negative Self-concept. Charlie O'Leary refers to these as 'bombs' (O'Leary, 1997) to denote the way they can lie, relatively unseen, for long periods before exploding to wreak their restorative havoc upon the negative Self-concept which threat-ened to change. The characteristic of configurations built around these subtle introjects is that they allow the person to make progress *up to a point*, after which the person *must* fail (Mearns, 1992, 1994: 88–93). New therapists may be surprised and confused by the action of these subtle introjects. All they are left with is confusion when their client falls into a sudden and dramatic regression after apparently experiencing a lot of gains, or perhaps they find that their client grasps failure from the jaws of success in 'falling off the wagon', just when things are showing the promise of change. However, if the therapist is engaged with her client at relational depth, that may undermine the protective function of such configurations. Jim's 'Guardian' was undermined by the 'touching', which the therapist was able to achieve with under-lying configurations. There was still a possibility that Jim's 'Guardian' could close that opening in the space between the first and second sessions – Jim spoke about his oscillation between wanting to attend the second session and wanting to cancel. A therapist familiar with the action of these subtle configurations and confident in the contact she had established in the first session might not be so easily dismissed even if the client cancelled the second session – she might follow that up with a telephone call or a carefully worded letter. The following are some examples of injunctions characteristic of these subtle self-protective introjects:

- The more I build myself up, the harder my fall will be.
- When I feel happy, then I really should be afraid.
- The more I try to do better, the worse I am.
- I can do very well, so long as I don't actually succeed.

- No matter how well I do, I will always sink to the level of my origins.
- Feeling good is evil.
- People can only tell me I am OK if they are lying.
- If the other person continues to think that I am OK, I must destroy them.
- If I begin to think that I am OK, then I must destroy myself.

In regard to configurations built around restorative self-protective introjects such as these, there are no clues to be found in the way the client experiences them – sometimes they are described as frightening or threatening, but at other times they are experienced as a source of comfort, warmth or security. The truth is of course, that, at an existential level, they can offer both *security* to those parts of the Self which embody the negativity and *threat* to those parts of the Self which might entertain the possibility of change.

Simple introjects on their own would not be particularly powerful in their action upon the Self. However, when they accumulate cognitive, affective and behavioural elements to form a configuration, then they can more strongly protect the definition they carry of the Self – earlier in this section we described the client who built up so much evidence of her own 'unattractiveness' that it had become irrefutable by the time she was 20. Physiological metaphors are often interesting in the psychological domain because there is always the possibility that there may be parallels between psychological and physiological processes. With that question lingering in the background, we might liken configurations built around self-protective introjects to leucocytes in the bloodstream. Leucocytes protect the body against the invasion of harmful intruders that might alter the physiological status quo. Crudely speaking, they attach themselves to the surface of the intruder to neutralise its effect. The parallel with configurations built around self-protective introjects is a perfect one. If our self concept is positive, it will be supported by configurations built around positively oriented self-protective introjects and we might be quite happy for their protection. If, however, our introject configurations are protecting a negative, abused, or otherwise damaged self-concept, they are actually protecting us from positive experiences which might serve to shake the negativity of that Self-concept. In the language of social psychology, the introject-based configurations offer an alternative means of dissonance reduction within the Self – they reduce the pressure to change. The example of Sally illustrates this process:

Sally: session 25

'When you have got to fail, to entertain succeeding is terrifying'. In this short sentence my client, Sally, symbolised her debilitation and showed that she was strong enough to face it down. This awareness came in an elusive 25th session.

After 24 sessions watching Sally 'face her devils one by one' (her phrase) and exorcise them herself, I thought that we were nearly finished. Then she did not turn up for session 25, made another appointment and cancelled, then didn't return my calls. I considered writing to her, but after crunching up 11 attempts I went round to her flat.

She was *amazed*. As it later transpired, the part of her which was protecting her had thought of everything else but this, unannounced, visit. Sally takes up the story:

'When I saw you at the door I was blown away. You were meant to give up on me – I was running away – retreating into an old, familiar and very effective part of me. But you coming round and literally knocking on my door was amazing – if you were willing to reach out this far, then so could I'.

Configurations which are established around dissonant self-experiences

In Rogers' theory of the development of the Self (Rogers, 1951, 1959) he pointed to two parallel processes:

- The *introjection* into the Self-structure of elements which had not been directly experienced by the person.
- The *denial* from the Self-structure of elements which had been direct self-experiences but which were inconsistent with the rest of the Self-structure.

Our earlier work on configurations built around introjects relates to the first of these processes – now we must address the second. Rogers' theory on this matter is consistent with the *unitary* emphasis of his time and, indeed, with *consistency* theories of that era in social psychology (Festinger, 1957; Heider, 1958). However, if we are not bound to thinking of the Self as a unitary phenomenon but as comprising a range of configurations whose inconsistencies are tolerated by their boundaries and dynamics, we have a system which may now be able to describe human experience more fully.

For example, Cooper (1999) observes that 'denial' is not the only response to dissonant self-experience – the human being can be much more sophisticated. He can encompass and encapsulate those dissonant experiences *within a part of the Self*. Hence, a man who has a rigid self-concept of portraying stoicism and is generally dismissive of 'over-effusiveness' with regard to emotion, might have alternative self-protective options when he finds himself sobbing towards the end of an evening's heavy drinking. He might dismiss the experience as 'just because of the drink' and in that way seek to preserve the integrity of the Self through denial, as depicted in Rogers' theory. Alternatively, his response might be to accept the experience into the concept of Self but to seek to contain it within a configuration – hence he might acknowledge: 'I know that there is a part of me which is very sad'. Such a client would not easily open this configuration to the sight of others because of its inconsistency with the rest of Self. Indeed, he might be loathe to open it to his own consideration. This is one of the reasons why the very special conditions created by meeting at relational depth are important – they offer a striking and unusual amount of safety for the client. We need a high degree of safety if we are to face our existential inconsistencies.

'Growthful' and 'not for growth' configurations

It is not any one configuration within the client's Self which is important but the whole constellation of the configurations and the dynamics which define their interrelationships. It is this dynamic integration which will result in an overall picture that reflects the person's Self. A frequently observed dynamic centres around the challenge towards 'growth' or, in person-centred language, the *actualising tendency*. Some configurations appear to be particular vehicles for the actualising tendency in that they manifest a continual striving to maintain, enhance and develop the functioning of the organism even in circumstances which are highly unfavourable for growth. People enduring grotesque privations will often speak of going into 'a part of' themselves for survival. Clients who feel 'stuck' in their present life may have configurations built around their inclination for *growth* – configurations with labels like 'the part of me that wants more out of life'; 'the bit of me that isn't satisfied' or 'the voice within me that screams, "is this all there is?" '. Person-centred therapists are particularly good at paying attention to these 'growthful' members of the intrapsychic family. They recognise the promptings of the actualising tendency as a force for life – a force which urges growth and fights against apathy and atrophy.

Arguably the most common mistake made by person-centred therapists is not to be as aware of those configurations which carry an opposite imperative – those which caution against change because of the disruption and loss which might result. It is important that the person-centred therapist offer an equally full therapeutic relationship to *not for growth* configurations, like: 'the "me" that just wants to curl up and do absolutely nothing'; 'the part that wants to go back'; and 'the bit of me that wants to destroy this therapist'. Person-centred therapists often have a mistaken understanding that therapy should always be pointing in a 'growthful' direction. In fact, therapy is about helping the person to view and review *all* aspects of their existence including 'growthful' and 'not for growth' imperatives. Indeed, getting the balance wrong by over-focusing on the 'growthful' dimensions of the client is likely to slow down, or even block the therapeutic and growth processes because it is offering a conditional relationship. Growth is most likely to occur when the client can openly review all their aspects and inclinations – when all the members of the intrapsychic family can be heard and valued in the therapy. If the therapist is seen to align with only certain members of the family, the therapeutic process is stifled or elongated because the 'not for growth' parts will still have their voices even if they are banned from the therapy – in fact, their powers of sabotage may be even greater if they have to go underground.

Paying attention to the 'not for growth' configurations of the client can be extremely challenging for the person-centred therapist. Consider the client, repeatedly abused by her partner, who says 'I know I *should* leave him, but a big part of me does not want to do that'. The challenge for the person-centred therapist is to offer as full a meeting at depth with this part of the client as with other parts – to offer this part high degrees of empathy, congruence and unconditional regard. The therapist must actively value this part of her client as well as understanding its nature and existence.

There is no space in this work for the injunction, which pervades much mental health work, that the helper should not focus on 'problematic' parts of the client in case that attention encourages their expression. Such policies are usually found in professions whose mode of intervention is much shallower than working at relational depth. If I am a client struggling with the dynamic of growth within my life then I must feel free and supported in exploring both sides of that conflict.

It can help the therapist to be more valuing of 'not for growth' dimensions if she understands more about them. Although during therapy they are often experienced as 'inhibiting' or 'blocking' by the client, whose strength is growing to overcome them, there was probably a time in the client's life when these same parts were of crucial importance in helping to stabilise and define his existence, not to mention protecting him against other dangers. Jim's 'Guardian' may have been serving a 'blocking' function in the present, but how important was that part in Jim's history? In the full course of therapy clients often go through a roller-coaster process in relation to important 'not for growth' configurations. At first they seek to destroy them, then they understand them better and later they accept and embrace them as valued senior members within the family of the Self. Chapter 7 includes extracts from therapeutic dialogues where the therapist must maintain a therapeutic relationship with both 'growthful' and 'not for growth' configurations. But first we must pull together the strands of theory we have been propagating.

A person-centred theory of configurations

Developing configurations within the Self is a way of becoming expert in social living and preserving sanity. In life's varied social contexts it would be only minimally adaptive if the human being had to rely on one consistent image of her Self. This person would have to limit her social contact to situations in which her Self was appropriate. Incongruence between persons would be a much bigger problem if we lacked the capacity to adjust the Self which we exhibited. It is not sufficient simply to consider ourselves using a range of attributes integrated within a consistent and unitary Self. Rather, life's many challenging contexts require many *contradictory* responses which a unitary self cannot provide. As well as responding to a range of *external* demands, the person also has to cope with diverse *internal* imperatives. We have fluctuating, sometimes contradictory, needs, many of which evolve with the process of life. To seek to hold an internal inconsistency within the concept of a unitary Self in the face of this range of external and internal demands would be a recipe for insanity. How much more sophisticated it is for us to respond both to diverse and contradictory external demands and internal imperatives if we can use a plurality of configurations within our Self to house and to a degree compartmentalise the range and the contradictions.[1]

So, as the young person is faced with challenging, diverse and sometimes contradictory *conditions of worth*, he adapts not the whole Self but parts of the Self. This is a dimension of the protective function of Self configurations. The configuration constructed around the negotiation of a condition of worth allows us simultaneously to develop an adapted response to that condition of worth and *also* to preserve, intact, the rest of the Self.

Equally, the Self which has endured, survived and adapted to pervasive and sometimes contradictory conditions of worth also needs to find ways to respond to *self-experiences* which are inconsistent with the rest of Self. Rogers pointed particularly to the protective mechanism of *denial* – whereby experiences dissonant with the rest of Self are disowned. However, an alternative protective response, as suggested by Cooper (1999), is to encompass and encapsulate those dissonant experiences within a part of the Self.

We may now want to reconsider Rogers' proposition XIII:

> Behavior may, in some instances, be brought about by organic experiences and needs which have not been symbolized. Such behavior may be inconsistent with the structure of the self, but in such instances the behaviour is not 'owned' by the individual. (1951: 509)

To Proposition XIII, we may want to add the following:

> In some cases the behaviour *may* be 'owned' but allocated to a part or *configuration* within the Self. Such a configuration may well be inconsistent with other parts of the Self and carry restricted access.

Thus far we have hypothesised two processes whereby configurations may develop in relation to introjected material and inconsistent self-experiences – there may be other pathways. However, even these represent merely the start of the developmental process for configurations. Once such a formative configuration becomes established it will voraciously *assimilate* other consistent elements. The configuration becomes an *organising principle* which can lend structure and function to individual thoughts, feelings and self-experiences. For example, a configuration established around the person's previously unforeseen ability to 'survive' huge privations may accrue other consistent elements such as their toleration of physical pain, their liking for demanding settings, their self-reliance, etc. Indeed, the organising principle function of the configuration may allow it to encompass other narratives about Self close enough to be reached by modest expansion. For example, a configuration carrying the narrative that the person is 'untrustworthy' may readily expand to include the message that they are also 'unlovable' on the basis of minimal evidence.

An additional means for the accrual of other elements relates to the *self-fulfilling* nature of configurations. Once a configuration actively participates in the existential life of the person it can bring about its own narrative, hence adding elements to expand its existence and veracity. For instance, a configuration may carry a 'narrative' of failure which may cause the person to behave with the expectation of failure and thereby enhance the possibility of failing.

Hence, the formation of configurations may, initially, represent a means to respond to external demands through conditions of worth, or to internal imperatives reflected in self-experiences which are inconsistent with the concept of Self. Thereafter, configurations can accrue other elements by assimilation and self-fulfilment to expand their evidential base and diversity.

If we were to stop at this point we might have something which resembles object relations theory (Fairbairn, 1952) or Transactional Analysis (Berne, 1961) in postulating fairly static and unchanging 'objects' or 'ego-states'. However, the human being is a dynamic, interactive event in evolution. The configurations within the Self are not permanently compartmentalised like psychic 'scabs'. Each of these 'parts' needs to have a developmental existence to serve its protective function more effectively. This development is facilitated by the *interrelating* of configurations within the Self. Hence, we open the door to a whole world of configuration evolution and configuration dynamics. The illustrative case material presented in the next chapter will give examples of configurations evolving into *derivatives*, sometimes with *bifurcations*. Furthermore, configuration dynamics describes the interrelationship between and among configurations where *alliances* and *conflicts* contribute to the ever-changing process.

This dynamic evolution and interaction of configurations provides a highly sophisticated means by which the Self can continue through the challenges of life maintaining a breadth of substance and responsiveness to function as a relational human being in that ever-changing social world. The more we look upon the human being the more we are amazed by her beauty.

Note

1 Here we can see, within this 'normal process' of adaptation, the same parameters that we find extended into dissociated form in Margaret Warner's 'dissociated process' (see Chapter 8 and Warner and Mearns, 2000).

7 Person-centred therapy with 'configurations' of self

In this chapter we shall explore the discipline of person-centred working with clients who articulate configurations within their Self. We shall start with an illustration of work with the client, Alexander. From the outset, it must be emphasised that the extracts reported are specifically chosen because of Alexander's references to configurations. This may give a misleading view of the work overall because there were many sessions when Alexander made no mention of 'parts' of himself.

Alexander

Alexander had been allocated numerous psychiatric labels during the last 15 of his 28 years. If anyone in his previous mental health history had been able to engage and sustain contact with him at an existential level, they would have been less inclined to apply such labels. While some of Alexander's outward behaviour might appear bizarre and even potentially dangerous to himself at least, it was perfectly coherent when the basic configurations of his Self were engaged. Within the field of mental health, labels are usually founded on our *lack* of understanding of the individual.

Alexander had briefly engaged in therapy a year earlier but, after three sessions of fairly fast work in which a good therapeutic relationship had been achieved, he decided that this was 'not the time for me'. A year later he came back to therapy in a panic – in his own words, he was 'losing it'. The quality of his despair had changed, it was no longer chronic and stable but now it was full of panic. His fear, which had always been deep-seated, was 'out-cropping' in almost every area of his life: his sleeping was disrupted, his drinking was less under control and he found himself subject to sudden bursts of annoyance, irritation, sadness and crying. He recounted a recent incident where he had sat on a bench and watched children play in the park. His sadness and sense of loss grew until he found himself sobbing uncontrollably. His sadness was not only related to the loss of his own childhood but, and this gave him greater surprise, he was also experiencing sadness that, according to the life track he had chosen, he would never have children of his own.

Therapists of most persuasions will recognise that the pattern of destabilisation experienced by Alexander *might* be heralding the possibility of an important psychological shift. In the person-centred approach we focus on the concept of Self. Alexander was experiencing a considerable increase in *dissonance* within his Self (Mearns, 1994: 88–93). Theoretically, such an increase in dissonance can make self-concept change more of a possibility but there are also other ways in which the dissonance may be reduced. For example, sometimes the self-concept 'fights back' through self-protective introjects and finds ways of reducing the dissonance other than changing the self-concept (Mearns, 1992, 1994: 88–93).

Let us look at a portion of dialogue during one of the early therapy sessions. The reader needs to know that in the previous therapy experience a year earlier Alexander had identified and labelled one part of his Self as 'the creep'. It is important for the person-centred therapist to recall features like this from her notes but also to be ready for the client re-configuring parts of his Self in the year gap.

> *Alexander:* I am breaking apart – I can't hold it together.
> *Therapist:* What are you trying to hold together, Alexander?
> *Alexander:* My life – my sanity – my Self as I know me.
>   [*Pause*]
> *Therapist:* My Self as I know me?
> *Alexander:* There is 'me as I have always known me' and 'another me'. It feels like a cancer.
> *Therapist:* That the 'another me' is eating away at 'me as I have always known me?'
> *Alexander:* Yes – I'm scared.
> *Therapist:* Yes, it sounds scary – real scary . . . real scary.
> *Alexander:* If I let go, I'll disintegrate . . . and I can't hold on.
> *Therapist:* I feel shivery when you say that.
> *Alexander:* Yeah, me too.
>   [*Pause*]
> *Alexander:* I am glad you are here.

> *Therapist*: What does it do for you – that I am here?
>
> *Alexander*: It helps me feel some warmth – otherwise I am stone cold . . .
>
> *Therapist*: 'Stone cold' . . . and 'some warmth'.
>
> *Alexander*: Part of me is *scared* that you are here.
>
> *Therapist*: That makes sense to me.
>
> *Alexander*: That part is *embarrassed* that you are here – if he was on his own he would tell you to 'fuck off'.
>
> *Therapist*: But he is not on his own.
>
> *Alexander*: No.
>
> *Therapist*: Who is with him?
>
> *Alexander*: 'The creep'.
>
> *Therapist*: So, *part of you is scared and embarrassed* that I am here but that part is not alone – there is that part you call 'the creep' here as well and the result is that, overall, 'you' are here and you're feeling some 'warmth' and a lot of 'cold'.
>
> *Alexander*: Yeah – funny how 'the creep' is helping.
>
> *Therapist*: Like . . . helping you to stay *in* this?
>
> *Alexander*: Yeah . . . the wee shite bag has his uses.
>
> *Therapist*: Yeah.

In this dialogue we have been introduced to three or four configurations within Alexander's Self. There is 'me as I have always known me', 'another me', 'the part of me who is scared and embarrassed you are here' and 'the creep'. It is likely that the 'part of me who is scared and embarrassed you are here' will prove to be the same as 'me as I have always known me' but it is important for the therapist not to close on that assumption and to continue to hold the two labels as possibly corresponding to different configurations until that is revised by the client. One of the major skills of person-centred work is illustrated: restraining *our* need to 'make sense' of the material and waiting for the 'sense' to come from the client.

A portion of dialogue from a later session also sees Alexander exploring configurations. In this extract we find the interesting phenomenon of the 'timelessness' of configurations. A configuration may have evolved over time, in line with the development of the Self, but it may *also* be available in its original form.

> *Alexander*: 'The creep' has been getting help from 'another me'. 'Another me' is a newer version of 'the creep' and more difficult to put down. 'Me as I have always known me' can't dominate like before – he is going to have to let go.

Therapist: What happens if he lets go?

Alexander: God knows . . . I don't know how I'd feel about that.

Therapist: Like, different parts might have different feelings?

Alexander: Yeah – 'the creep' would say 'great – kill the shit'. 'Another me' would say 'freedom at last'!

Therapist: And what would 'me as I have always known me' say?

Alexander: [*Pause*] . . . that I am really, really scared . . . that if I let go of us we can be . . . 'abused'.

Therapist: 'Abused' . . . is that *your* word?

Alexander: No, it's the word others use . . . it's the polite word.

Therapist: What is *your* word?

Alexander: I don't really have one – it all started so early that it became *part* of me. I didn't have a word because it was all *inside* me. It is only if it comes out that you need a word . . . Maybe the closest word is 'fucked' – that I live in fear of being 'fucked' . . . that my whole life is spent making sure I don't get fucked. That 'fucked' isn't a sexual thing . . . it is how you feel when someone deliberately hits yesterday's bruise with his baton, like my father would do . . . it's like . . . being *totally beaten* – when someone fucks you with their *absolute power*.

This dialogue led Alexander on to explore another configuration which he called 'fucked me'. Later in the therapy, Alexander reflects:

Alexander: I have changed a lot over these months.

Therapist: Tell me how.

Alexander: I am not scared anymore . . . I suppose 'me as I have always known me' is giving way to 'me as I was', though he can come back. He keeps putting his oar in – trying to sabotage things – but he is on his way out.

Therapist: How does it feel to be him, *now*?

Alexander: [*Pause*] . . . Gosh, he hasn't been asked that for a while . . . God – he feels *sad*! He really feels 'sad' – what a turn-up! He *never* feels sad – other bits feel sad, but not him – he is the *hard man* [*Alexander begins to cry*]

Therapist: He is crying? or, you're crying for him?

Alexander: Both . . . he was just doing his best and I was putting him down – sending him away. He had kept me safe, like an 'elder brother' all these years . . . he kept me 'alive' . . . he stopped me getting 'fucked' any more. And now that I think

I don't need him any more, I want to kick him out – kick him out of *me* – like *I* want to 'fuck' him too!

Figure 7.1 is representative of Alexander's symbolised configurations including their derivatives and the dynamics among them. *All* the configurations within the Self are important and it is incumbent upon the therapist to listen to all the parts and to value each of them unconditionally, even if the client is not valuing them. It is not the place of the therapist to collude with parts of the client to ignore or judge other parts. The person-centred family therapist would not accept the father's view that the adolescent was 'not worth listening to' and was only to be valued 'if he behaves appropriately'. Similarly, the individual therapist attends to all the configurations within the client's Self. For Alexander, 'me as I have always known me' had been a crucially

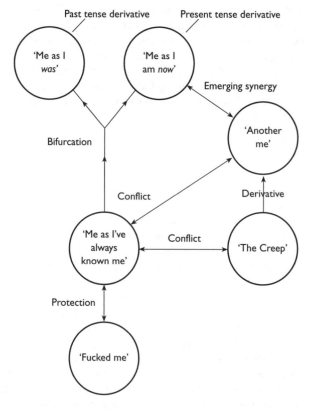

Figure 7.1   *Alexander's configurations*

important part of him. In this part resided many of his strengths and it had helped him to be the 'hard man' when that had been his only defence. Alexander likened 'me as I have always known me' to a protective elder brother of the earlier abused part which he referred to as 'fucked me'. Alexander may not need 'me as I have always known me' in his current existence but that elder brother could be allowed to leave home with grace – he did not need to be ejected – he did not need to be 'fucked'. A very interesting configuration is 'the creep' which had carried out an enduring conflict with 'me as I have always known me'. In terms of person-centred theory 'the creep' may have been the vehicle for the actualising tendency at that earlier time. 'The creep' kept alive the possibility of a more expansive, 'growthful' existence, albeit in a fairly delinquent fashion against the backdrop of the ever-controlling 'me as I have always known me'. In the present time 'the creep' was giving way to its derivative, 'another me'. This may be a newer 'home' for the actualising tendency and one which promises to be more effective within Alexander's current life. 'Another me' is better adapted to adult living and more able to challenge 'me as I have always known me'. Initially these dynamics had thrown Alexander's life into apparent crisis because of the huge dissonance being created within the Self. 'Me as I have always known me' was receding in the face of the conflict with 'another me'. It later transpired (see Figure 7.1) that 'me as I have always known me' was giving way to the bifurcated derivatives 'me as I was' which could hold, and honour, the historical content and a very new, and still undefined, configuration, 'me as I am now'. Interestingly, constructive dialogue and mutual respect became established between 'me as I am now' and 'another me'. This may represent a fundamental synthesis within the Self.

The configuration 'fucked me' was never given a voice after the initial reference to his father's beatings. At times it was referred to by Alexander, but Alexander did not speak *from* that configuration. Therapists from other traditions, with specific expectations as to appropriate therapeutic process for clients, would likely push for more from 'fucked me'. Part of the discipline of the person-centred approach is not to make assumptions about the client's appropriate process, but to follow the process laid out by the client. If the therapeutic relationship is strong, then that is providing maximum safety for the client to raise what for him is most important. At a later 'review' session, the therapist observed that little more had been said about 'fucked me'. Alexander said that this part had not been relevant to his current struggle – that this part of him was there and would always be there 'as a kind of "touchstone" to me – a part of me I can touch to remember where I have been and where I have come from – in a way, it is a great source of *power* for me – and it will also help me not to abuse others!'

The access level of configurations

Even if we have not thought of our Self in configurational terms, we might be readily aware of certain 'ways of being' which we adopt in particular circumstances. If these are properly to be called 'configurations', these 'ways of being' are fairly substantial in the repertoire they can call upon. It is not simply a matter of displaying a facet of our personality or adopting a specific role – if we are relating with another person from one of our configurations we will have a broad repertoire of feelings, thoughts and readily accessible behaviours associated with that configuration. As Cooper (1999) observes, going into a specific part of the Self is like 'method acting' – we are not following a tightly written script but we are opening out a whole dimension of our existence filled with layers of sophisticated ways of responding, yet all linked to the central theme of that part of our existence. Every time we go into a social situation and adopt a starting position for our Self, we are probably entering a familiar configuration. Dave Mearns gives a personal example:

On being my 'apprentice'

When I am seeking the guidance of some person more expert than I, I find it works best if I first pause to put myself into 'me as an apprentice'. I am a very good 'apprentice'. In that mode I have absolutely nothing to defend – I presume no prior learning or expertise, so I can ask even the most stupid questions without feeling that it reflects upon me in any way. Also, I listen carefully to my tutor and I am not scared to seek her judgement on my work as it progresses.

If I enter these learning situations in any other mode, such as 'I probably am already an expert in this', then I am more intent on showing my tutor what I know, hiding my lack of knowledge from her and certainly failing to ask those questions that are very important but which might reveal my naiveté.

My 'apprentice' has succeeded in building a gigantic wood shed, fencing a large garden, slating a roof and learning how to write books. On the other hand, my 'expert' has managed to put engine oil into a car radiator, set fire to a tent with a Primus stove and drive a speed boat for a whole day in reverse gear!

We will each have a number of configurations to which we have easy access. In entering each new social situation we will make a judgement on what mode of being is appropriate and select a configuration that fits. But we are always ready to switch. A client, Linda, describes her first day with a new colleague:

I got myself all ready to meet him with my 'sophisticated woman who knows the job'. But he was such a PIG that within half an hour I was sunk without trace in my 'totally lost little girl'. Fortunately, I retrieved the situation by getting into my 'vixen' mode!

It would be interesting to research the way clients approach first sessions with their therapist. It is likely that they initially present familiar configurations as part of the early 'rehearsed material' (Rogers, 1977). However, these easily accessed configurations may be quite different from those dimly symbolised configurations which are entered when the client moves on to 'edge of awareness' material (Gendlin, 1981, 1984, 1996). At that point our client is extremely vulnerable to invasion and distortion from a therapist who is insensitive to the delicacy of those parts of the Self. Here, the discipline of the person-centred therapist in staying close to the client's symbolisation is crucial.

Staying close to the client's symbolisation

The skill of the person-centred therapist is to help the client to unravel the uniqueness of his own structures and dynamics of Self. And so, the person-centred therapist *listens* as openly as possible to all the different parts, meanings and conflicts gradually unveiled by the client. Some of those parts will be very familiar to the client and might even have been given names. Others will be very dim figures in the background, only just reaching the early stages of symbolisation. Perhaps they are so early in the symbolisation process that the client cannot give them names which carry much meaning. The discipline of the person-centred therapist is not to contaminate the client's meaning with his own and so the therapist will be skilful in recalling and re-using the working labels given by the client to parts of her Self. For example, a client talks about different parts of her Self:

> Of course, there has always been the part of me which is the *dutiful daughter* and the other one which is the *delinquent* but there is another sense of me as well . . . I can't grasp it . . . it is *something to do with sadness* . . .

Whatever response the person-centred therapist makes to this statement, she would have stored this interim label 'something to do with sadness' as the client's current symbolisation of that aspect of the Self. The person-centred therapist would not do anything else with that construction until the client had moved it on.

Naive therapists can do considerable damage to clients who are vulnerable in regard to their *locus of evaluation* (Mearns, 1994: 80–3) by re-structuring the client's experience. If the client has a highly externalised locus of evaluation, finding it difficult to trust the meanings which she ascribes to parts of her Self, the therapist who willingly offers her own labels is a menace. For example:

> *Client*: there is a part of me that is dreadfully vulnerable and sad . . . she has only a very small voice . . . so I don't hear her very often.
> *Therapist*: So I wonder what this 'hurt little girl' has to say to us?
> *Client*: I don't know . . . I don't know . . .
> *Therapist*: From what you said before it sounds as though she is not just a 'hurt little girl' but an 'abused little girl'?
> *Client*: I don't know . . . I don't know . . .

It is no wonder that this client has been silenced – that may be a healthy response to the therapist's incompetence. Translating the client's construction of part of her Self 'that is dreadfully vulnerable and sad' into a 'hurt little girl' and then an 'abused little girl' is unacceptable because it is fitting the client's experiencing into the therapist's theoretical construction and then imposing that theoretical construction back on the client. If the work is with a client whose locus of evaluation is profoundly externalised, this is a most dangerous procedure akin to what has become known as 'therapist induced false memories'. The finishing point for the client in her symbolisation of this part of herself was 'dreadfully vulnerable and sad'. This therefore becomes the starting point for the competent therapist in her continued communication with the client.

Sometimes the therapist has even less to work with than this initial verbal symbolisation. There was the client who went for weeks with a screwing up of his face and the expression 'ugh!' to describe a part of his Self which he sensed was important but which was not 'coming-out'. Throughout those sessions the client and the therapist both referred to this part of his Self as 'ugh!', until he was able to refine it further.

Indeed, some of the most absorbing person-centred work occurs when the client is at a presymbolic stage in relation to a configuration of Self. Here, the client and therapist can not talk *about* the configuration, they can only be *in* the configuration. The client is dimly and partially expressing himself from the configuration but the material is not neatly organised. For the therapist whose listening requires coherence there is only confusion. What is required is a listening which hears the *person* rather than the content. The listening is to the existence and expressing of the person. It is the expressing which is being listened to rather than the expression. This is the kind of companionship which offers a *meeting at relational depth* described in Chapter 5 and elsewhere (Mearns, 1996, 1997a). It is extremely difficult to exemplify this communication in the written word, partly due to the conceptual incoherence of the content, but chiefly because this level of communication results from the relating which has gone before. Nevertheless, the following attempts to present an example.

Listening to the expressing

Tony was in pain. He had been sitting on the floor in a corner of the group room all morning, crying. This was new for Tony – crying was new. More characteristic for Tony was *either* extreme gregariousness, *or* complete silence. Tony was twenty-three years of age and a 'veteran' of two tours in Vietnam. He had not spoken about his experiences in war.

Tony's therapist, Bill, was sitting on the floor beside him, very close but not touching. For an hour nothing had been said between them and the communication had been intense. Now Tony spoke for the first time:

Tony: I can't, I can't, I can't, I can't, I can't . . .

Bill: No, . . . you can't.

Tony: No-one can.

Bill: [*Silence*]

Tony: [*Thumping his fist on the floor and screaming*] I need to kill myself.

Bill: [*Silence*]

Tony: I need to go . . . I must go . . . I must go away from me.

Bill: [*Silence*]

Tony: I don't know how to do it.

Bill: It's hard, Tony . . . It's hard . . . there's no way . . .

Tony: No way . . . no way . . . how do people do it?

Bill: God knows Tony.

Tony: Can you warm me Bill?

Bill: [*Puts his arm round Tony*]

Much later Bill comments on this meeting:

It's an example of how you can be *with* someone and have conversation without having any idea what it's about. Yet all the time you can *feel* them – and be with them feeling. It was weeks later that I found out the 'content' of this meeting. Tony was 'being' the part of him which had done some bad stuff. In war people can do bad stuff that they can't live with later. Tony was *feeling* that part – he wanted to get rid of it – to kill it or for it to go away – to 'exorcise' it might be a good metaphor. But, of course, there was no way to do it – that's what we were in.

Not changing the client's symbolisation of parts of his Self is respectful but it is also functional. The symbolisation, however poorly it is formed, expresses the closest the client can get to its meaning in his existential world at that time. The skill of the person-centred therapist is to work *without* offering external constructions – that is not an easy matter, for such external constructions can help therapists to feel both secure and smart. That is why the person-centred approach is such an unsatisfying home for therapists who like to feel 'smart'.

Where a client has declared the existence of a configuration, this information becomes a significant part of the person-centred counsellor's record-keeping. It is not sufficient to have a 'rough memory' of the way the client has talked about parts of themselves in the past – it is important to remember the actual labels he has used because those represent the client's symbolisation to that point. There should be no question about the counsellor's diligence on this matter – these are very important characters within the Self of the client. As well as recalling names and descriptive terms it is important to remember interrelationships and dynamics among configurations and be ready for all these to change.

Nothing is done with this record during supervision between sessions. The person-centred counsellor is not concerned to use supervision as a means of further analysing the client and his configurations. When person-centred supervision resorts to this kind of 'analysing the client' activity it generally means that the supervisor and counsellor have lost an immediacy in their relating. Supervision in the person-centred approach is not about 'detective work' on client material but, instead, it focuses upon the counsellor's congruence in relation to the client and whatever factors are affecting the counsellor in the work, including monitoring the configurations which the counsellor is using in her relating with the client. Elke Lambers explores the essence of person-centred supervision in Chapter 10.

Although person-centred therapists would agree with the importance of staying close to the client's symbolisation they might have varying views on whether the therapist should only address configurations which the client has presented in that session. The alternative view is that therapy should not be compartmentalised into discrete sessions and that it is appropriate to address configurations previously declared. The specific example represented by Alexander suggested that it was appropriate the therapist did not directly address the heavily protected configuration 'fucked me', though there was indirect reference in a review session when the therapist sought to investigate the current importance of this configuration to Alexander. In the case of Alexander it was appropriate that the therapist was sensitive to the need for caution in addressing this configuration directly – to ask about 'fucked me' openly could have been so invasive as to be actually abusive, particularly with that kind of configuration. However, we must be wary of arguing theory from individual cases, particularly since person-centred therapy, like any approach, contains a range of views (Bohart, 1995). For instance, a *process-experiential* orientation within the person-centred approach (Rennie, 1998) would be less wary than ourselves in offering 'process direction' to the client. In Chapter 9 we offer a fairly

integrative theoretical framework in suggesting that such apparent differences within the approach might be less marked when
we actually address the specifics of each client. We contend that
our theory needs to take greater account of differences among
clients. Hence, both we and those with a process-experiential
orientation might be wary of offering process-direction to clients
who are highly vulnerable with respect to their 'locus of evaluation'.

Avoiding 'zero-sum' responding

Therapists are familiar with 'the client who cancels himself out'
with opposing imperatives. Here, we are not simply talking about
an important decision to be made and strong arguments pointing
in both directions, but a real conflict within the person where one
part of his Self points in one direction and another part in the
opposite. In this situation it is easy to fall into what might be
called 'zero-sum responding' where the therapist's empathy simply reflects the zero-sum of the parts of the client. For example,
the therapist's response below is only partially empathic:

> *Client*: Part of me feels X . . . and part of me feels not X.
> *Therapist*: So, you are conflicted about how you feel?

The therapist's response sums the two elements presented by the
client. The sum of these two poles is zero – but that is certainly not
how the client feels! In this situation it is not uncommon for
person-centred therapists to seek to focus on the conflict or the
'stuckness' the client is feeling. The interesting thing is that this
'conflict' or 'stuckness' often does not *focus* for the client – it is
difficult to feel the full substance of conflict or stuckness. The
previous conventional wisdom of 'staying with the stuckness'
rarely leads to anything underlying in the client. Hence, we must
ask the question whether the stuckness is an actual experience or
simply a cognitive construction. Interestingly, when the therapist
responds in the way illustrated she has actually missed *both* things
the client has said. The client feels X. Also, the client feels not X.
Each of these will 'focus' for the client because each is grounded
within his Self. If we can find ways, empathically, to reflect each of
these elements with something like the power with which they are
felt by the client then our empathic response is more accurate. Our
client cannot focus and respond to our reflection of the conflict or

stuckness because these are not coming directly from parts of his Self – they are simply dynamics of the interaction of parts. However, if we can reflect each of the parts in such a way that he attends to them directly, then fuller access may be gained to those configurations and the possibility of movement is established.

In Carl Rogers' early transcribed interviews he had a tendency to offer zero-sum empathic responses, probably because the emphasis at that time was more on *reflection*. (There are fewer such examples in his later work where his strong 'presence' appears to be a greater emphasis.) For example, from the case of Mary Jane Tilden in 1946:

> *Mary Jane*: (Pause) See, that's just it, I – I can do something, or I can go through an experience, and I feel, well, I haven't done so badly, and then the next minute, 'Oh, no'. Immediately something inside attacks me and tears me down. And it discourages me, discourages me to the point where I don't want to repeat it.
>
> *C.R.*: In other words, your own evaluation of yourself fluctuates so that it is very discouraging. (Farber et al., 1996: 165)

Here, Carl's 'summative' empathy has missed the power the client is expressing in the parts. In the next example, taken from a later interview with the same client, Carl reflects both parts, but we do not know whether his tone of voice is 'summative' or emphasises the distinctive parts:

> *Mary Jane*: Yes, that's true. The only thing is that I can't help but feel that I work against myself. I mean it's just so obvious to me that I do work against myself. And it seems rather silly to be one minute trying to do something about it, and then it seems so certain that there's something present that doesn't want to do anything about it (Pause). It's such a contrary thing – the whole problem is just –
>
> *C.R.*: So that the very time that one part of you is perhaps really taking hold of this whole situation, another part of you is just sabotaging the whole business. (Farber et al., 1996: 174)

A clearer example of Carl avoiding a summative response and honouring each part is given in a later interview with Mary Jane.

> *C.R.*: You feel that your doubting force is definitely stronger that your constructive force.
>
> *Mary Jane*: Yes. (very long pause) That's just it. (Pause) I guess I've always believed the other one because I've built it up so high

and then I believe that it's true because it's so big. (Very long pause) That's something I never thought about. (Very long pause) It seems that the more I ever try to drive it out, the louder it yells. Every time I want it to say no, it just yells louder. And then the more the other doubts came – I mean, it seemed so much more positive – so much more positive than the littler one – I just accepted it.

C.R.: You just felt that the armies of doubt are definitely unbeatable armies.

Mary Jane: M-hm. Yeah.

C.R.: And that the other is a pretty weak and struggling thing. (Farber et al., 1996: 179)

The discipline of avoiding zero-sum responding is simply illustrated in the following extract from work with 'Sandie'. Here, the therapist does not 'sum' Sandie's conflicting statements but empathises with each of them.

Sandie

In this extract the client, Sandie, is reflecting upon herself during a recent and verbally violent dispute with a colleague at work:

Sandie: . . . it was bizarre, it was like standing 'outside', watching myself. I was skilfully defensive – I was so *good* at it – so confident in it. It was like I could hear his arguments as he was voicing them and have my 'definitive' statements prepared before he was even finished. I was really *good*.

Therapist: How did it *feel*?

Sandie: Great! . . . No, *not* great . . . it felt *terrible*!

Therapist: Sounds as though those were *both* strong – it felt *great* – really *great* . . . and, also, it felt *terrible*.

Sandie: It did – and also . . . I felt *guilty* . . . but I just couldn't *stop* myself. It was as though there was a bit of me watching me take him on, and feeling terrible. And another bit that felt guilty. But they were just 'observers', they couldn't stop me.

Therapist: Those bits could see what was happening and felt bad about it . . . But they couldn't stop you.

Sandie: I was 'unstoppable' – I was powerful. I didn't recognise myself. I was a 'killer'.

Therapist: That *does* sound powerful . . . I wasn't expecting just such a powerful word. I was picturing a scene in which you felt threatened, and you became defensive – very powerfully and effectively defensive . . . but you are saying more than that . . . a 'killer'.

Sandie: I could take him apart – I could 'dismember him' . . . like pulling the wings off a butterfly. I could smile at him and nail down his coffin, nail by nail. Everything he said I could use as a nail in his own coffin. [*smiles and shivers*]

Therapist: You smiled . . . *and* you shivered . . .

Sandie: It's scary to hear me talk.

Therapist: Like you are enjoying it *now* – enjoying the memory . . . and that is also scary?

Sandie: Part of me *is* enjoying it . . . but part of me is frightened and disgusted by me.

Therapist: Part of you is enjoying it and part of you is 'frightened' and 'disgusted'.

Sandie: And part of me just feels so *guilty*.

Therapist: That part which feels 'guilty' – that is a different part from the one which feels 'frightened and disgusted'?

Sandie: Yes, it really *feels* different. The 'guilty' part *just* feels 'guilty'. It is a constant presence whenever I do or feel *anything* unusual. It is a constant voice with a repetitive message. It's been there all my life. But the part that is 'frightened' feels more *real* to me.

Therapist: 'The part that is frightened' has a different quality to it?

Sandie: Yes, it's coming more from the *inside* of me – whereas, 'guilt', is someone else's voice, essentially. That's one thing that is changing for me – 'guilt' is still around but it is less internal.

Therapist: It feels like there is so much to respond to you here – like I would want to say at least three different things to different parts of you. What would *you* like me to say?

Sandie: [*Pause*] I would like you to be close to my 'frightened' part – she needs some warmth. I also would like you not to dismiss my 'strong' part, even though she is cruel. Somehow, she is important but I don't know how . . .

Therapist: Staying close to *her* is important too – giving *her* part of my warmth is important too.

Sandie: [*Becoming agitated and with a tear in her eye*] . . . Yes . . . Yes . . . but watch her mind – she will be wanting to destroy you. Do anything out of line and she will pull the wings off you.

Therapist: Will I have a chance with her?

Sandie: She hopes so.

Working with the configurational 'family'

When considering this area of configurations it can be helpful to employ the language of the 'family'. Indeed, most of the workers in this area find themselves using phrases like 'the family of selves' (Rowan and Cooper, 1999). Richard Schwartz noted the same experience when, as a family therapist, he entered the intrapsychic world of an individual client. He found himself working with the 'parts' in the same way that he would work with members of a family (Schwartz, 1987, 1997).

Even if the similarity is only metaphorical, it can be useful for the therapist to carry it with her in relating with the separate configurations of a client. For example, it is important to remember, as would the family therapist, that every member of the family who is present in the room needs to be offered the same, strong, consistent therapeutic relationship. As person-centred family therapists will attest (O'Leary, 1999) this is quite a challenge. Just as the teenager in the family might feel rejected when the therapist is evidently empathising with and prizing the parents, so too might one configuration feel rejected by the very fact that another is receiving such quality attention. Nor is it simply a matter of the therapist being 'fair' – those who are familiar with working in families will know that 'fair' means giving me more than them! Perceptions of 'fair' are grossly affected by the extent of our need.

A rich concept from family therapy is that of *multi-directional partiality* (Boszormenyi-Nagy et al., 1991; O'Leary, 1999). This is a challenging concept, particularly for the person-centred family therapist. Essentially, it takes the view that in working with a family it is not sufficient to be 'impartial' or 'fair'. Ivan Boszormenyi-Nagy suggests that it is important to offer strong engagement with *all* the family members – in other words to be 'partial' – but in all directions! So, the family therapist might express that by way of the following example.

> *Therapist*: Right, I can see your position in this, Dad. You really *love* this boy of yours – in fact, you love him *so damned much* that you are shit scared that he is going to get into trouble – so you just can't help going on and on at him. I can understand that – that makes sense to me. Also you, Robert – you are on the other end of that – you *don't* see any 'love' coming from Dad – of course not – all you see is this guy

continually getting *on top of you*. He never listens to a damned word you say – he just comes out with the usual stuff. If I were in your shoes, that sure wouldn't look like someone who loves me!

'Multi-directional partiality' is a good family therapy equivalent to 'unconditional positive regard' and emphasises the concept not just as some kind of 'impartial acceptance' but as a strong understanding and prizing bond made with *every* member of the family. Exactly the same 'multi-directional partiality' is important in relation to the different parts of the client's Self. The same kind of therapist statement as was illustrated above, could well be applied to the different parts of the client's Self which may be in conflict. However, the individual therapist has the added difficulty that contact with the other parts may have to be negotiated through the part which is dominant at that time – this can even lead to the therapist challenging that dominant part, for instance:

> *Therapist:* It seems to me that most of this session, so far, we have been hearing from that part of you which you called 'the strong part of me' but, earlier in the session, you also identified another part of you that was quite different from 'the strong part of me' – you called it the 'frightened part of me'. Is it meaningful to check in with that part – what do you think?
>
> *Client:* Fuck it – it's in the past – it's history.
>
> *Therapist:* Right, let me catch up – this is new. Is it like that part, is, really, 'history', or is it that you would *want* it be history?
>
> *Client:* Fuck you – you won't let it go will you.
>
> *Therapist:* I am not going to let it go if it is a part of you – I am not going to dismiss any of you.
>
> *Client:* Who pays you anyway! [*with humour*]
>
> *Therapist:* Good point . . . actually, I don't know who pays me. Who pays me?
>
> *Client:* Clever Bastard.

In working with a family, the therapist would be clear on establishing his right to respect everyone. Similarly, every part of the client's Self is prized by the therapist. Family therapists (O'Leary, 1999) note that even the dominant member of the family likes the therapist to respect all of their family members, even if that dominant member is in conflict with them. That is also true of the parts of the Self in therapy. Even in conflict, the parts are deeply related with each other and at some level they value each other and consider it to be appropriate that the therapist shares that valuing. The family would not be in therapy if there was not at least some respect among its members. Similarly, the Self would not be in therapy if there was not at least some respect for all its parts.

What about the therapist's configurations?

If the notion of 'configuration' is meaningful then the therapist will have configurations within their Self as well as their clients. Perhaps we might expect the dynamics among the therapist's configurations to be more creative than disabling and, also, we might reasonably expect a level of awareness in the therapist about her configurations and configuration dynamics. We would stop considerably short of expecting a full 'configurations analysis' and would sincerely hope that our work does not lead to the growth of 'configurations analysts'! Yet, the person-centred therapist in training might wish to explore the relevance of this notion of 'configurations' to their own existence. To this end, the simple reflective exercise offered below may offer a useful start.

A configurations exercise

Exploring our 'configurations' requires little more than our introspective attention allied to the encouragement of a supportive partner. The best situation is a training course where the entry skills of members and also the supportive background can be relied upon to help the individuals to relate to whatever personal 'discoveries' result. The most irresponsible use is with a group of clients who may not yet have symbolised 'parts' to their own existence – exercises such as this are, by their nature, powerfully 'suggestive'.

Basically, all that is required for this exercise is a session of between two and four hours, one sheet of A1 'flip chart' paper and a selection of felt tip pens.

The time is divided equally between reflection on one's own and discussion with a chosen partner. In the reflection period people are asked to find a quiet space to consider the relevance of the notion of 'configurations' to themselves and to use the paper to create some representation of their own configurations and any interrelationships these may have. It is best to give people as little structuring as possible because whatever is given may cut across the existing structuring of their configurations. The audience may already have been introduced to the notion of 'configurations' and this should be enough to enable them to begin. In other circumstances the following questions offer sufficient structure:

- What might be different 'parts' within my 'Self'? – what do they 'say'?
- What were my 'parts' at earlier times in my life? – what did they 'say' then?
- How do/did these different parts relate together?

Our experience of this exercise, which bears similarities to the 'personality mapping' exercise in person-centred training (Mearns, 1997a: 100–1), is that most people find it highly generative. Even some who are initially sceptical discover that the process of reflecting upon themselves rapidly bears fruit.

More important than an in-depth analysis is that the therapist is at ease with her configurations and their dynamics – that she values all these dimensions to her existence. In other words, we expect that she has achieved a degree of self-acceptance, currently recognised as the core person-centred training and development aim (Mearns, 1997a).

If the language of configurations is meaningful to the therapist, then she may want to attend to that in her own supervision. One of the distinguishing features of person-centred supervision (see Chapter 10) is that it is about the therapist rather than the client. The therapist is the person in the supervision room – not the client. It is pointless to devote supervision time to the therapist's second-hand account of the client's experience except in so far as we are working on the therapist's experiencing. Hence, supervision time is not wasted on building configuration maps of clients though attention may be given to how the therapist is experiencing different configurations of the client and the difficulties she may be having in responding to those various parts. Also, it is relevant in supervision to beg questions of the therapist's configurations in relation to the work. In summary, the following questions can be usefully addressed in supervision:

- How is the therapist maintaining awareness of the client's symbolisation of configurations and their dynamics?
- Is the therapist 'adding values' in her understanding of the client's different configurations? Therapists sometimes ascribe

values to the client's configurations because of their own individual valuing system. For example, the therapist may add their own 'value' words to parts of the client's Self, such as: the 'poor' little girl/the 'defenceless' young man/the 'vile' abuser, etc.

- Is the therapist equally 'open' to all the client's configurations? For instance, the person-centred therapist may be falling into the trap of valuing the 'growthful' more than the 'not for growth' configurations.
- Is the therapist aware of the parts played by her own configurations in the therapy room?

The person-centred approach has consistently emphasised the full involvement of the therapist. It is interesting to trace what this might mean in terms of configurations. If the client has more than one configuration present in the therapeutic relationship, what about the therapist? Does the therapist simply employ a single configuration entitled 'therapist'? This would be surprising indeed. Ned Gaylin takes a view closer to our own:

> Therapist congruence implies that the many subselves of the therapist are integrated in some way during the hour. The therapist must be able to draw upon these many subselves as a frame of reference in listening, empathizing, and responding to clients as they explore their own subself complex. (Gaylin, 1996: 388)

Looking at the therapist's personal involvement in the relationship from the perspective of configurations can be fascinating – it could well have constituted a third chapter on configurations. For example, is there a configuration within our Self which we tend to enter when we are meeting the client at relational depth? (Lambers, 1999). The question of how counsellors become existentially (or spiritually) equipped to work at relational depth has never been fully explored: is there a part of our Self which is our 'touchstone', or is it, as Dave described in Chapter 3, that we have within our Self many places which we can enter to meet our client? Instead of embarking upon a third chapter, we shall simply end our introduction to configurations by illustrating how the therapist's configurations may become involved in the work. We are aware that therapists from some other approaches would regard this as de facto evidence of 'over-involvement', but the person-centred approach *does* get more involved with people, like the client, Clair.

Clair

Two extracts are presented from work with the client, Clair. In the first, we discover that sufficient depth of relating had not been achieved with Clair so that one important configuration was not 'coming out' into the relationship. The second extract shows how the therapist's contribution was aided by involving more of his own configurations.

The therapy with Clair had apparently been going well, with Clair negotiating a number of changes in her life. The therapeutic relationship had appeared to be characterised by openness and intimacy, yet not *all* of Clair had been declared present in the therapy room. This came to light in one session when Clair announced that she was going to leave her professional job – she 'can't stand the pressure of it any longer' – the 'continual demands are draining me'. The therapist was surprised by the strength and apparent finality of this decision. He had not seen it coming at all – indeed this decision of Clair's was quite incongruous to him – it did not seem to fit 'the frame' he had for her. The only thing to do was to open that frame. When he did this, he was introduced to a powerful configuration within Clair. This configuration had been relating in an unspoken way with the therapist and had been the essential driving force behind her decision to leave her job.

Extract I

> *Dave:* I really don't understand why you are leaving the job.
>
> *Clair:* No, I knew you wouldn't.
>
> *Dave:* You mean you *knew* that I wouldn't understand it?
>
> *Clair:* Yes . . . I've seen it for ages. We are OK when we are working on my 'strong Self' – that work has been great – I wouldn't take anything away from it. But my 'little girl' isn't so sure about you.
>
> *Dave:* She doesn't trust me.
>
> *Clair:* She doesn't think you want to know her . . . she is pretty scared you know.
>
> *Dave:* [*Pause*] I suppose we haven't spent enough time on her.
>
> [*Pause*] I guess I didn't hear her very well – I didn't realise how bad she felt. I see now that I didn't hear her very well.

Clair: I didn't let her come out very often with you. Maybe I thought you wouldn't like me if I really showed you her.

Dave: And perhaps I wasn't as open to her as I could have been . . .

Clair: Well, she has got to come out now. She needs to become a big girl now. So I am holding her hand and walking her out.

Dave: And what are *you* feeling, little girl?

Clair: I am scared . . . and I am *angry*. I am not sure if I can trust you . . . But I want to trust you.

Dave: I want to apologise to you for not *really* listening to you until now.

Extract 2 (two sessions later)

Clair: It is better now, in here. It feels as though there are four of us working together.

Dave: You mean, two of you and two of me?

Clair: Yes.

Dave: The two parts of you, you have called your 'strong Self' and your 'little girl'. But you also sense two parts to me here?

Clair: Yes, don't you?

Dave: Yes, but I haven't given them names yet – in here at least – what is *your* sense of them?

Clair: One is watching over everything that is happening. He is pretty competent, but he is also nervous. The other is not so used to being here but he has been invited. He has got a softness and a vulnerability which is really good for me. He helps me to be 'soft' with myself.

Dave: He helps you to be soft with yourself?

Clair: When it was only your 'strong, competent' self that was here – then *my* strong self just got together with you and there was no space for 'softies' – no space for 'softies' in *either* of us.

Dave: And it is important that we touch that 'softness' in you?

Clair: It is important that we are all here, together. My parts *both* have strength – but they need to 'get along' together, like yours do.

Dave: Maybe I am more 'tentative' than I look. My 'soft' part kind of feels OK with this but he is a bit unsure.

Clair: That's what 'soft parts' are like, silly! Being 'unsure' is part of being 'soft'!

Dave: I think you are more experienced at this than me, Clair.

Clair: Never mind, we'll help each other along!

8 Person-centred therapy at the difficult edge: a developmentally based model of fragile and dissociated process

Margaret S. Warner

Given their emphasis on the positive potential and personal uniqueness of human beings, person-centred therapists have hesitated to conceptualise clients as having 'characterological' disorders such as narcissistic personality, borderline personality or dissociative identity disorder. Yet, like other therapists, person-centred practitioners find that some clients have an extremely difficult time moderating the felt intensity of their experience, dealing with internal reactions of self-criticism and shame or controlling destructive impulses. Some clients feel such extremes of closeness and dependency, or of distance and mistrust, that they have difficulties in working within the usual limits of a therapeutic relationship. Some clients experience dissociative shifts into 'parts' which see themselves as separate from each other and from the main personality of the client, altering client perceptions, beliefs and physiological responses in the process.

This chapter will combine person-centred theories of process with recent work in developmental psychology to offer an alternative model for understanding extreme affective and relational sensitivity. Most clients who experience such extremes of affective and relational sensitivity are experiencing some combination of 'fragile' or 'dissociated' process and that the core conditions of person-centred therapy are necessary and sufficient for work with these styles of process.[1]

'Fragile' process is a style of process in which clients have difficulty modulating the intensity of core experiences, beginning or ending emotional reactions when socially expected, or taking the points of view of other people without breaking contact with their own experience. Clients in the middle of a fragile process often feel particularly high levels of shame and self-criticism about their experience.

'Dissociated' process[2] is a style of process in which aspects of the person's experience are separated into 'parts' – personified clusters of experience which may be partially or totally unaware of each other's presence. These parts have trance-like qualities, allowing the person to alter perceptions, to alter physiological states and to hold contradictory beliefs without discomfort. Such parts seem to have been created in early childhood as a way to keep the person from being overwhelmed by experiences of incest or other abuse. They may influence behaviour while remaining out of the awareness of the rest of the personality. They may come into the person's consciousness as 'others' whose images and voices have an impact on the person. Or, they may emerge as temporarily dominant personalities who take control of the person's consciousness for a period of time.

Diagnoses of people experiencing these difficult forms of process tend to be misleading since such diagnoses attempt to characterise the whole person. Difficult styles of processing can develop individually, or in varying combinations with each other. For example, a person may experience fragile process alone or as an aspect of dissociated process or psychotic process.[3] Styles of process may be experienced at different levels of intensity and may apply to some aspects of a person's experience but not others.

These two difficult styles of processing tend to emerge when a child's earliest experience is not adequately accepted, protected and responded to by parenting figures. When crucial capacities have been thwarted in their early development, adults continue to try to make sense of experience, but their attempts are much more emotionally and relationally painful. To understand these more difficult styles of process, let us first explore person-centred theories relating to optimal ways of processing experience. We can then consider ways that early childhood difficulties may impede the development of important processing capacities, leading to experiences of fragile and dissociated process in adults.

Theories of optimal processing

In a basic sense everyone who is alive 'processes', since all people have experiences that go through changes over time. Person-centred therapists believe that human beings have a tendency toward actualisation which is fostered in relationships characterised by empathy, genuineness and prizing (Rogers, 1957a, 1959). One crucial aspect of this actualisation tendency is the capacity and desire to process experience in productive ways and to develop personally meaningful interpretations of one's own life history.

A number of person-centred theorists have developed models as to how this natural tendency to process experience tends to work under optimal circumstances (Gendlin, 1964, 1968, 1974; Rice, 1974; Wexler, 1974). A core intrapsychic ability is required for optimal processing as described in each of these models – an ability to hold experience in empathic attention at a workable level of intensity. Processing theorists suggest that as a person holds an experience in this sort of attention, new experiences tend to come into awareness. They note that productive reorganisations of experience are particularly likely to occur when clients attend to aspects of their experience which they have not yet clearly articulated to themselves.

Each theorist has emphasised a different sort of unclearness: the bodily felt senses clients have about situations (Gendlin, 1964, 1968, 1974), vivid scenes or images which arise in clients (Rice, 1974) and themes and facets which clients have not fully worked out within themselves (Wexler, 1974).[4] During processing, related, but previously unattended memories, thoughts, feelings and images emerge and transform themselves into more clearly understandable forms. As such new material is attended to, the individuals are likely to construe their situations in new and more meaningful ways. When emotions are evoked in the process, they often intensify, go through transformations and ultimately resolve themselves into experiences of much less intensity (as when sadness becomes grief and sobbing and ultimately resolves into a feeling of peace).

Given the tasks described in these process theories, a number of *experiential capacities* seem likely to be central to the individual's ability to process experience:

- The capacity to hold experience in attention at moderate levels of arousal.
- The capacity to modulate the intensity of experiential states.
- The capacity to relate words to experience.

Let us look at the development of these capacities in relation to fragile process and go on to consider some of the issues involved in working therapeutically with clients. Thereafter, we shall similarly examine the developmental and therapeutic dimensions of 'dissociated process'.

Fragile process

Development of the capacity to hold experience in attention

Human beings initially hold experience in attention and moderate its intensity within parent–child dyads. This relational partnership provides a developmental basis from which they internalise increasingly autonomous capacities for experiential processing.

Initially, an infant's experience can be seen as entirely constituted by Gendlin's directly felt, implicit meanings, since the infant has no ability to symbolise in words.

> . . . the 'implicit' or 'felt' datum of experiencing is a sensing of bodily life. As such it may have countless organized aspects, but this does not mean that they are conceptually formed . . . we complete and form them when we explicate. (Gendlin, 1964: 113–14)

Still, the infant engaged in such implicit experiencing relates and undergoes change within relationship:

> . . . it is often the case that there is an ongoing experiencing process without verbal symbols. In fact, most situations and behaviors involve feeling in interaction with non-verbal events. (Gendlin, 1964: 130)

Thus, it can be said that:

> Interpersonal events occur before there is a self. Others respond to us before we come to respond to ourselves. If these responses were not in interaction with feeling, if there were nothing but other people's responses as such, the self could become nothing but the learned responses of others. (Gendlin, 1964: 135)

Certainly, in this initial 'implicit' relating, an infant is active in initiating and responding to interactions with adults. Daniel Stern (1985) eloquently describes the non-verbal *affect attunement* central to early phases of infancy which cultivates a sense of efficacy in relating to another. Also, the carers' overall ability to eliminate trauma and to create a benign ratio between positive and negative experiences undoubtedly contributes to an infant's overall association of his or her experiences with 'goodness' or 'badness'.

Development of the capacity to modulate the intensity of experiential states

Based on studies of heart rate and gaze aversion, Fogel (1982) finds that over the first year of life, secure infants gradually learn to moderate levels of arousal while staying engaged in pleasurable interactions with carers for longer periods of time. Studies with animals have demonstrated how experiences within the caregiving system actually tune the central nervous system to tolerate high arousal (Hofer, 1990; Kraemer, 1992). Through repeated experiences of increased arousal and subsequent modulation, the brain itself becomes better adapted for dampening high arousal and for emotional regulation in general (Schore, 1994).

Less securely attached infants do not seem to acquire these abilities. In fact they seem to come to an opposite set of learnings: that it is difficult to maintain emotionally engaged attention in a way that leads to sustained positive experiences, that situations of high arousal are likely to lead to overload and disorganisation and that carers are not very effective in soothing distress when it does occur. Sroufe (1996) suggests that under these circumstances, fearfulness and anger are chronic experiences in response to new situations, leading infants to take one of two opposite strategies – seeking out continual carer contact or cutting off from attachment feelings altogether.

While toddlers show substantially greater ranges of exploratory play and capacity for self-regulation than infants, in research studies they present parallel patterns of attachment to those of infants. In the absence of secure attachment, toddlers are highly vulnerable to being overwhelmed by shame, frustration and rage. Sroufe (1996) suggests that under these circumstances, toddlers are likely to adopt styles of chronic dysregulation or rigid self-control.

Longitudinal studies document the continuation of attachment styles into school years, with less securely attached children being seen as being negativistic, as lacking in self control and as not being well liked by their peers (Egeland et al., 1993; Sroufe, 1996).

Development of the capacity to relate words to experience

Early on, most parents engage in a particular sort of empathic interaction in which they begin to name an infant's experiences and to offer hypothesised reasons for these experiences, perhaps saying that the baby is 'tired' when she cries or that she thinks 'spinach is disgusting' when she spits it out. Essentially, parents are offering verbal symbols that could carry the infant's implicitly felt experience forward into explicit meaning if the infant had words. At some point children come to recognise a matching or mismatching between these words and their own felt experience.

Of course, there is great variation in the quality of parental empathy in this early naming of infant experience and the clarity of reasons offered for such experiences. Some parents are relatively inattentive or have difficulty leaving their own perspectives. Hence, experiences may go unnamed or be systematically misnamed. Particular sorts of experiences such as unhappiness or anger may be threatening in some families and may be routinely labelled as something else. Or, children of a very volatile or insecure parent may learn to label their experience in the way they find most calming or least threatening to that parent. As the result of such empathic failure, children may never develop a capacity to hold experience in attention to check the felt rightness of its meaning. In the process they are likely to rely on more external or socially conventional cues as criteria for labelling experiences. Their personal senses of experiential recognition, or the lack of it, may be unattended to or actively avoided and disparaged.[5]

Main (1991) suggests that a particular kind of 'metacognitive' functioning, in which a person reflects on the validity, nature and source of experiences, plays a significant role both as a precursor and as an outcome of secure attachment. This capacity allows individuals to attend to and resolve contradictions in their experiences thus generating a single, reasonably integrated, narrative for organising their life experience. Main (1991) found that the overall coherence of the carer's presentation of his or her own attachment history was the single strongest correlate of secure infant attachment. Further, in a longitudinal study following nine children from infancy, she found that, by ages 10 to 11, 80 per cent of children who had shown a stable pattern of secure attachment since infancy were able to offer a 10-minute spoken autobiography, often with spontaneous instances of metacognitive processing. This was only true of 25 per cent of children with a history of insecure attachment, none of whom showed instances of metacognitive processing in their comments.

The absence of the sort of secure attachment that tends to be created within a safe, empathic parental environment, seems to have the result of creating both an inability and a disinclination to attend to the immediacy of experience in ways likely to generate a reorganisation of understanding. Children appear to have difficulties in maintaining a focus on experience or moderating its intensity. Given such negative experiences, the immediacy of their process is likely to feel dangerous and somehow shameful. Further, they are likely to have developed a deep belief that the presence of others who connect to their experience will make already problematic experiences worse.

Therapy with clients whose process is 'fragile'

Clients who have suffered empathic failure in childhood seem to experience a 'fragile' style of processing as adults. I will describe this process in some detail as I have observed it in my own, fairly classical, practice of person-centred therapy. Clients who have a fragile style of processing tend to experience core issues at very low or high levels of intensity. They tend to have difficulty starting and stopping experiences that are personally significant or emotionally connected. In addition, they are likely to have difficulty taking in the point of view of another person while remaining in contact with such experiences.

For example, a client may talk circumstantially for most of a therapy hour and only connect with an underlying feeling of rage at the very end. At this point he may feel unable to turn the rage off in a way which will allow him to return to work. He may then spend hours walking in the park trying to handle the intensity of the feeling. The client may be able to talk about feelings of rage with the therapist and very much want them understood and affirmed. Yet, therapist comments to explain the situation or disagree with the client will be felt as attempts by the therapist to annihilate his experience.

Empathic understanding responses are often the only sorts of responses people can receive while in the middle of fragile process without feeling traumatised or disconnected from their experience. The ongoing presence of a soothing, empathic person is often essential to the person's ability to stay connected without feeling overwhelmed. In a certain sense, clients in the middle of fragile process are asking if their way of experiencing themselves at that moment has a right to exist in the world. Any misnaming of the experience or suggestion that they look at the experience in a different way is experienced as an answer of 'no' to the question.

Clients with low-intensity fragile process are likely to experience personal reactions as subtle emotional shadings, as threads of experience that they can barely catch and hold on to. If distracted or contradicted, they are likely to give up on the idea that such experiences have any significance. Therapist comments intended to offer helpful advice or insight are likely to cause the client to disconnect. Clients experiencing a high-intensity fragile process feel their experience very strongly and often want to be understood and affirmed in the rightness of the experience. However, even slight misnaming or misunderstanding of the experience is likely to make the client feel violated. For example, a client who says that he feels 'irritated' may feel deeply misunderstood if the therapist says that she understands that he is 'angry' (hence, the importance of 'staying close to the client's symbolisation', emphasised in Chapter 7). Other sorts of interpretive comments or advice are likely to be experienced as invalidating the experience altogether.

The physical arrangements of therapy sessions are likely to affect clients' abilities to stay connected to a fragile process. Knowing that sessions will take place at the same time of the day and week, that they will begin in the same way and that the physical arrangement of the room will remain the same, often helps clients stay with a fragile process. Changes that might be insignificant under other circumstances can completely disrupt a client's ability to work therapeutically. For instance, meeting in a different office, rearranging furniture in the office, or meeting at a different time may be experienced by the client as destroying the therapeutic context without any certainty that it can be restored. On the other hand, clients who experience fragile process often feel the need to have considerable control over the arrangement of sessions. Being able to adjust the length of sessions, have sessions at a certain time of day, or arrange the room in a way that feels comfortable, may allow a client to connect with process that would be inaccessible otherwise. As was discussed in Chapter 2, the 'therapeutic context' is an active variable in the therapeutic process.

Clients who have a fragile style of processing often experience their lives as chaotic or empty. If clients with high-intensity fragile process choose to stay connected with their experience in personal relationships, they are likely to feel violated and misunderstood a great deal of the time. When they express their feelings, other people in their lives are likely to see them as unreasonably angry, touchy and stubborn. These others are likely to become angry and rejecting in return, reinforcing the client's sense that there is something fundamentally poisonous about their existence. Clients who continue to express their feelings are likely to have ongoing volatile relationships, or a succession of relationships that start out well and then go sour. If, on the other hand, they give up on connecting or expressing their personal reactions they are likely to feel frozen or dead inside. Many alternate, holding back their reactions while feeling increasingly uncomfortable and then exploding with rage at those around them.

Clients with low-intensity fragile process are likely to have difficulty becoming aware of or taking their personal reactions seriously. When they do express reactions they often do so in subtle and indirect ways. They are likely to feel rebuffed and withdraw personal connection before others are aware that a serious issue was involved. They may simply stay detached for most of the time, living lives that are outwardly functional, but lacking in a sense of vitality. Clients with low-intensity fragile process may not know that there is an alternative to a low-key, slightly depressive existence.

Ideally, therapy with adults who have a fragile style of processing creates the kind of empathic holding that was missing in the clients' early childhood experiences. If the therapist stays empathically connected to significant client experiences, the clients are likely to feel the satisfaction that comes from staying with their experiences in an accepting way. Initially this tends to be a very ambivalent sort of pleasure, since the experiences themselves are often painful. Moreover, clients may regard the experiences as shameful and likely to result in harm to themselves and others. Clients may feel the need to test the therapist in various ways, before trusting that the therapist can relate to their experience or believing that their experience could have any value. They may be afraid that expressing their experience will make them vulnerable to manipulation and control by the therapist, or that their experience has the power to overwhelm and harm the therapist. Over time, however, clients are likely to find that their reactions make more sense than they thought and that seemingly inexorable feelings go through various sorts of positive change and resolution.

Effective therapy with fragile process requires high quality listening skills. Clients typically need more than an accepting presence. They need to know that their experience has been understood with exactness and sensitivity as to its emotional vulnerability. They also often need to have some control as to how that understanding is expressed. They may need to hear their moment-to-moment reactions reflected almost word for word in order to know that their therapists have grasped exactly what they were feeling and trying to express.

As was described in Chapter 7, therapists need to be particularly attentive when clients have a sense of experiences for which they do not yet have words. If therapists make space for the lack of clarity, clients are likely to find their own words for the experience. For example, the therapist might say 'Something about that feels really uncomfortable, but you're not quite clear what it is'. The client may then say, 'Yes, it's kind of a sad hopeless feeling.' On the other hand, if the therapist fills in the meaning, the client is likely to feel misunderstood and angry or give up searching for the right words to express the experience. Many clients ask for some sort of physical touch to help them feel safe enough to remain connected to their experience in the moment. This is not a trivial request when we understand the terror which might previously have accompanied the act of remaining connected to their experience.

The following therapy segment shows the moment to moment attunement typical of this work as a client begins to hold deeply felt experiences in attention. In this session, the client had asked to place her head in the therapist's lap with the therapist's hand on her stomach, a position that the client often chose for herself. Earlier, she had spent several minutes crying and hitting her knee.

> *Client:* I don't even know why it's so hard. All I was working with . . . I always turn my head. And I don't have a judgement about that. But I was working a little with turning my head

> toward you instead of turning away. I can get so far and it's
> too scary.
> *Therapist:* Fear just at that moment.
> *Client:* Not that in itself it's important. I think it's just a
> reflection. [*Cries to herself for a minute*] I don't even know
> what my hitting is. I don't know why. It's not like I remember
> anything.
> *Therapist:* It's right there in your body.
> *Client:* It's this incredibly terrifying something, like I'm looking
> at my house burning down.
> *Therapist:* Horror.
> *Client:* I want your hand here now. [*Points to her upper chest, the
> therapist moves her hand. Client cries again and hits her knee*]

Most therapists believe that they listen well, when they are
actually quite inattentive and inaccurate in their understanding of
moment-to-moment client interaction. Therapists often have to
listen to tapes of their own interactions to realise how little they
have understood of clients' immediate concerns and how ineffectively they have expressed that understanding to their clients. In
addition to listening poorly, therapists may offer a considerable
number of comments, interpretations or questions to their clients
without adequate thought about their possible effect. Such interventions may seem quite mild to the therapist but be experienced
as annihilating to a client in the middle of fragile process. For
example, a client may say that she feels upset when she thinks
that she has to come to therapy sessions and the therapist may ask
why she feels that she has to come. The client in the middle of a
fragile process may be just starting to feel that she can hold her
feeling of upsetness and feel that she is all right in the process.
Under those circumstances, the therapist's question is likely to be
experienced as a message that the client's experiences are wrong
and that she has no right to have them. Yet, if the client expresses
anger at the therapist, the therapist is likely to feel puzzled and a
little annoyed by the client's reaction.

Clients typically have some themes or life situations that are
much more fragile than others. They are likely to express themselves in ways that are much more clear, forceful, and seemingly
rational around aspects of their lives that are less fragile. When
issues are fragile, they will express themselves more indirectly – in
side comments while leaving the session, or in themes buried
within long stories, or by comments made very tentatively and
then quickly denied. Such indirectness is one reason that clients

who have a fragile process often feel misunderstood. Therapists can easily miss attempts by their clients to communicate about experiences that are fragile then find that the clients leave therapy or do not seem to be making any progress.

When clients come to be able to hold and process fragile experiences in therapy they are likely to feel very reliant on the therapist for a period of time. At this stage, the empathic presence of the therapist is essential to the client's ability to hold her experiences without feeling traumatised. It is as if the therapist holds an oxygen mask for the client who spends the rest of the week struggling to breathe. Quite sensibly, the client may hate to leave sessions and resent the time that they have to spend out of contact with the therapist. Gradually, though, the client comes to be able to hold their experience for longer and longer periods of time between sessions. Often, having several sessions a week helps the client to bridge between sessions without losing their sense of connectedness. In this in between phase, clients can often reconnect with their experience by calling up the image of the therapist in various ways. Brief phone contact, hearing tape recordings of the therapist's voice, holding an object that belongs to the therapist, or sitting outside of the therapist's office may help to maintain connection with their experience.

Fragile process and self psychology

Many ideas of Heinz Kohut (1971, 1984), already mentioned in Chapter 2, fit well with a model of fragile process. A number of writers have noted that Kohut's emphasis on empathy in work with narcissistic clients comes remarkably close to the attitudes of empathy, congruence and unconditional positive regard that Carl Rogers had earlier advocated in therapy with all clients (Kahn, 1996). Kohut's (1971, 1984) discussions of 'selfobject' transferences capture the intense dependency which clients feel while they are in the middle of fragile processes. Kohut was the first theorist to really understand the way clients may need to use the therapist as an auxiliary ego for a period of time. His discussions of empathy vividly capture the sense of violation which clients experiencing fragile process feel when they are misunderstood by their therapists.

These contributions by Kohut have been very helpful to many person-centred therapists in coming to a deeper understanding of their clients' processes. On the other hand, Kohut's theory is much less elaborated than the person-centred tradition on the nature of empathy, on exploring ways empathy can be expressed most effectively, and on the sorts of client processing likely to be fostered in an empathic understanding relationship.

While Kohut saw his thinking as an extension of psycho-analysis, his ideas fit somewhat uncomfortably within the psycho-analytic model. Most psychoanalysts try to avoid gratifying the infantile wishes of their clients and rely on interpretation to engender awareness and change. Kohut was suggesting that when pre-oedipal issues are involved, the therapist needs to replicate a number of parental 'selfobject' functions that the client missed earlier in life by fostering similar selfobject transferences with the therapist.

By suggesting that positive elements of the therapist's style of interaction potentiate natural, self-directing processes in the client, Kohut (1971, 1984, 1985) is expressing ideas that are much more compatible with a person-centred model of therapy than a tradi-tionally psychoanalytic one. Of course, he moderated this position by suggesting that this non-interpretive, empathic stance should only be taken while the client was dealing with pre-oedipal issues and should be abandoned with more advanced clients. In some ways, Kohut's attempts to make his thinking compatible with drive theory impeded his development of an internally consistent approach to therapy with clients whose experience is fragile.

Interpretations of fragile process as archaic defence

Many therapists interpret negative therapist reactions as result-ing from unconscious communication on the part of clients, who they see as using the archaic defence of *projective identification* (Kernberg, 1976). Initially, therapists often feel uncomfortable being with clients who are in the middle of fragile process. They may feel that the clients are detached and boring, that they are perversely unwilling to receive helpful interventions or that they are unreasonably angry about minor dislocations in the therapy process. Using an object relations model, they may then conclude that the client unconsciously wants the therapist to feel bored or frustrated so that the therapist can understand how bored and frustrated the client is or has been feeling in her life.

It is wise to be conservative about such judgements when clients are experiencing fragile process. They are usually just trying to hold on to their own experiences and keep them from going out of control. They generally have no particular wish for the therapist to feel frustrated and out of control in the process. In fact, they often feel a terror of burdening or harming therapists by their relationships with them. Therapist discomfort usually arises for one of two reasons. Firstly, the therapist may not understand the client's process and therefore experiences him or her as perversely frustrating and unreasonable, or secondly, the therapist has his or her own control or dependency issues that are activated by the intensity of the client's needs. Jumping to the conclusion that clients unconsciously want to create uncomfortable feelings in the therapist can easily stop therapists from trying to understand their own and their clients' reactions and can impede the very empathy that is so essential to these clients.

Occasionally, clients in the middle of fragile process *are* trying to create negative feelings in their therapists. These are better understood as interpersonal strategies secondary to fragile process, rather than manifestations of unconscious defence. When this happens, clients are usually trying to find ways to handle their intense needs for therapist support. They may try to test the therapist with negative behaviour to find out if the therapist is likely to leave them, before risking the intense dependence which will occur if they open up fragile processes. Once they are in a close relationship with the therapist, they may try to find indirect ways to get more help from the therapist when their experiences feel overwhelming. Or, they may want to express their resentment at the fact that they suffer so much in the relationship while the therapist does not seem to suffer at all.

Many psychodynamically oriented therapists interpret the intense reactions of clients in the middle of fragile process as *splitting* and assume that the client is having trouble integrating good and bad qualities into a single image. They then feel that it is important to point out the other side of each issue – noting, for example, that people idealised by the client are fallible and that the people clients are angry with also have good qualities (Kernberg, 1976). Descriptively, it is accurate that clients experiencing fragile process often react in strong and unilateral ways. For example, clients are quite likely to idealise a therapist who is successfully connecting with fragile process. They are also likely to feel very angry with other people in their lives by whom they feel misunderstood and mistreated. On the other hand, they are likely to switch to feeling extremely angry at the therapist when they feel misunderstood and mistreated by small missteps in that relationship. However, therapist attempts to balance clients' points of view are unnecessary and potentially quite harmful to clients in so far as they are actually recapitulating the external judgemental ingredients inherent in the development of fragile process.

The primary difficulty that clients with fragile process have is one of not being able to hold their experience, rather than a difficulty in integrating good and bad images into a single gestalt. When the experience of fragile process is understood, strongly positive and negative reactions expressed by clients often make a great deal of sense. Once clients gain a sense of security in their ability to hold good and bad reactions in an accepting way, other processing skills develop without any intervention on the part of the therapist. Clients become more interested in understanding the experience of others and they become more able to use that experience to modify their understanding of their own situations. In doing this, they spontaneously move into the sort of metacognitive processing described by Mary Main (1991) and, as a result, they develop more integrated good and bad images of themselves and others. As they become more able to hold and affirm their reactions, they are less likely to feel thrown off and violated by other people's reactions to them. They become more able to switch back and forth between their own points of view and those of others, or to postpone interactions that could be dealt with more effectively at later times.

Dissociated process

Trauma and the development of affective regulation

Dissociated process seems to arise almost exclusively as a response to early childhood trauma. Experiences of physical and sexual abuse are likely to overwhelm children's abilities to modulate arousal, whatever their attachment histories. Preliminary research (Coe et al., 1995) indicates that there is significant overlap between issues of attachment and issues of trauma. The same personal difficulties generating a lack of attunement to an infant's needs seem likely to leave parents vulnerable to perpetrating physically or sexually abusive behaviours as well.

Several theorists have noted that young children who are physically or sexually abused are particularly vulnerable to emotional flooding since they have not developed the verbal and logical capacities to make sense of the experience. Before the ages of two or three children are not able to name emotional experiences (Dupont, 1994). Additionally, before the shift to concrete operations (approximately age seven), they are unable to integrate positive and negative emotions into a single schema or to retain awareness of properties that contradict those in immediate awareness (Van der Kolk et al., 1994). With this all-or-nothing quality to their thinking, children experience shame, and believe in retribution without being able to have an integrated sense of how parents who are sometimes caring could be abusive at other times (Dupont, 1994). Without the mental ability to have a complex sense of causation they are highly likely to experience traumatic events as shameful and themselves as bad.

Van der Kolk et al. note that conceptual processes are essential to the ability to contain affect.

> One of the great mysteries of the processing of traumatic experience is that as long as the trauma is experienced as speechless terror, the body continues to keep score and react to conditioned stimuli as the return of the trauma. When the mind is able to create symbolic representations of these past experiences, however, there often seems to be a taming of the terror, and a related desomatization of experience. (1994: 727)

Further, they note that young children who are traumatised tend to freeze the development of capacities to modulate affect at the age at which the trauma occurred, and assert their belief that therapeutic modalities which negotiate interpersonal safety and recreate aspects of early attachment relationships are most likely to be effective.

Van der Kolk et al. (1994) go on to report that, in a study of a large sample of patients with a variety of personality disorders who were given a Traumatic Antecedents Questionnaire, more than half of those diagnosed as borderline had histories of severe sexual or physical abuse before the age of six years, and 87 per cent reported such abuse at some time in their childhood.

The development of trauma-driven dissociation

In recent years, several person-centred therapists at the Chicago Counseling Center have done intensive work with clients experiencing dissociative identity disorder and various other trauma-related dissociative states. Their experiences in therapy offer a subjective account of the development of dissociated process.

The clients we have seen who worked through dissociative experiences all came to remember experiences of sexual or physical trauma before the age of seven. At such early ages children have high levels of hypnotic suggestibility. Faced with overwhelming trauma and lacking the more complex ways of coping with experiences available to older children, our clients seem to have stumbled on dissociation as a solution. One client, for example, found that when she stared at dots on the wallpaper she could separate herself out from the terror and anguish of being raped by her father. Some clients describe experiencing themselves as out of their bodies and watching the events from the ceiling.

Understandably, dissociation under these circumstances is extremely reinforcing. Children go from an extreme of anguish to a lack of intense pain and an ability to put the whole thing out of their minds the next day. This capacity makes family life seem tolerable and for some allows the illusion that they have a normal, happy family life. Clients seem to take a larger lesson from the apparent effectiveness of these early dissociation experiences – that emotional pain is destructive and that the way to live successfully is to make painful experiences disappear.

Such early childhood dissociation seldom seems to stop with separation from the experience, as is typical of adult post-traumatic stress disorders. Children almost always divide the dissociated aspects of their experiences into a number of compartments that are separate from each other. This may happen because young children have a number of intense reactions that seem irreconcilable with each other and they do not yet have the mental capacities to integrate such contradictions.

Typically our clients describe having feelings of helplessness, terror, pain and anguish which were so intense that they felt that they could die from those feelings. They simultaneously felt afraid of dying and wished that they could die. They felt intense rage and wished that they could do violence to the perpetrator. Yet they wished that they could hold on to the times when their parents seemed loving or nurturing.

In the helpless part of their feelings they were terrified of the violence of their angry feelings. From the angry part of their feelings, they felt disgust and shame at their reactions of helplessness. In their desire to hold on to some normal life, they wished that both the angry and the helpless, anguished reactions would disappear. Probably as a result of these contradictions, a number of different clusters of experience separated out within their dissociated experiences. Each cluster of experience came to have a distinctive 'person-like' nature, with its own feelings, history and way of looking at the world.

These 'parts' bear resemblance to the notion of 'configurations' outlined in Chapter 6, but the psychology of configurations seeks to describe fairly 'normal' self-development. As outlined in Chapter 6 and in Ross (1999) there are important qualitative differences between configurations and dissociated 'parts'.

A number of dissociated parts typically take on self-abusive or suicidal qualities. These impulses seem to arise when the pain of dissociated memories threatens to return. Typically, though not always, this anguish is held by a young child part who is terrified and alone and wishes someone would come to help. Angry abusive parts are also frightened children and have their own disturbing memories that they may be trying to get away from. In either case, when memories threaten to return, one or more parts would rather die than let that happen. Clients perhaps stumble on the fact that a wide number of self-destructive behaviours are effective in containing memories. By adulthood, clients are likely to be engaged in eating disorders, impulses to cut themselves, substance abuse, suicidal ideation, and/or various compulsive sexual, athletic or work behaviours. They may hear disparaging voices which tell them that they are worthless or which press them to cut themselves or take pills. Some clients keep these behaviours quite hidden from themselves and others. Others present to therapists with an astonishing array of out-of-control, seemingly impulsive behaviours. As a result, they are often mistakenly diagnosed as borderline or schizophrenic, and subjected to symptom-specific inpatient treatments.

Clients may have one or more parts which take on qualities of the perpetrator – wanting to dominate and harm others, or being attracted to sadistic or masochistic sexual experiences. One woman commented that she felt so awful being a helpless victim that she preferred seeing herself as an active participant, feeling that she was her father's real 'wife' and that she was superior to her mother.

Distinctive characteristics of dissociated parts

Therapists and clients differ as to whether to call these dissociated experiences – 'personalities' or 'parts' or 'ego-states'.[6] Clearly they differ significantly from the full everyday personalities of clients. Yet, they are a great deal more personified than ordinary mood states or even 'configurations'. The dissociated parts have a number of qualities that distinguish them from other states of mind.

Dissociated parts have the ability to alter perceptions in much the same way as a person in a trance. For example, while a part is present, a client looking in the mirror may see herself with the characteristics of that part – as older or younger, fatter or thinner, a different age or sex. Parts may even feel no pain under the most excruciating circumstances or create sensations with no external cause. The degree of distortion can be considerable – for instance, one client, on leaving our session, experienced herself as an older man driving a red sports car to an unknown destination.

Parts are quite untroubled by the idea that there are several of them in one body, that they were born when the client was a particular age, or that they exist in some part of the client's body (such as the right side). They often believe that they could kill the client without killing themselves. Parts often think quite concretely, believing that their feelings could literally contaminate and harm the therapist or that angry thoughts could make the therapist's plane crash.

Along with the ability to alter perceptions, parts have quite amazing power to generate physiological changes in the client's body. Clinically demonstrable signs of illness may disappear within hours, only to reappear at another time or in another location. One client had an ear infection on the left side which had moved to the right side by the time of her next medical exam a few days later, much to the confusion of her doctors.

Client experiences of dissociated parts

Most clients do not experience the presence of dissociated parts all of the time. In fact, the point of dissociation is to minimise painful, out-of-control experiences, and various part-related experiences are likely to feel quite disturbing to clients. They are likely to come to therapy asking the therapist to help them get rid of the various manifestations of dissociated parts that they cannot keep out of their consciousness – bad dreams, impulses to cut themselves, 'funny' states of consciousness.

The parts seem to emerge when trauma memories are pressing to the surface. This can happen when some life experience, such as going to a violent movie or seeing a child being hurt, stimulates feelings related to the original trauma. Some clients find themselves helplessly recreating their victimisation and have memories triggered in current abusive relationships. On the other hand, clients may find that the memories begin to press to the surface when they are becoming emotionally healthy in many other ways. Clients who have been making progress in therapy often begin to sense that the memories need to be faced for them to become whole.

The parts are experienced in quite different ways when they are at different distances from the client's immediate awareness. Some clients go for years with very little awareness of the parts. To stay away from part experiences, though, they generally need to lead quite restricted lives. Sometimes clients work incessantly, never leaving a space when any out-of-control experience could come into their awareness. They may stop any relationship before it becomes vulnerable enough to raise feelings of helplessness. Often they have bouts of unexplained anxiety or depression.

When part experiences are a step closer to the client's subjective awareness, clients experience them as disowned thoughts, actions or feelings. One client made arrangements to go to a motel to kill herself with no sense of why she was doing this. Another had feelings of overwhelming anguish and terror with no idea where these feelings came from. A third, who had always had a strong preference for wearing pants and sweaters, found that she had bought several dresses without any sense of why she had done this.

With another step closer to awareness, many clients experience parts as frightening presences. One had the experience of a young girl coming to her in a dream wanting to tell her something, but the feeling of anguish was so frightening that the client started to take sleeping pills to make the girl go away. She then said that she had the feeling that the girl was angry with her. Another experienced a 'monster' in her awareness who would threaten her and tell her that he would not stop until she took an overdose of pills.

With still another step closer to awareness, clients may experience the presence of a dissociated part in consciousness without having the part take over their personality. Clients then sense the parts as personalities with distinctive intentions, thoughts, feelings and memories that motivate their actions. Under these circumstances many previously puzzling feelings and behaviours come to make more sense. The dissociated parts often follow a peculiar logic, but it is quite consistent and often aimed at protecting the client in some way. For example, one client who had been suicidally depressed precipitously went home to see her father who had raped her as a child. When asked about it she checked with parts inside. She said that 'Lucky' felt that her father had succeeded in life because he had no feelings and if she went to visit him she could learn to be as cold as he was and then she would be able to kill herself without remorse.

At certain points clients *switch* and dissociated parts take over control of their consciousness and behaviour. This can happen dramatically with a named other personality. For example, one client named 'Ann' suddenly started talking about what a wimp 'Ann' is and how 'Ann' couldn't do anything if she, 'Claudia', was not around to hold things together. At other times the switch can be more subtle with the client sliding unobtrusively into another part that is not within the control of the client's everyday personality.

When clients 'switch', they often cannot remember what happened afterwards. One client remembered beginning to get angry at work and the next thing she knew it was an hour later and people were treating her with cautious reserve. She made a comment about how they were all under stress, hoping to get some sense of what might have happened in the interim. Another client who had been threatening to slit her throat, woke up in the hospital in restraints with no idea of how she had got there.

Clients typically have parts that try to intervene to keep the 'switching' from being too obvious to outsiders. If behaviour begins to get out of control, the person may say she is feeling sick and leave or invent some other cover story. Blatantly obvious switching in front of strangers or acquaintances often indicates that the client is extremely overwhelmed and can no longer keep herself from being flooded by traumatic memories.

Client experience of the therapeutic process

The process of regaining memories almost always feels chaotic and painful to clients. They often wish that they could forget about the experience and return to their former lives, however restricted or symptomatic. However, clients may sense intuitively that the process is important and that they need to stay with it if their lives are to have any sense of vitality or wholeness in the future. While some clients stop, others find that they are unable and unwilling to pull away from the process once memories begin to emerge in an empathic environment.

The work that we are doing with clients who experience dissociation follows classic person-centred principles. As with many other client groups, we have found that therapeutic relationships grounded in empathy, authenticity and prizing of clients tend to foster latent capacities for self-directed change. Given the particularly intense wishes and fears of clients having dissociative experiences, the balance between therapeutic effectiveness and ineffectiveness is often tipped by the accuracy and sensitivity of the therapist's empathy. While basic empathic skills are essential, empathic understanding is greatly enhanced when therapists have some background understanding of dissociative processes as commonly experienced by clients. Particular empathic sensitivity needs to be developed for communicating understanding to clients who experience several personality parts that operate independently, since understanding expressed to one part may feel like a disparagement or a threat to another part. (We found a similar challenge for the therapist working with the 'family' of configurations in Chapter 7.)

In my experience, very few clients come to therapy describing dissociative experiences in ways that are obvious to therapists who are not experienced in work with dissociation. A minority will immediately show drastic puzzling mood shifts in therapy sessions or even talk about separate personalities. Most clients, however, begin by describing more commonplace symptoms. They may discuss relationship issues, work blocks, global anxiety, depression, self-destructive impulses, or eating disorders. Sometimes they describe troubled, or incestuous family backgrounds, sometimes they describe memories of idyllic families that are virtually problem free.

Some clients do a considerable amount of therapeutic work without addressing the dissociation at all. They may appear to make great progress for a while but hit a plateau in which problems seem puzzlingly intractable and their behaviours perversely contradictory.

Clients come to a point beyond which they cannot progress further without remembering and processing the original childhood trauma. They cannot connect with these issues without acknowledging aspects of the dissociative experiences to themselves and to their therapists. In this sense, it is often a sign of progress in therapy when clients become more 'multiple-like'. As memories start to press more urgently to the surface, clients are likely to become more obviously fragmented and aware of dissociated parts that are trying desperately to keep the experience in control. One advanced graduate student spent years in a seemingly productive analytically oriented therapy. She knew that she had memories of being molested by her brother as a teenager, but had no feelings attached to the memories. She suddenly found that she was having intensive suicidal impulses, was losing track of hours at a time, and was sometimes finding herself feeling like a five-year-old unsure of how to get home. For a while she frequently said that she knew that there was something that she needed to know but that she didn't want to know it. One evening she felt particularly frightened and went home with a friend. Once there she shifted into a vivid flashback in which she remembered her brother raping her while her father looked on. The experience was enormously painful but she also felt great relief in finally knowing. The out of control dissociative experiences diminished immediately.

When clients begin to trust their therapists more they are likely to begin to describe some of the various oddnesses occurring in their experience, or allow themselves to 'switch' in the therapist's presence. This level of trust may come within weeks or only after years of work with a therapist. Many therapists stop clients when they try to talk about such dissociated aspects of their experience. This happens for a number of reasons. Some therapists believe that such dissociated experiences are 'regressive' or 'non-reality-oriented' and will tell clients that it is best not to talk about them in therapy. Frequently, however, therapists who want to welcome the full range of their clients' experiences unintentionally misunderstand and block clients in their attempts to communicate about dissociated experiences. Since clients are often afraid that they will be rejected or labelled as crazy if they talk about such experiences, they often begin by presenting them in ways that are oblique or seemingly casual to see how the therapist will react. These oblique 'clues' may be missed altogether by a therapist unfamiliar with dissociated experiences, or the therapist may assume that their client is speaking metaphorically. One client of mine was switching in sessions and felt hurt that I did not sense what was going on. While in her everyday self she did not want to be touched at all, she had switched during several sessions into a very vulnerable part and wished that I knew that she needed to be held. She even tried to draw a picture for me of how her consciousness was organised, though she did not explain that that was what the picture was about. For several months she kept saying 'I've put the pieces on the table. You have to pick them up'. Only while I was away on summer vacation did it occur to me that she might be trying to tell me that she had been having dissociative experiences in our sessions. After I returned she commented that it was both a relief and a little scary how well I now understood what she was saying to me.

Connecting with dissociated parts

I have found the following simple responses helpful when I am not sure whether a client might be dissociating. All of these responses have the underlying aim of making it easy for clients to speak of dissociated experiences without advocating or pressuring them to do so. I will describe each of these responses briefly.

Sensitising myself to possible clues to dissociation. I make a mental note whenever clients report anything about their life experiences that might be consistent with dissociation. These include any incest experiences in the immediate or extended family, histories of self-abusive, impulsive or substance abusing behaviour, reported memory lapses, nightmares, headaches or odd states of consciousness and demeaning or suicidally oriented voices. I try not to assume that a client is dissociating, but if a number of these signs manifest themselves, I do begin to listen closely to client communication that might refer to dissociative experiences.

Listening concretely to client expressions that might easily be assumed to be metaphoric. When clients describe experiences that are odd, disconnected or divided into parts, I am likely to let the client know that I have heard them, expressing my understanding in almost the same words that the client used. In doing this, I am trying to reflect in a way that does not make a pre-judgement as to whether particular comments are meant literally or metaphorically. So, if a client says 'I feel that I am only here with my head and like my body is in some other place', I am likely to say, 'So it does feel like your head is here and the rest of your body is somewhere else'. Paraphrasing or loose reflection that would work perfectly well under other circumstances, is often experienced by clients as an unwillingness or inability to understand. For example, a therapist might unintentionally miss the 'parts' aspect of the communication by saying, 'You're not quite here yet' or 'It's hard to get started today'. Here we have another parallel with configurations work in 'normal process' – the inadequacy of 'zero-sum responding' (Chapter 7).

WELCOMING PARTS EXPLICITLY. Communicating an openness to dissociative experiences is particularly delicate when clients describe experiencing monstrous presences in their consciousness or disconnected impulses to cut or harm themselves. Clients are likely to express the wish that the therapist would help them to get rid of these experiences. I have found that if I simply express my understanding that the client wants help in making these experiences go away, the persecuting parts often feel that I want them destroyed. They are then likely to escalate their threatening actions while remaining out of awareness. One such client ended up in the hospital after serious threats to slit her throat. Later when I became aware that parts were operating, that personality commented 'That was the first time I ever tried to talk to you and you wouldn't listen to me and I ended up in the hospital in restraints'.

Given these experiences, I now try to say something to indicate that the part would be welcomed by me whenever I think that a part may be present in the client's experience. Again, I try to say this in a way that does not press the client into dissociative experiences if none are present, or push the client to talk about things she does not want to share. So, I might say something like the following: 'I know that you are afraid of the impulses to cut yourself and I don't want you to be physically hurt in any way. But I also wonder whether there may be some part of you that has reasons for wanting to do that'.

Such welcoming statements often make no sense to the client at the time. She might say 'How can you say that? What could be good about cutting myself?' I do not press the issue or try to clarify it much further than 'I don't know if it's true of you. It's just been my experience that when people want to hurt themselves, there is sometimes a part of them that has reasons for feeling that way'. If a persecutory part is present, no matter how outwardly menacing, it is likely to feel scared, lonely and misunderstood inside. The idea that I might be able to understand is very tempting, though also frightening since the client has experienced betrayal so many times in the past.[7]

If persecutory parts are present, this amount of understanding often takes the urgency out of their need to act on their abusive impulses. Once they feel that they are welcome, they are likely to emerge more clearly, if not at that moment, sometime in the next few sessions. One such part, which carried the client's rage, said to me, 'I was the only one left around when the abuse was happening. All the rest of them left me alone to handle it. We wouldn't have survived if it wasn't for me. I don't understand why they're all so mad at me'. When persecutory parts are not present I have found that open-ended welcoming comments pass fairly harmlessly, leading the client to explore different sides of their feelings about the self-abusive impulses.

EXPLAINING DISSOCIATION WHEN ASKED BY CLIENTS. Clients who are experiencing upsurges of dissociative experiences are often afraid that they are having a psychotic break, or that they will be seen as crazy by others. This fear is exacerbated by the terror many incest survivors have that they caused the trauma to happen, or that they are fundamentally and irretrievably damaged as a result of the trauma. If clients sense that I am able to connect to their dissociatively related experiences, they are likely to ask what it is that I think is going on with them. I will often explain that dissociation is a protective coping mechanism that is common to young children undergoing trauma somewhat like self-hypnosis. Many clients are relieved to know that dissociation does not involve any fundamental or irretrievable defect in their processing capabilities. On the contrary, the emergence of dissociative symptoms often indicates that a client is ready to allow herself to process experiences that were too overwhelming to handle at earlier times in her life.

The person-centred discipline and dissociated process

As with fragile process, the person-centred discipline is well suited for work with clients who are dissociating. The key process of empathy, well developed in the person-centred approach, is crucial to the whole endeavour of distinguishing parts from metaphors. The attitude of unconditional positive regard is integral to forming relationships with all the presenting parts (just as was described in Chapter 7) and the congruent ability of the therapist to express the variety within her own self offers a richness to the different parts of the client.

Also important is the genuine commitment and flexibility offered by the person-centred therapist compared with workers from many other disciplines. Clients with dissociated process often ask for a bit more than others who are not so tortured. A moderate level of flexibility is often extremely helpful to clients. Alterations of the length or timing or format of sessions can facilitate the client's ability to handle intense experiences. The knowledge that some flexibility is available can foster the client's sense of being personally valued in the therapeutic relationship. There are, however, great dangers for both the client and the therapist if the therapist becomes over-extended. If a client feels that the therapist has given an excessive amount, she may feel guilty and burdened. She may feel inhibited from expressing the full range of negative feelings that inevitably arise. A therapist may feel moved by her client's struggle in a crisis and extend herself unrealistically without realising that she will not be able to keep up that level of involvement on an ongoing basis. Once a therapist is over-extended she is likely to be particularly vulnerable to feeling wounded by further client demands and angry entitlement. Therapists can easily work themselves into a situation in which they feel that they have to terminate therapeutic relationships altogether. Here we recall the client, 'Joe' from Chapter 2 and his therapist's crucial sentence: 'I never offered him more than I could sustain . . . and I tried not to offer him less'.

Arguably, the most important dimension of the person-centred approach for work with this clientele is the attention we pay to fostering the client's symbolisation while not inserting 'suggestive' material of our own. This orientation is critical at a time when therapists are accused of inducing 'false memories' of childhood abuse. I am struck by the fact that therapists at the Chicago Counseling Center have found that the distinctive syndrome of 'parts' and traumatic memories can be creatively and effectively addressed by faithfully using a client-directed style that does not involve the kinds of directed questioning or confrontation which many critics see as likely to elicit false memories (Brown, 1995). In this sense, a person-centred style of therapy seems to offer an approach that is effective in recovering and reworking trauma memories while minimising the chance that false memories will be induced in the process. The person-centred approach, which fosters a relatively equal, person-to-person therapeutic relationship and leaves the primary control over core therapeutic decision-making in clients' hands, is often particularly appreciated by clients who have been abused by previous authority figures in their lives.

Notes

1 Earlier versions of this model have been published in Warner (1991, 1997, 1998).

2 Dissociated process operates in quite distinctive ways in the context of person-centred therapy. However, my understanding of the phenomenon itself as presented in this chapter, parallels that of more directively oriented theorists of dissociative identity disorder such as Putnam (1989), Ross (1989) and Kluft (1985).

3 Psychotic process is a third sort of difficult process that will not be addressed in this chapter. For a theoretical and clinical account of person-centred work with psychotic clients see Prouty (1994).

4 A similar synthesis of person-centred process theorists was developed independently by Vanaerschot (1993).

5 Stern (1985) elaborates on this process in his chapter on 'The Verbal Self', in *The Interpersonal World of the Infant*, pp. 162–82.

6 For the purposes of this chapter, I am using the terms 'part', 'dissociated part', and 'personality' interchangeably in referring to dissociated states derived from early childhood trauma.

7 In this conflict for the client about wanting the therapist's understanding yet fearing betrayal, the reader can see parallels with case illustrations from many parts of this book, including 'Jim' (Chapter 6), 'Alexander' (Chapter 7) and particularly 'Bobby' (Chapter 3). Perhaps the most striking parallel is Bruno Bethelheim's 'Sandy' quoted in Elke Lambers' paper on a person-centred approach to work with personality disordered clients (1994: 119).

9 Advancing person-centred theory

Dave's fantasy

When I was with Carl Rogers in my capacity as Visiting Fellow to the Center for Studies of the Person in La Jolla in 1972/73 I was a young psychologist of 25 years. I lacked knowledge but I was an enthusiastic learner – now that my age is reversed I know a lot more and hope I still have the enthusiasm! At 25 years of age I suspect that I used my 'organismic valuing process' rather than theoretical acumen to judge the work of my elderly colleague. I knew that there was something important in his theory although I did not quite know why. One enduring fantasy I have is to meet Carl again, but this time with my more developed theoretical knowledge. The meeting would begin with me saying 'Right Carl, what about this theory? What needs to be done to move it from 1963 to the new millennium?' Unless he had changed in the 13 years since his death, Carl would certainly respond, 'Sounds like you have some ideas!' Then we would take off to explore the actualising tendency and where he was really going with it in 1963; whether the theory would benefit from taking a more 'pluralist' view of Self and whether 'personal growth' had become too dominant a value within the theory during the 1960s and 1970s.

Carl would delight in this process. Theory for him was dialogue, not doctrine or dogma. It is disciples who convert dialogue into dogma. Carl had plenty of disciples – but he also had people around him who enjoyed the tussle over ideas – pity I can't meet him now.

This is going to be an ambitious chapter in its effort to develop person-centred theory into a more dialogical form. There have been contributions to theory already in this book, particularly in Chapters 3, 5, 6, 7 and 8. The chapter will make reference back to these parts without reproducing them. Instead, the centre-piece of the chapter will be an attempt to re-present Rogers' Self theory in a fashion which more fully embraces the social dimension of existence.

Rogers' theory had three main aspects: his theory of personality, often called his 'Self theory'; his theory of therapy and his theory of inter-personal relationships. Since the present book restricts its focus to person-centred therapy, we shall limit our attention to offering contributions to the Self theory and the theory of therapy.

The 'Self theory'

On two occasions in his working life Carl took up the challenge to present his theory of the Self (Rogers, 1951, 1959). These were both significant papers pieced together over long periods and carefully worded in the psychological language of their day. Although that language does not make them easily accessible to students and further clarification has been useful (Brodley, 1999; Ford, 1991; Ford and Maas, 1989), it is worth re-reading them after a number of years experience in the approach. Each statement is carefully weighed and each assertion explained and exemplified. Eighteen pages are devoted to the definition of terms (Rogers, 1959: 194–212) and every major feature which should be contained within such a theory is considered: the concept of the person; motivation; the creation of disturbance; psychological defence and the process of psychological change.

Reviewing the theoretical propositions on 'configurations' within the self

In Chapter 6 we offered a series of theoretical propositions reflective of a more pluralist conception of Self. None of this theory contradicts Carl's but it does seek to offer further development. Here we shall summarise these theoretical propositions:

- Specific 'configurations' of Self may be established around introjections in response to conditions of worth.
- Specific configurations of Self may be established around dissonant Self-experiences.
- The notion of *pluralism* offers an adaptive versatility within the Self. It is a means of containing internal dissonance and also of retaining a range of integrated 'Selves' for use in different

social contexts (this is not the same notion as that of 'role' playing – each 'configuration' is a congruent dimension of the person's existence).

• The formative configuration provides an 'organising principle' which can then offer structure and function to other elements and narratives within the Self and, by that means of assimilation, the configuration may further develop.

• The 'Self-fulfilling' principle can be another means of growth as well as validation for the configuration.

• Finally, in Chapter 6, we posited the interrelating of configurations and their continued development-in-relationship. These configuration dynamics interact with the evolving phenomenal experience of the person in relation to her social world, resulting in a pressure towards reconfiguration – that pressure towards reconfiguration is generally the motivating experience to enter therapy. There are likely to be numerous theoretical propositions resulting from this dynamic conception.

Reconfiguring Rogers' concept of the Self

Rogers equated the terms 'self', 'self-concept' and 'self-structure' (Rogers, 1959: 200). To equate Self and Self-concept was a radical step that placed Rogers firmly outside the psychoanalytic tradition which emphasised the importance of unconscious dimensions of Self. More importantly, it created a context meaningful to the research parameters of its time. Even within his paragraph of definition Rogers was attentive to the operational needs of research:

> It [the self] is a fluid and changing gestalt, a process, but at any given moment it is a specific entity which is at least partially definable in operational terms by means of a Q sort or other instrument or measure. (Rogers, 1959: 200)

Rogers was quite clear about the pragmatic nature of his decision to limit the definition of Self to that which was available to the conscious awareness of the person. He wanted to restrict his attention to that which could be researched within the research parameters of his day:

> It should be recognised that any construct is a more or less arbitrary abstraction from experience. Thus the self could be defined in many different ways. Hilgard, for example, has proposed that it be defined in such a way as to include unconscious material, not available to awareness, as well as conscious material. Although we recognise that this is certainly a legitimate way of abstracting from the phenomenon,

we believe it is not a useful way because it produces a concept which cannot at this point be given operational definition. One cannot obtain sufficient agreement as to the content of the individual's unconscious to make research possible. Hence, we believe that it is more fruitful to define the self-concept as a gestalt which is available to awareness. This has permitted and encouraged a flood of important research. (Rogers, 1959: 202–3)

Although he does not include them within his definition of the Self, Rogers acknowledges the influences upon behaviour of other dimensions of the person's existence: 'Behavior is regulated at times by the self and at times by those aspects of the organism's experience which are not included in the self' (Rogers, 1959: 226). Indeed, within his definition of *anxiety*, Rogers marks the boundary of his concept of Self and gives us the useful term, *subception*:

When experience is *obviously* discrepant from the self-concept, a defensive response to threat becomes increasingly difficult. Anxiety is the response of the organism to the 'subception' that such discrepancy may enter awareness, thus forcing a change in the self-concept. (Rogers, 1959: 204)

We propose a slight, but important, re-configuration of Rogers' concept of Self to include such 'subceived' material. Extending the notion of 'Self' to include this 'edge of awareness' material, even that which is not yet accepted by the person as a part of their self-concept, is much less constraining for theoretical purposes. Rogers initially sought that constraint of definition to make the subject more available to the science of his time which had lurched away from anything that smelled of introspectionism. However, in the past 40 years our more radical social scientists and philosophers of science have generated appropriate qualitative methodologies (for example, Moustakas, 1994) and pluralist methodologies (Goss and Mearns, 1997a, 1997b) to make meaningful research in the area of subceived material perfectly possible.

It may seem to be a trifling and an obvious step to widen the definition of Self such that the Self = Self-concept + edge of awareness material, but it is an important step. At a stroke we have become theoretically inclusive of 'focusing' as a dimension of person-centred therapy. Furthermore, it makes it possible for us to consider emerging 'configurations' of Self described in Chapters 6 and 7. However, it is also a fairly radical and potentially dangerous step. It is radical because to distinguish between the Self and the Self-concept could detract from the essentially phenomenological nature of person-centred therapy. Equating Self and Self-concept was a distinctly phenomenological step. In effect, Rogers was saying that our starting point for considering Self only needs to be that material which the person already considers to be a part of his Self, that is, his Self-concept. This simplicity helps to reinforce the discipline of the person-centred approach in carefully *following* our client's symbolisations.

Widening the conception of Self, then, brings both *opportunity* and *danger*. The *opportunity* lies in the tension which this difference creates between the client and the therapist. The therapist has an eye not only to what the client is currently expressing as the contents of his Self but to those emerging elements not yet fully symbolised. Implicitly, then, the therapist will continually be inclined to probe the edges: 'Is there anything else there . . .?', 'What do you experience when you consider X?'. The *danger* is that this widening conception of Self could lose its discipline in holding to the edge of awareness and wander into the unconscious. We want to hold this new line very firmly. An important and distinguishing feature of person-centred therapy is that it does not drift into the unconscious but works within the awareness and, we are suggesting, the *emerging* awareness of the client. Some practitioners of other approaches might consider this limitation within person-centred therapy to be naive – believing that there is a wealth of material to be uncovered within the unconscious. In fact, the decision is certainly not naive but well-considered. Much is lost by disappearing into the unconscious. By definition we have entered areas which cannot yet be known by the client and where, also by definition, the client cannot be 'expert'. From the person-centred perspective, operating from a therapeutic frame where the client cannot be expert in relation to his existence brings enormous dangers of disempowerment, which at best may hugely lengthen the therapeutic process and at worst may further externalise the client's locus of evaluation. The unconscious world of the client as it is 'explored' in therapy is, in fact, a combination of the *therapist's* theoretical constructions and the *therapist's* imagination. Perhaps this is what makes it so attractive to therapists – it allows the therapist unbridled power to exercise theory and imagination without possibility of contradiction. For those who seek such power, therapeutic approaches which purport to work with unconscious material will be much more satisfying than person-centred therapy which insists on holding the disciplined line of the client's awareness and, in our extension to the theory, his 'edge of awareness'.

A dialogical person-centred theory of the Self

The inspiration for this attempt to broaden person-centred Self theory comes from work with many clients who symbolise a part of their Self that expresses caution when faced with the urge to move or change. In Chapter 6, these were simply described as 'not for growth' parts. In configurational work the discipline is to value each part equally and fully. The result is that parts like these are given the chance to blossom into 'figure' rather than remaining in 'ground'. There has been a tendency in the popularisation of the person-centred approach to honour these parts less than growth promoting dimensions which more obviously reflect the actualising tendency (Rogers, 1963). Yet, when we get to know them, these 'resistant' parts prove not only to be most interesting facets of the Self, but have also usually been of fundamental importance to earlier survival and development. Paradoxically, the 'not for growth' aspects have actually helped to maintain a balance to allow optimum growth to occur in very difficult circumstances. Although the 'not for growth' imperative is often experienced as unduly restrictive and conservative in its influence, it is also possible to find examples where such restraint helps the person to mediate the pace of growth and to keep contact with the social structures of life which, if maintained, can offer considerable orchestration for future growth. Hence, the fragments of hypotheses develop: perhaps the 'not for growth' imperative is important in the dialogical relationship it forms with the actualising tendency; perhaps this is a sophisticated dialogical system whereby growth is mediated and social structures are maintained; perhaps psychological 'health' is not a matter of overcoming this restrictive force but one of restoring an appropriate balance between the forces of the actualising tendency and social mediation. These are the hypotheses but it is time to go back and to cover the ground more methodically.

Significant changes are apparent in Rogers' thinking from 1963 onwards, though the ideas were certainly formulated before that time. In 1963 the actualising tendency was characterised as the positive force and the factors which would restrain it were regarded 'negatively' to say the least:

> I have gradually come to see this dissociation, rift, estrangement, [between self structure and experience] as something learned, a perverse channeling of some of the actualizing tendency into behaviors which do not actualize . . . In this respect my thinking has changed

during the past decade. Ten years ago I was endeavouring to explain the rift between self and experience, between conscious goals and organismic directions, as something natural and necessary, albeit unfortunate. Now I believe that individuals are culturally conditioned, rewarded, reinforced, for behaviors which are in fact perversions of the natural directions of the unitary actualizing tendency. (Rogers, 1963: 19–20)

And later:

. . . the extremely common estrangement of conscious man from his directional organismic processes is not a necessary part of man's nature. It is instead something learned, and to an especially high degree in our Western culture. It is characterised by behaviors which are guided by rigid concepts and constructs, interrupted at times by behaviors guided by the organismic processes. The satisfaction or fulfilment of the actualizing tendency has become bifurcated into incompatible behavioral systems, of which one may be dominant at one moment and the other dominant at another moment, but at a continual cost of strain and inefficiency. This dissociation which exists in most of us is the pattern and the basis of all psychological pathology in man, and the basis of all his social pathology as well. This, at least, is my view. (Rogers, 1963: 20–1)

This represented a profound change in Rogers' thinking – we now had a unitary theory of existence with poles which were not too far away from notions of 'good' and 'evil' (although, it must be said, Rogers would not have used those labels). As the approach entered its so-called 'California' period with Rogers' move to the west coast, it continued in this more polarised direction. Anything which appeared to be in the direction of the actualising tendency was valued and anything which resembled restraint or social mediation was discounted – in fact, it was pathologised. This new value bias was generalised into a preference for 'feelings' over 'thoughts'; for non-self-conscious 'being' over 'considered' action; for 'free expression' over 'censoring'; for 'radical' choices over 'conservative' choices and for 'volume-up' expression of feeling over 'volume-down' expression of feeling.

Interestingly, this time also marked the end of Rogers' contribution to Self-theory. Perhaps he had actually fallen into the theoretician's trap of believing that he had found answers rather than further questions. His theory had found resonance within the American counter-culture of the 1960s and 1970s. Indeed, the approach came to epitomise the value of making 'growthful' choices. When people are freed from forces of restraint or social mediation they do indeed follow growthful choices for the organism in that moment. This worked well enough in a therapeutic context because the majority of private practice clients had personal processes which were imbalanced in the direction of social restraint. Any movement in the direction of the urgings of the actualising tendency would also be working towards a better 'balance' unless they lurched too far to the extreme and ignored, devalued or demonised other tendencies towards social mediation.

There were few dissonant voices within the person-centred approach. One notable exception was Bill Coulson who had worked closely with Rogers for a number of years but who resisted strongly the drift which he found in Rogers' 'California' period. Theory needs to prize its critics because they are the means by which it can discover its blindness. Unfortunately, the influence of Coulson's critique has largely been lost because of its perceived vehemence. Coulson cautioned against the unitary conception of growth – that the way to health is through the unrestricted expression of the actualising tendency. In a paper entitled 'Reclaiming client-centered counseling from the person-centered movement' (1987), he points to some interesting findings from the Wisconsin project – a major research initiative to explore client-centred therapy with a schizophrenic population (Rogers et al., 1967). Coulson comments:

> . . . the hospitalized schizophrenic individuals were completely unmotivated to accept help. All were patients of the nearby state hospital, and many resided on locked wards. Carl Rogers and a small number of his most gifted associates were able to overcome their lack of motivation, but most of the therapists employed in the project were not . . . the schizophrenic patients of the state hospital had long since become resigned to never developing their potential. 'Becoming a person' was not a prospect they would even conceive any more . . . What if they began to like it? What would they do when the research project was over and the sensitive therapists left? Who would accompany them? I think they believed they would have been foolish to accept the offer of therapy. Perhaps the therapists knew it as well, at least tacitly so; in any case, it is to their credit that they did not push. (Coulson, 1987: 1)

Coulson goes on to explore the interesting fact that the 'normal' comparison group within the Wisconsin study had to be dropped from the research because, typically, they would have one or two therapy sessions but then stop. Coulson's analysis of this is that the 'normals' (Rogers' term) realised that therapy could be disruptive to their settled life unlike the Chicago 'neurotics' (Rogers' term), in earlier studies, who grabbed the opportunity of therapy as a means of getting their lives back on track.

These are interesting observations which feed into a theoretical construction that may offer an alternative to the unitary conception of the 'good' actualising tendency and the 'bad' forces of social mediation which is what the theory was becoming from 1963. Perhaps it is the *balance* in the person's life which is important – that they are achieving a balance between the drive of the actualising tendency and the restraint of social mediation which allows them an optimum of growth opportunities in the present and retains for them sufficient social contexts for future growth.

It is informative to observe the therapeutic process of our clients. Within most, but not all, therapeutic settings, it would be fair to say that the majority of clients suffer from an imbalance which errs severely on the side of social meditation. The establishment and continued maintenance of oppressive conditions of worth reduces scope for the promptings of the actualising tendency. Typically, such clients would benefit from therapy through the dissonance which it creates within the Self-concept (Mearns, 1994: 88–93) and the possibility that that dissonance will lead to a restructuring which offers greater potential for growth. It is common for these clients to 'overdose' on growth potential once that is becoming realised. Indeed, the balance can swing wildly towards the other extreme with the client making radical changes in his life, even divesting himself of previously important but restraining relationships. However, this is not usually the end of the process. Whether it continues within therapy or after therapy has ended, the client will generally swing back towards a less extreme point of balance. Once the forces of action and reaction have become dissipated, a new balance can be achieved which is more realistic to the person in his life circumstances.

If this model of client movement has any veracity, then perhaps we can learn from our clients that a successful outcome cannot be measured by a unitary criterion. It is not simply a matter of swinging wildly to the other extreme and giving maximum expression to the actualising tendency. This pattern begs for a dialogical model where both the forces towards growth, and the restraint of social mediation, are valued as contributing to the fundamental dialectic of the social being. Interestingly, in extending the approach to families and couples, O'Leary (1999) also emphasises the dialogical. Essentially, we are returning the theory to Rogers' 1959 expression and seeking to take further the dialectic which he observed between the actualising tendency and the Self-as-it-has-actualised. Our focus is the whole *actualising process* which contains not only the actualising tendency but the dialogue between it and the restraints of social mediation. This leads us to frame four general propositions describing a dialogical conception of Self within person-centred therapy.

THE ACTUALISING TENDENCY IS THE SOLE MOTIVATIONAL FORCE. The notion of the actualising tendency has been central to person-centred theory since Rogers' earliest formal framing of his self theory (Rogers, 1951). Indeed, we can also find its roots in his very first book, *The Clinical Treatment of the Problem Child*:

> . . . most children, if given a reasonably normal environment which meets their own emotional, intellectual, and social needs, have within themselves sufficient drive towards health to respond and make a comfortable adjustment to life. (Rogers, 1939: 274)

We see no reason to contest this basic ingredient of Rogers' theory. There has always been a simple elegance to this single motivational concept. Also, there is logic in the notion that there should be a fundamental drive in life to maintain, develop and enhance the functioning of the organism and that this tendency can manifest itself in many different guises. Although comparison with other living things can be nothing more than metaphorical, it is nevertheless interesting to witness the many instances where biological 'growth' is maintained despite unfruitful conditions. Although it is a simple concept, the actualising tendency tends to be misunderstood, particularly by critics, for example May (1982) and Geller (1982). Such misunderstandings clearly stem from the California period when the movement which was announced in Rogers' 1963 paper gained huge momentum with the popularisation of the approach. The actualising tendency was endowed with a moral directive – it was the force towards 'good', fighting against the oppression of the social environment. In true 'modernist' fashion the script could have been borrowed from a John Wayne movie with the actualising tendency playing the 'lead'.

Of course, the actualising tendency is not 'good', nor is it 'bad' – it is an amoral concept. The actualising tendency is a basic *biological* concept – it is a 'growth tendency' similar to that which is embodied in many living entities but also distinctive in that it carries the potential for social expression. This needs to be carefully described. The actualising tendency is not, itself, a social phenomenon – social phenomena are only exceptionally biological. It simply has the capacity to be expressed in social contexts, indeed, much of its expression *is* in our social world. It is a fundamental drive within us to make the most we can of our living process and much of that living process is social in nature. It is this capacity to be expressed in social contexts which gives rise to the notion that the actualising tendency is essentially 'constructive' in nature (Brodley, 1999; Rogers, 1982). Again, this is an easily misunderstood term because the reader tends to add a moral assumptive frame (May, 1982). It simply means that the drive of the actualising tendency will tend to make the best use it can of social circumstances, including forming mutually enhancing social relationships when the conditions permit. When conditions do not permit such an expansive reciprocity the actualising tendency will attempt to find expression in other ways, always seeking to maintain and enhance the functioning of the organism. As Barbara Brodley reminds us: 'The AT is *a tendency, it is not a guarantee* of full health or full realization or good behavior' (1999: 113).

THE PROMPTINGS OF THE ACTUALISING TENDENCY INSPIRE THEIR OWN RESISTANCE WITHIN THE SOCIAL LIFE SPACE OF THE PERSON. AN INTERIM TERM FOR THIS RESISTANCE IS THE FORCE OF 'SOCIAL MEDIATION'. The actualising tendency, with its pro-social capacity (Brodley, 1999), finds expression in relation to the person's phenomenal social existence where it can, potentially, obtain its most effective articulation. But there will be limits to this expression – and these will vary considerably from one individual to another. There will be times when the pressure of the actualising tendency will inspire a resistance. Such resistance is intimately related both to the actualising tendency and to the person's current existence as a social being. The effect of the resistance serves to maintain a balance which allows for a degree of expression for the actualising tendency while taking care to preserve the viability of the social context within the person's 'life space'. Here, the term 'life space' is taken directly from Kurt Lewin (1939, 1946) to denote, in this case, the phenomenological reality of the person's social existence. As a phenomenological concept, the person's social life space may appear quite different when viewed from the perceptual frames of other people.

The pressure of social mediation is not of itself an inherent motivational force like the actualising tendency, but a force which is directly derived from the action of the actualising tendency on the social life space. Yet, it is an integrated, congruent force within the Self. It is not simply composed of parental injunctions and introjections, although these will have their impact upon the person's symbolisation of their social existence. The forces of social mediation form a coherent and functional part of our existence as social beings, allowing us expression of the actualising tendency but exerting an imperative which cautions against the endangering of the social life space.

In therapy, there are plenty of examples where clients show an awareness not only of the actualising tendency but of the reactive forces. Although a phenomenological perspective is essential, examples of the reactive forces might be reflected in client responses like the following:

- I could do more with my life but I am scared to lose what I have.
- I need to stop this road – I can see where it points and I don't want it – not yet anyway.
- I fought my way out of a relationship previously, and I lost more than I ever imagined.
- Part of me says 'go for it' and part of me says 'watch it' – I need to stay with 'watch it' for now.
- I look at what other people have got and I want it like a child wants everything. But my child isn't going to make all my decisions.
- Everything seemed to point in the direction of leaving the job – I needed to be free of it. But my family would have lost too much – and that would mean *me* losing too much. So I rolled up my sleeves and made the best of it.

A unitary conception of the actualising tendency might easily result in notable directionality on the part of the therapist who regarded such cautions merely as reflections of earlier conditions of worth or as 'a perverse channeling of some of the actualising tendency into behaviors which do not actualize' (Rogers, 1963: 19). As we discussed in relation to 'growthful' and 'not for growth' configurations in Chapter 6, the therapist needs to remain open and engaging with both parts of the dynamic and to respect them equally and fully. Only then is the therapist truly open to her client for whom the social imperative as well as the actualising tendency is important.

A PSYCHOLOGICAL 'HOMEOSTASIS' DEVELOPS WHERE THE BALANCE IS UNDER 'DUAL CONTROL', WITH THE DRIVE OF THE ACTUALISING TENDENCY AND THE RESTRAINT OF THE SOCIAL IMPERATIVE BOTH ABLE TO EXERCISE POWER. This concept of a fluid homeostatic balance of at least two forces with opposite vectors offers an exciting and sensitive reactivity to changing needs and circumstances. In nature, dual control is much preferred to unitary control because two opposing forces can give a more sensitive and revisionable balance. Although physiological comparisons can be regarded as nothing more than metaphors, we should note the preponderance of dual control homeostatic systems within every evolved life form.

This combines well with the theory of configurations, allowing for different 'balances' to be struck in different social contexts. In some areas of our client's life the balance might favour giving more scope to the actualising tendency, while in other areas a different balance of configurations would take care not to be too disruptive to the social environment.

In this revision of the theory the central concept becomes the *actualising process* which is described by the homeostasis of the imperatives of the actualising tendency and social mediation within different areas of the person's social life space and the reconfiguring of that homeostasis to respond to changing circumstances.

'DISORDER' IS CAUSED WHEN THE PERSON BECOMES CHRONICALLY STUCK WITHIN HIS OWN PROCESS SUCH THAT THE HOMEOSTATIC BALANCE CANNOT RECONFIGURE TO RESPOND TO CHANGING CIRCUMSTANCES. This is quite a different framing from that of Rogers (1963) where he considered disorder being caused by the relevant social forces inhibiting and derailing the urgings of the actualising tendency. Interestingly, it shares some similarities with Bohart's notion of *dysfunctionality* (1995: 94). The emphasis is on the fluidity of the process to respond to changing circumstances. For example, we may have derived a balance which fitted a particularly threatening social context, but that balance can change, allowing us to symbolise more of our potentialities and possibilities when the social context becomes less threatening. This is illustrated in Chapter 7, where Alexander gradually reconfigured 'me as I have always known me' into 'me as I was' and 'me as I am now'. While reconfiguring is often painful it is, of itself, a healthy process rather than one which is disordered. In this orientation the person-centred concept of disorder is close to that of R.D. Laing (1965).

While we have worked to re-present Rogers' Self-theory in dialogical rather than in unitary form and found it necessary to challenge his own drift with the theory from 1963, it is important to note that Rogers' theory up to 1959 was not very different from what we have outlined. He acknowledged the forces of the social imperative and up to, and including 1959, he did not pathologise these.

Our reworking of the theory might not make a great deal of difference for the person-centred therapist in practice. In so far as the majority of clients coming to therapy are revising their balance in favour of the actualising tendency vector, the client's process will be the same in both theories. However, a distinct advantage of the revised theory is that it avoids creating a 'tyranny of growth' and warns the therapist against differentially reinforcing the prompting of the actualising tendency against the forces of social mediation.

Furthermore, although they are a rarer phenomenon in therapy, we sometimes find clients who are seeking to change the balance in the opposite direction. It is important not to deify any concept in psychology and while Rogers gave the actualising tendency a very positive press, he also noted that it was not infallible: 'In nature, the working out of the actualizing tendency shows a surprising efficiency. The organism makes errors, to be sure, but these are corrected on the basis of feedback' (Rogers, 1963: 16). This caution alerts us to the fact that we can become stuck within a frame of favouring our own valuing process rigidly and not being able to consider feedback. One client, Mary, describes this position:

> After countless years of going against my instinct and fitting into other people's wishes I finally broke free. For a time after that I was impossible to live with – I couldn't compromise at all. It's like I couldn't go against my view of events and what was right for me in the moment. Having finally got hold of myself I wasn't going to let go – I suppose I was scared I would lose myself again.

Rogers encouraged people to place more faith in their organismic valuing process. That advice was generally well placed because culturally we tend to develop an estrangement between our behaviour and our experiencing. However, this is not to say that our sense of Self is accurate in every respect, particularly in regard to our social functioning. Just as an organismic valuing process relies on feedback from our body, so, too, do we rely on feedback from our social world. It is just as much a tyranny always to presume that the feedback from our social world is wrong if it conflicts with our own sense, as to be trapped in the opposite reality where we always favour the social imperative over our own. It can be difficult to struggle between these realities, as is exemplified by the trainee, James:

> I can see that my sense of myself isn't working. Other people are giving back a different view of myself, and they are pretty unanimous. They say that I look 'cold and detached' when I feel 'warm'. It is difficult to know who to trust. Either they share the same illusion or I have a huge blind spot that I can't see past. It is really difficult to go against my sense of myself – I have no sense of being wrong. But these are good people – I need to pause awhile.

Earlier in this section we described an apocryphal client process. The client is initially trapped by other people's definition of himself and then, during therapy, swings to the opposite extreme, just as rigidly trying to hold on to his own judgements over those of others before reverting to a position of greater balance where he is able to weigh up all the evidence. Interestingly, if we look at the theoretical suggestions we are making, this same process is being recapitulated. Rogers helped us to be aware of the huge bias within our culture towards favouring strong social constraints rather than the promptings of the actualising tendency. Then, during the 1960s and 1970s, Rogers' suggestion that we might place greater trust in our own 'organismic valuing process' combined well with the counter-culture of its day, resulting in a swing in that direction. Our present theoretical offerings seek to restore a balance where both the actualising tendency within the individual and also the forces of social mediation are respected, with neither being given a domination over the other and with therapy, as well as a fruitful adolescence and other facilitative human events, encouraging us not only to strike a balance but to be able to be fluid in that balance.

The cultural 'boundedness' of the Self theory

The shifting of person-centred Self theory from a unitary to a dialogical framework may assist its application in a wider range of cultures and sub-cultures. At a stroke, the proviso that the imperative of the actualising tendency should always be valued positively is no longer required.

As we have seen in Chapter 4, Len Holdstock, more than any other writer, has urged the person-centred approach to consider the cross-cultural dimension in relation to the concept of Self. Essentially, Holdstock, unlike Carl Rogers (see Wood, 1997), takes a 'transpersonal' orientation towards Self. In relation to Rogers' self theory he points out that 'others are attributed a secondary and not a primary role in the life of the individual' (Holdstock, 1996b: 399). He goes on to say: '. . . even in the social outreach of the theory, empowering the individual remained the focus through which societal change was thought to be brought about' (1996b: 399). Holdstock's work is rich in the referencing it offers on cross-cultural theorising in respect of the Self (Holdstock, 1993, 1996b) and urges a revision in the person-centred concept of Self:

> The major task confronting humanity is to create a new self, better suited than the model adhered to at present by psychology, in order to deal with the issues of our global and postmodern society. Whether person-centred theory can rise to the challenge of revisioning its individuocentric approach to the self remains an open question. (Holdstock, 1993: 45)

Our attempt to revise the theory might help a little in improving its wider cultural applicability. Certainly, we have found a way to mark the importance of social forces as part of an ongoing dialectic with the actualising tendency – a dialectic which is constructive in helping the person to stay connected with the social world in such a way that would maximise his possibilities for actualisation. However, although a dialogical theory contains more potential than a unitary theory for describing the social dimension in interaction with the individual, in our model the actualising tendency is still to the fore and our theory is as vulnerable as Rogers' in respect to the cross-cultural applicability of that concept.

In the final analysis, the central question remains whether, in the actualising tendency, Rogers is observing a universal phenomenon or one which is culturally 'bounded'. It is extremely difficult to come to a conclusion on this, either way. Certainly we can note, as in Holdstock (1993), numerous other cultures where extensive social enmeshment is the valued norm. In such cultures it is difficult to imagine the greater autonomy and 'interdependency' reflective of the actualising tendency finding much of a basis. But does this mean that such cultures are reflecting the fundamental human condition *or* have they created a pervasive cultural neurosis to protect the community at the expense of the individual? Such issues of comparative psychology cannot be 'solved' because there can be no fixed cultural perspective from which to define reality. For example, the revered shaman, viewed from the perspective of western psychiatry, might be a hopeless psychotic. Similarly, the client who struggles to become more autonomous in her previously dependent relationship with her partner might be seen as 'assertive' by the therapeutic world and 'irresponsible' by her family. One is reminded of the huge body of largely male inspired research which emphasised the 'higher' skill of perceptional *differentiation* whereby men, more than women, displayed the ability to discriminate sensory input from different modalities. Only after many years of research was it observed that the opposite process, that of 'synaesthesia' – the ability to *integrate* sensory information from different modalities, might be the valued position!

A culture may exert its influence through a process of 'values attribution'. If we take the concept of Self as an example, a culture might give messages on the 'right' kind of Self to possess. The messages might be consistent and pervasive in declaring the kind of Self which is to be valued. In this culture, exceptions would exist but they would be dishonoured and even pathologised. For example, a culture which placed a high value on heteronomy would express that message through its education, religion, politics and psychology. Exceptions could be logically possible but they would be severely inhibited by sanctions of various kinds.

A different process of cultural influence exists where the 'symbolisation parameters' of the culture dictate the *only* kind of Self which is possible. This represents a much greater level of cultural construction and constriction. Here the 'right' kind of Self is so embedded in the culture that there can be no exceptions. At this level of embeddedness it is not seen as a value and a choice – the nature of Self is defined by that which can be symbolised. For instance, on the issue of autonomy versus heteronomy, in this culture heteronomy is not simply 'valued', but it is so fully embedded that no alternative can be conceptualised – there is not even the seed of an alternative to be fostered.

When considering the cross-cultural applicability of a theory we must not only examine the nature of the theory but also the culture. A theory cannot be tested where the cultural symbolisation parameters do not at least acknowledge its possibility.

However, the theory *can* be explored in a context where the cultural influence is at the level of values attribution, even if those values appear to run counter to the drift of the theory. Here, there exists at least the language of the alternative. Hence Rogers' theory can meaningfully be tested in cultures which seem to contradict the notion of an actualising tendency so long as the difference is at the level of values attribution rather than symbolisation. In summary, the realignment we have suggested for the theory might widen its cultural applicability but we should not expect anything approaching universality: as well as theories being 'culturally bounded', some cultures are 'theoretically bounded' by their symbolisation parameters.

Rogers' theory of therapy

This will be a shorter part of this chapter because, as he said himself, Rogers left his theory of therapy much more fully formed and tested in research than his Self theory (Rogers, 1959). However, it is worth reviewing recent developments to see which aspects of the theory of therapy are being highlighted. Thereafter, we shall explore the basic issue of 'directivity' and suggest that the approach, thus far, has taken a particularly 'counsellor-centred' rather than 'client-centred' orientation.

Highlighting aspects of the theory of therapy

In Chapters 3 and 5 of this book we have not so much sought to 'advance' the theory of therapy but we have vigorously restated its core. We have reasserted that the quality of relationship offered by the therapeutic conditions requires their integrated presence to a high degree. We suggest that it is meaningless and misleading to separate the conditions and consider their partiality. Original attempts at separation represented an effort to respond to the reductionistic research parameters of the time. Our wish is to put the therapeutic conditions back together again so that the person-centred therapist can offer the client a meeting at *relational depth*. It is the quality of that meeting which marks the essence of the person-centred approach and distinguishes it from others.

Again, in Chapters 3 and 5, we assert that to achieve this depth and openness of relating requires a distinctive personal commitment on the part of the therapist. Reviewed either in the language of spirituality or in existential terms, the therapist is freely tapping her essence as a human being without defence or pretence. That essence is a constant touchstone for the person-centred therapist. As the profession of counselling develops there is a danger that counsellors will be encouraged to offer a less personally involved relationship with the client (Chapter 2). While we support moves towards professionalisation we need to take care not to dilute the spiritual/existential quality of the work and our hunch is that this will require increasing courage and strength of conviction.

Chapter 7 explored work with *configurations* of Self but found no need to suggest alterations to the theory of therapy. However, once again, specific features were highlighted, such as the importance of closely following the client's *symbolisation* of parts of Self and listening to the client's *expressing* rather than merely his expression. We pointed to the fact that making empathic summaries could represent a kind of *zero-sum responding* where conflicting configurations cancel each other out. Perhaps the most important part of this chapter in regard to the theory of therapy was the suggestion that we needed to offer a distinctive therapeutic relationship with each configuration which emerges – we want to be aware of the dangers of being 'partial' to some configurations and not to others. Most particularly, we suggested that the therapist needed to attend equally to those parts of the client which might be expressing a 'not for growth' imperative. These are 'family members' who might not take a large part in the process because therapy would be perceived as potentially dangerous for the balance they are trying to maintain within the Self. Other configurations which are more representative of the growth-promoting actualising tendency will be more orientated to therapy and the danger is that we regard these as more attractive family members and align with them more than with others. This emphasis on aligning with *all* the parts of the client, even with those which appear to be growth-restricting, is also indicated by our contribution to the theory of the Self earlier in this chapter.

A functional view of directivity

The historical and philosophical cornerstone of the person-centred approach is seen to be its rootedness in *non-directivity*. As well as Rogers' own contributions to this theme (Rogers, 1942, 1951) there have been offerings by Cain (1989, 1990), Grant (1990), Lambers

(1993) and Lietaer (1998) among others. The general view on directivity is that the counsellor should not direct the client either in terms of product or of process within the therapy – the client should neither be directed on what to consider in therapy nor on how to consider it. Critical attention is not simply paid to straight-forward directive processes but also to various forms of sugges-tion and selective reinforcement of client responses. The rationale for rejecting directivity is sound – the central aim of the approach is to help the client find his own direction and empower himself in the process. That is not to be achieved by being the expert in relation to his product or process.

Unfortunately, in our attention to this fundamental concept of the approach we have been decidedly naive over the last 60 years. We have tended to take an essentially *structural* (see Chapter 2) and 'therapist-centred' view of directivity. Let us turn that round for a moment and seek to take a *functional*, 'client-centred' per-spective on directivity. The importance of directivity is not in what the counsellor *does* but in what the client *experiences*. Whether my behaviour as a therapist looks directive or non-directive to my peers is entirely irrelevant – what matters are the functions of my behaviour. The question which should be asked is not 'is the therapist behaving directively?', but 'is the client being directed?'. It is astounding that client-centred therapy has failed to take a client-centred perspective on directivity. The importance of a functional view of directivity is illustrated by the contrasting examples presented by Jeri and Joan.

Jeri

> *Jeri*: Okay, Dave – tell me what I should do – should I take this job or not?
>
> *Dave*: Take it. Ring them now before they change their minds. It's a great job.
>
> *Jeri*: [*Pauses*] . . . No, it doesn't feel right . . . I don't know what's wrong about it yet . . . but it's not right.

Joan

> *Joan*: Early in our work together I needed to make you tell me what I should feel. It is so scary not to know what to feel.

My 'breakdown' meant that I couldn't trust anything about myself. I needed you to tell me when to breathe but you wouldn't do it. So, I would . . . kind of . . . try to work out what you wanted me to do. If you paused after I said something then I would think that you didn't want me to do that. If you smiled or were warm after I had said something, then that was the right thing to say. If you asked me a question then I would work out some message from the question. I needed you so much to tell me what to do and what to feel that I 'made' you do it.

The major difference between Jeri and Joan was that Jeri had an internalised *locus of evaluation* (Mearns, 1994: 80–3) while Joan's was profoundly externalised. This made Jeri relatively invulnerable to the 'directivity' of the therapist while Joan was so vulnerable that she created directivity even where it did not exist.

Different disciplines are required in responding to these two clients. Jeri likes a firm engagement with the therapist. It does not matter to her what his opinion is but it is important to her that he gives it. She is entirely uninfluenced by the therapist's opinion but she can make good use of it as a means of 'focusing'. When the therapist says 'take it' his specific opinion is unimportant, but it allows Jeri to imagine her Self, in that moment, telephoning to accept the job. People whose locus of evaluation is firmly internalised make good 'focusers' and immediately she experiences the reaction which tells her that something is not right. She makes good use of the therapist's 'advice'. On the other hand the statement by Joan (taken from the audio-tape of her final session) is a poignant illustration of just how vulnerable a client may be. Joan is in that most scary of existential positions where she cannot trust any aspect of her own functioning. Recognising this vulnerability, her therapist had been extremely careful to eliminate anything which might be suggestive of actions she might take, feelings she might have or processes she might consider. In summary, with Jeri the therapist was highly directive and the client was not directed, and with Joan the therapist was highly non-directive and the client was directed.

In his important 1959 paper Carl Rogers said:

It has been our experience to date that although the therapeutic relationship is used differently by different clients, it is not necessary nor helpful to manipulate the relationship in specific ways for specific kinds of clients. (Rogers, 1959: 213–14)

In disagreeing with this statement of Rogers', we need to be fair to him in acknowledging that his was an interim assessment. Indeed, in a footnote he acknowledged the possibility that this position might have to be revised in the light of the evidence from a future piece of research. However, despite the tentative nature of all of Carl's formulations in this 1959 paper, few practitioners have proposed a different view. Certainly Swildens (1980) expresses the opinion that the therapeutic relationship becomes more egalitarian as it unfolds and Van Kalmthout presents a clear contradiction to Carl's position in suggesting that: '. . . (depending on the client's interpersonal pattern – for example, too distant or too close), the therapist should relate more intimately or in a more disengaged manner' (1998: 57). Apart from these isolated examples, which might be debated in their own terms, the approach has stoically avoided theoretical consideration of circumstances where the therapist should vary her behaviour in relation to different clients, and the client variables which should demand that variation. It is one of the most astounding aspects of the 'client-centred' approach that the emphasis has almost entirely been on the therapist's behaviour! The plethora of research into the therapeutic conditions is focused entirely upon counsellor values, attitudes and behaviours with little regard paid to the communicability of these conditions to a variety of clients although this 'communicability' was one of the fundamental six conditions (Rogers, 1957a). To learn more about the subject of directivity we need to switch our attention away from counsellor behaviours and on to client reception.

Therapists need to work out different ways of working with Jeri and Joan. It would be both insensitive and unintelligent for the therapist to work in the same way with Joan as she does with Jeri or vice versa. For example, the discipline which the therapist evolved in work with Joan made use of 'review' phases within *every* therapeutic meeting. These 'reviews' explored the structuring which Joan had taken from the session thus far. In a sense, these review sections tapped elements of the 'unspoken relationship' (Mearns, 1994: 64–74) between Joan and her therapist and enabled both of them to pick up many of the inferences which Joan was making due to her pathological need for directivity. These could then be reflected back to Joan, not only as a way of checking on the directivity she had derived, but also in a fashion which showed her how much aptitude she was using in coming to those inferences. In a paradoxical fashion Joan's locus of evaluation was helped to internalise slightly by this process of meta-communication (Greenberg et al., 1993; Rennie, 1998).

In the early framing of his theory of therapy Rogers was absolutely correct to emphasise non-directivity because the vast majority of clients would display an externalised locus of evaluation – but there is also a danger of that becoming routinised within the behaviour of the therapist. We repeat, it is not the behaviour of the therapist which is important but the impact upon the client.

There is a difficulty in this more functional analysis of directivity: it begs the question, 'how accurate is the therapist's assessment of the client's locus of evaluation?'. This matter is further complicated when we step into configuration theory because some configurations within the client's Self may have an internalised locus of evaluation, while, for others, the locus is externalised. A sophisticated, highly empathic therapeutic relationship will relate differently with these different parts, taking great care with one part to offer no process direction or reframing, while, with another part, the dialogue need not be so cautious because the configuration contains an established self-evaluative function. As was described in Chapter 7 under 'Staying close to the client's symbolisation', when configurations are emerging into the therapeutic relationship, their nature is not known and a cautious, non-directive approach is the discipline.

If the therapeutic relationship does not contain the dimension of 'meeting at relational depth', it will be virtually impossible to assess the client's locus of evaluation. In superficial encounters the client is likely to portray a more unitary picture of Self which could misrepresent the parts considerably. An example of this was the work with 'Clair', presented in Chapter 7. Clair appeared to present a fairly internalised locus of evaluation but, because relating had not occurred at sufficient depth, the therapist was missing the vulnerable 'little girl' whose locus of evaluation was distinctly externalised. The person-centred therapist appropriately tends to err on the side of caution with respect to directivity as she grows to know her client.

This analysis begs the question of whether the therapist changes her behaviour as the client's locus of evaluation internalises. Of course, she does. This may be the kind of changing anticipated by Swildens (1980). Indeed, that changing may not even be a matter of conscious decision-making for the experienced therapist, but will be a consequence which flows from her experiencing of the client-in-relationship: a function of both the therapist's sensitivity and her relatedness to the client.

In this chapter we have tried to revise aspects of Rogers' Self theory and highlight dimensions of his theory of therapy. There are still many issues which require our theoretical attention. Some of this work has begun but is not far enough advanced for the present book. Notably, we want to explore one particular area within Rogers' Self theory which has never been seriously questioned and which demands examination. It is summarised by the two questions: 'why does the person have a need for positive regard?' and, also, 'why does this require to be transformed into a need for Self-regard?' These have been accepted as basic premises since Rogers' tentative statement of his theory (1951, 1959) – indeed, we can find their roots in his very first, and seldom quoted book, where he said that one of two 'vital needs' for the human organism was 'the need for affectional response from others' (Rogers, 1939: 11). Perhaps it is time that we explored these premises thoroughly.

In presenting this chapter we hope that we have responded reflectively to some of the ideas which Carl Rogers articulated many years ago. In taking on the task we have sought to follow the spirit of the man who framed his theoretical propositions carefully but always invited a challenging response. Even though it is only a fantasy, we look forward to next week's seminar when Carl might, in turn, respond to our paper!

10 Supervision in person-centred therapy: facilitating congruence

Elke Lambers

As counselling and psychotherapy have become more profession-
alised over the past 30 years, supervision has become accepted as
an integral part of ethical practice and as an essential support for
the therapist. The requirement for all practising therapists to be in
regular supervision throughout their working life means that
large numbers of therapists are working as supervisors. In the
absence of a career structure in counselling and psychotherapy, for
many therapists becoming a supervisor represents a step on a
(short) career ladder.

There has been a growing view that supervision is distinct
from therapy and that therapy training and experience do not
equip the therapist to become a supervisor. Carroll (1996) suggests
that supervision requires a theoretical understanding in its
own right and that supervision demands different skills from
counselling. He goes even further when he declares his intention
to 'move individuals away from counselling-bound models of
supervision (ie in which supervision is closely allied to the
counselling orientation of the supervisor) to developmental
and social role models of supervision (which start with the
learning situation of the supervisee)' (Carroll, 1996: 4). Much of
the current literature on counselling supervision takes a similar
approach, emphasising the need for an overarching framework
for the supervision process (Page and Wosket, 1994: 33) and
encouraging a movement away from 'approach-oriented' supervision which would only be of use to the 'purist' therapist (Page
and Wosket, 1994: 30). The inference is that supervision based on a
generic model of supervision is preferable to an approach-specific

model and indicates a higher level of professional functioning.

Although supervision is accepted as part of the therapist's professional life, there is ongoing debate about the nature and purpose of supervision; the training and qualification of supervisors; the supervision relationship; the responsibility of the supervisor and the amount of supervision required. In the current climate of fear of complaint and litigation, the link between supervision and ethical practice, professional development and monitoring of the therapist's competence may be contributing towards an understanding of supervision as a 'policing' activity. The supervisor operating from this perspective is likely to focus on ethics, contracts and boundaries; she will feel responsible for the client's welfare and may even be worried about being implicated in the supervisee's mistakes. This will inevitably lead to a less accepting attitude on the part of the supervisor, resulting in a more defensive or dependent attitude in the supervisee.

Both these trends, away from 'approach-oriented' supervision and towards a 'policing function' for supervision, could endanger the distinctive contribution which person-centred supervision can make to practitioners in the approach. The view of the supervisor as an outsider looking in, as an external source of evaluation, is in conflict with two of the fundamental principles of the person-centred philosophy: the development of the 'internal locus of evaluation' and the facilitation of congruence.

In person-centred supervision, the supervision relationship can be conceptualised as parallel to the therapy relationship: offering a context where the therapist can become aware of the processes taking place in herself in the relationship with the client and enabling her to become more congruent in that relationship. This is a developmental view of supervision in an accurate sense, the supervisor has no other concern, no other agenda than to facilitate the therapist's ability to be open to her experience so that she can become fully present and engaged in the relationship with the client. The person-centred supervisor accepts the supervisee as a person *in process* and trusts the supervisee's potential for growth. The person-centred therapist who is willing to fully engage with the client on an existential level will be changed by the experience – the supervisor is a witness to that change.

In this chapter I will explore supervision as a relationship which supports the therapist in the development of her *congruence* in relation to her client.

Previous work

In marked contrast with the vast amount of literature on person-centred therapy, relatively little has been written about supervision from a person-centred perspective. Rogers identifies the need for 'a resource person, available for consultation . . . an interested but non-coercive and non-judgemental source of stimulation' (Rogers, 1951: 475). Patterson (1964, 1983) and Rice (1980) emphasise the importance of the supervisor's attitude and describe the process and relationship dimensions in client-centred supervision. Hackney and Goodyear (1984) examine Rogers' views on supervision and analyse a supervision session conducted by him. They are particularly interested in the distinction between supervision and therapy and in the teaching element in Rogers' supervision. Mearns (1991) writes about the supervision relationship as one which fosters professional growth, drawing attention to the 'unspoken relationship' in supervision. Conradi (1996) describes how, as a person-centred supervisor, she encourages exploration of the supervisee's experience arising out of the relationship with the client. Maria Bowen explores the supervision relationship from the perspective of the therapeutic principles of person-centred therapy, in particular the trust in the supervisee's inner resources and the capacity for self-direction (Villas-Bowen, 1986). Baljon (1999) explores the concept of supervision as a place for 'learning congruence'.

The briefest possible summary of person-centred therapy is that it is a process which facilitates the client's congruence. In the empathic and unconditionally accepting therapeutic relationship it becomes possible for the client to symbolise experience into awareness accurately and assimilate this awareness into the self-structure (Rogers, 1959). In order for this process to become possible, the therapist needs to be congruently present in the relationship (Rogers, 1957b). Gaylin puts it well:

> The therapist needs to be available: continuously in touch with his or her feelings and reactions to the client. If these conditions are met – if the therapist is congruent, integrated, fully present and genuine – the therapist becomes intuitively free to react to the total person of the client. (Gaylin, 1996: 388)

The therapist requires an integrated awareness of herself in her relationship with the client in order to be able to experience and communicate her empathic understanding and her unconditional positive regard (Wyatt, 1998: 17). Of course, no therapist is constantly congruent and integrated in the relationship. Congruence is not a static quality but rather one which varies, due to the complex dynamics of the therapeutic relationship and the therapeutic process (Gaylin, 1996: 390–1).

The meaning of the core conditions in supervision

Writing about the training of therapists, Rogers states that by providing the supervisee with an accepting, empathic and genuine atmosphere, the supervisor creates a climate in which the supervisee can freely explore the feelings, blocks and difficulties while learning to become a therapist (Rogers, 1951). Although in this approach to supervision the therapeutic core conditions have a central place, this does not mean that supervision equals therapy. Maria Bowen identifies a major distinction between therapy and supervision:

> In psychotherapy the client has absolute freedom to talk about any realm of experience, but in supervision there is a primary focus – the interaction between the supervisee and the client. (Villas-Bowen, 1986: 298)

Patterson goes even further when he boldly states that 'to do therapy with a supervisee is to impose counselling on a captive client' (Patterson, 1964: 48).

Supervisor and supervisee must be clear from the outset what the supervision relationship is about and both need to take responsibility for maintaining and managing the boundaries of the relationship. Where past or current issues in the therapist's life contribute to the therapist's incongruence, they need to be fully acknowledged without entering into a therapeutic exploration. The supervisor needs to trust that the supervisee will take care of herself and that she will be able to identify what support she may need, both personally and professionally.

Empathy

Empathy is the willingness and ability to enter the experiential world of the other person, leaving aside our own frame of reference. Empathy is a process, a way of being in relation to the client, which evolves in the course of the relationship (Mearns and Thorne, 1999: 41–4).

Setting aside her own frame of reference, the supervisor endeavours to be open to the supervisee's experience and to listen without evaluation. The supervisor who is free from feelings of responsibility and judgement is best placed to support the supervisee in her effort to give expression to her experience, her thoughts and concerns.

Supervisees may bring issues which are not yet clearly symbolised in awareness. They may present a vague feeling of disquiet or concern, or appear detached or preoccupied with 'details'. The supervisor's empathic presence can help the supervisee to settle and to focus on what she is bringing, as she becomes aware of the complexity of what is going on for her.

A session with Tina

Tina finished her counselling training 6 months ago and is now working part time in a 'drop-in' counselling centre. The supervisor has worked with her for two years.

Tina sits down, sighs, takes her notepad from her bag but, unlike normally, does not open it:

Tina: Nothing much to talk about really. Things are ticking over with my clients . . . nothing stands out for me . . . Perhaps we can talk about this article I read about anti-depressants?

Supervisor: Talking about the article would mean that we would be using our time constructively? There is not much that feels interesting?

Tina: Actually, I feel pretty flat about my work over the past two weeks. I am not happy with it [*Looks down, seems uncomfortable*]

Supervisor: You're not happy with how you are in your work . . . you sound as though talking about it would be an effort, like it is something you don't want to do . . .

Tina: I feel I *should* talk about it . . . I don't understand it. I can't be bothered listening to my clients, I get bored . . .

Here the supervisor shows her willingness to understand what is going on for Tina yet she is also careful to remain within the agreed boundary of the supervision relationship by reflecting Tina's statement about her unhappiness in relation to her work rather than take her somewhere else. The power of empathy is well known and it is important that the supervisor does not use her empathic skills in a parental fashion to 'draw out' the supervisee. The supervision relationship is an *adult* one, but the person-centred supervisor will always be mindful of issues of power which may be unspoken. Particularly when working with a therapist in training, or with a less experienced therapist, the supervisor may be perceived either as a powerful positive model or as a powerful judge, or both. The supervisor needs to respect the supervisee's boundaries, respect her ability to make a judgement about what she is ready to share and trust the supervisee to make appropriate use of the relationship.

It is a common misconception about person-centred work that the only useful, valid focus should be the exploration of feeling. Empathy is then narrowly defined as relating only to the affective realm of experience. The supervisor operating from this position of favouring feeling may in effect be creating a condition of worth for the supervisee: 'If I want to be accepted by the supervisor I will need to talk about feelings'. Empathy in supervision needs to extend to the whole range of the supervisee's experience: feelings, thoughts, theoretical questions, moral and ethical concerns. The supervisee who comes with an ethical or theoretical question may feel more fully empathically met by the supervisor who engages with her in her exploration of such issues than by the supervisor who seeks to discover the 'real feeling' behind the questions.

Acceptance

Acceptance is the consistent willingness to value and respect the other as a person of worth, without conditions and without being deflected by the person's behaviour.

In therapy, the therapist's unconditional positive regard makes it possible for the client to allow into awareness experience which normally needs to be denied or distorted in order to meet conditions of worth. The combination of empathy and unconditional positive regard in therapy facilitates the movement towards congruence.

Perhaps the difference between therapy and supervision is most clearly visible in relation to acceptance. Although in therapy the therapist may find herself struggling with her value judgements or, perhaps more rarely, may find herself concerned about the welfare of a third party, in supervision there is an expectation that the supervisor will (at least) challenge the supervisee about her behaviour. However, preoccupation with acceptance and judgement can take the supervisor away from the real challenge in supervision: 'Can I understand, respect and value this therapist and trust her to find her own unique way of relating to her client?'

As Maria Bowen states:

> Just as therapists' perceptions and responses are inevitably shaped by their 'personality, past history and so forth' (Rogers, 1985), it follows that the supervisee is going to perceive and act differently from the supervisor. It is important that the supervisor respects these differences and trusts that the supervisees have the resources necessary to develop their own effective ways of doing therapy. The function of the supervisor, then, is to create the atmosphere that will enable the supervisee to find her or his own style of being a therapist. By doing so the supervisor also models the growth promoting environment of congruence, acceptance and empathy. (Villas-Bowen, 1986: 296)

Bowen identifies a paradox in what she describes as *form-oriented* supervision: in her commitment to 'pure forms' the supervisor discourages styles of expression that do not fit the supervisor's model of person-centred therapy.

> In doing so a basic philosophical principle of the person-centred approach seems to be missing: the trust in the supervisee's capacity for self-direction and self-determination – that is the belief that the supervisee has the inner resources to develop his or her own style of being an effective therapist. (Villas-Bowen, 1986: 293)

In supervision training, much time is spent discussing this condition, particularly the aspect of unconditionality and the non-judgemental attitude. Is it possible for the person-centred supervisor to be non-judgemental? Is it appropriate to extend this condition to the supervision relationship? Can a supervisor genuinely accept a supervisee who through her incongruence could be damaging to her client? As well as feeling challenged from within her own value system, the supervisor may feel under pressure from the outside world – colleagues, agency, training course, professional organisation – to make a judgement about the therapist's practice and competence. To deal with such concerns constructively, sensitively and respectfully can be a real challenge – and will be all the more challenging for the supervisor who has difficulty with recognising and accepting herself as 'judgemental'. Kilborn concludes from her recent research into supervisees' experience of 'challenge' that:

> supervisees not only need to feel understood and accepted, they also need to know where the supervisor stands . . . Challenge within a

supervisory relationship is accepted by supervisees, indeed it can be experienced as stimulating and enriching. (Kilborn, 1999: 89)

Later in the session with Tina

We have talked about Tina's flatness, her current lack of enthusiasm with her work and she has touched on some issues with one of her clients with whom she feels stuck.

Tina: I have been thinking recently, maybe I shouldn't be counselling . . . maybe I am not suited to it . . . maybe I have not got the right personality for it . . .

Supervisor: You have a lot of doubts about yourself as a counsellor at the moment, you are asking yourself really difficult questions. I can see you are very serious about this . . .

Tina: [*looking down at her hands, sits very still. Long silence, then, in a different voice*] I feel *used* sometimes, it makes me angry. I don't need to take that from anyone, not even clients! Last Thursday I told P [*a client*] that I did not want to hear him go over the same stuff again, it is just not good for me. So I stopped the session halfway through. [*Voice raised*] Well, if it is not good for me, if I can't be there for him, it's better to be honest about it! I thought it was about time I used my congruence!

Supervisor: [*is silent for a short while*] I am wondering how to respond to you about all this, Tina. I hear something is really not OK for you in relation to P, that you feel used and that you felt you had to do something to stop that. I have never heard you talk like that before about P or about any client and I wonder what is going on for you there. I am also concerned about the way in which you dealt with this in the session with P – it sounds to me as though you stopped being his therapist there. How can we begin to talk about all this?

Here the supervisor is faced with a complex situation. The supervisor knows Tina and she is aware that this response to her client is unusual – clearly there is something going on for the supervisee. As well as feeling concern for Tina, she is aware of the client too. She may also be wondering about Tina's understanding of congruence and she may be thinking about ethics. Her response indicates her willingness to stay with Tina and to understand her

– she invites her ('. . . let's talk . . .') and continues to trust that she will take responsibility in the supervision relationship ('. . . how can we begin to talk about this?'). The supervisor is not deflected by Tina's behaviour and remains consistent in her respect and acceptance. Coming in with judgement or critical confrontation is likely to inhibit Tina's processing of the experience. The interests of supervisee and client are most likely to be served by helping Tina to explore the issues. It is of paramount importance that the supervisor is not simply using a 'technique' but that she is *congruent* in her invitation to dialogue. The essential challenge for the person-centred supervisor is to maintain her 'adult' orientation towards her supervisee's processing and not to degenerate into a judgemental parental figure.

Congruence

Congruence is the accurate symbolisation and integration of self-experience into awareness and the accurate expression of this integrated experience in behaviour.

The concept of congruence is a source of confusion and debate. Rarely do I hear supervisees question their expression of empathy or the meaning of acceptance in the same way as they ask questions about congruence. Perhaps one of the difficulties with congruence is that it cannot easily be operationalised in terms of behaviour. How can we tell if a person is congruent? How can we demonstrate or communicate that we are congruent?

We live in a culture which favours incongruence and as a result, many of us carry conditions of worth which stop us from knowing our experience, never mind expressing it. It is no wonder that therapists struggle with the concept, despite all the hard work put in through personal development to become more open to experience. Congruence is often equated with the direct expression of feeling. In person-centred gatherings the person who shows feeling (particularly of sadness or pain) is often praised as being 'real' and 'congruent'. This is a simplistic and inadequate understanding of congruence. It focuses on 'expression' more than 'experiencing'. The essence of congruence is the therapist's ongoing awareness of her *experiencing*, with that experiencing being available in the interaction between therapist and client. In this way, congruence is a state of being which is so continuous within the therapeutic relationship that it does not stand out as something

different or striking. Where the therapist carries the misunderstanding that congruence is all about *expression* of feeling, there is
a tendency for it to be experienced as discontinuous with the
process – indeed such powerful expressions are generally indica-
tive of the therapist's sudden awareness of her *incongruence*,
described disparagingly by Mearns and Thorne as 'splurging
congruence':

> . . . we need to draw attention to the danger of the counsellor . . .
> slipping into the phenomenon which we call 'splurging congruence'.
> This depicts a pattern where the counsellor is customarily incongruent
> with her client over long periods of time then discharges all that pent-
> up unexpressed feeling in one large lump of projective material. The
> splurging may be done in the name of 'being congruent', but the
> motivation is generally punitive and is certainly experienced that way.
> (Mearns and Thorne, 1999: 92)

The supervisor who has a limited understanding of congruence is
likely to support the supervisee in her effort to become more self-
expressive, perhaps encouraging her to 'take risks and bring her
feelings into the relationship with the client'. In doing so, she will
be focusing on the therapist's expression rather than on facilitating the therapist's awareness of her experiencing.

Tina's session continues

> *Tina*: [*Tearful*] I really don't think I can face talking to you about
> it now – I am too upset. I feel I have made a mess of it and
> I am worried about what you think of me. Maybe you think
> I should stop counselling. I really couldn't face another
> session with P – I always end up feeling I am no good.
>
> *Supervisor*: I see that you are upset and you keep saying that
> you are no good as a counsellor and you are scared of my
> judgement . . . This must be hard for you, but I would really
> like to look at all of this with you . . . I think I am trying to
> convince you here that I am not an ogre.
>
> *Tina*: . . . I just feel so embarrassed, I know I should not have
> said it to P – I suppose it was not professional. I wonder if he
> will come back. Do you think I should write him a note?

Is the supervisor congruent here? She is reaching out to the
supervisee, looking for a way of responding that shows she is
genuinely interested and willing to understand her, both in relation to her feelings about her work and in her feelings in relation

to the supervisor. The supervisor is not aware of her own defensiveness initially, but then spots it and acknowledges it ('I think I am trying to convince you here that I am not an ogre'). Perhaps this made it possible for the supervisee to own her feeling of embarrassment.

Just as the therapist's congruence is the bedrock for empathy and acceptance in the therapeutic relationship, so too is the supervisor's congruence an essential condition in the supervision relationship. The supervisor's full engagement with the supervisee is only possible if the supervisor is open to her own experience – her congruence gives depth and meaning to her empathy and acceptance. Congruent engagement not only makes it possible for the supervisee to become more congruent herself, it also presents her with a powerful model for her own practice. The supervisor's congruent acceptance supports the supervisee's self-acceptance and the supervisor's courage to be present may inspire the supervisee to trust herself to do likewise with her client. The supervisor does not show the supervisee how to 'do' person-centred therapy but through her experience in the supervision relationship the supervisee is empowered to become *herself* as a therapist.

In the same way that the therapist needs to reflect on herself in relation to her client, the supervisor needs to monitor herself so that she can remain congruent in her engagement with the supervisee. She needs to learn to recognise signs of under-involvement and over-involvement and she needs to pay attention to the power dynamic. She needs to be mindful of her own needs in the supervision relationship: her need to be seen as knowledgeable and competent, her need to be liked, her personal commitment to the person-centred approach, her pride in seeing 'her' supervisee develop and grow, can all be vulnerabilities which may make the supervisor incongruent.

So important is congruence to the supervision endeavour that the supervisor may even choose to give it a special focus. She may reflect and communicate about her experiencing in the supervision relationship in a much more systematic fashion than would happen in therapy. This kind of 'metacommunication' (Rennie, 1998) quickly brings into the open issues in the relationship which could become problematic if they had remained 'unspoken'. Mearns (1991: 118) talks about the often restrictive norms which can creep into a supervision relationship and reminds the supervisor of the importance of exploring the 'unspoken' in order to keep the relationship healthy. This more frequent self-reflection and expression on the part of the supervisor is just one way in which supervision can actively develop the supervisee's learning.

Theory in supervision

Many theories about supervision emphasise its educational aspect as distinct from the element of personal development. Proctor (1988) talks about the *formative function*, Carroll (1996) identifies the *teaching task* as one of the seven tasks of supervision, Feltham and Dryden (1994) write about using the *developmental opportunities* of supervision, while Page and Wosket (1994) prefer to see the supervisor as a *mentor* or *guide* rather than as a teacher. Bowen states that one of the functions of the supervisor is to create an environment which will facilitate the supervisee's openness to *growth* and *learning*, where she can learn to be the judge of her own performance (Villas-Bowen, 1986).

The person-centred supervisor aims to create a context for both affective and cognitive learning and development. In this learning climate a variety of methods may be used: notes, role-play, exploration of the literature, listening to taped counselling sessions or theoretical discussion. Any of these activities may help the supervisee to deepen her understanding of the therapeutic process and to increase her ability to make use of both her feelings and her thoughts in relation to the work with her client.

Faced with a supervisee who appeals for help, who asks for instructions or suggestions on what to do with a client, the supervisor may feel tempted to come to the rescue, offering prescriptions, suggestions, perhaps a theoretical explanation. By offering such a 'shortcut' through the supervisee's exploratory process, the supervisor is likely to maintain the supervisee in a position of powerlessness, giving in to her need to rely on the authority and power of the supervisor, instead of helping her to acknowledge her feelings of helplessness, stuckness, perhaps incompetence. Often, the exploration of such feelings leads to interesting discoveries about the supervisee's therapeutic work, allowing then a joint exploration of what would help the supervisee in her crisis or dilemma.

In my practice as a supervisor I sometimes refer to literature, offer a copy of a paper, or look up the Code of Ethics. I admit to even giving the odd mini-lecture. I love theory and I like talking about it; I find it stimulating and I know I can get carried away a bit sometimes. Invariably I find that when such offerings come from *my* needs they are, at best, of limited use to the supervisee. At worst, the supervisee feels that I do not understand her – it can disrupt our contact.

Supervision offers both the therapist in training and the experienced practitioner an opportunity to explore relevant aspects of person-centred theory. In his chapter on 'Understanding Theory', Mearns summarises the development of person-centred theory and argues the importance of a thorough theory curriculum in the training of person-centred practitioners. He illustrates how the person-centred therapist can use theory to help her understand the client's experience, not to diagnose, predict or influence the client but:

> to help the counsellor formulate a tentative and hypothetical understanding of the client which will be of sufficient help to the counsellor to stay open to the client's experience and thereby to work at relational depth with the client. (Mearns, 1997a: 146)

Therapists in training often try to link theory with practice and experienced practitioners enjoy revisiting theory to find a deeper level of understanding in themselves. Both in my own therapy practice and in my supervision work, the question I like to ask is: 'Is there anything in person-centred theory which can help me (you) to think about what is happening, or can help me (you) to understand the client?' The exploration of this question usually results in the therapist's deeper understanding of *herself* in the therapy relationship, so that she is more equipped to meet the client. It can also help her develop her ability to communicate her theoretical understanding, which is an important skill for the therapist working within a multi-disciplinary setting.

Professional issues and ethics

In my experience with supervisors in training, the ethical responsibilities in supervision are the subject of a great deal of discussion and the cause of considerable anxiety. The most often expressed concern is about the statement in the BAC Code of Ethics and Practice for Supervisors (BAC, 1996b: B1.11): 'Supervisors are responsible for taking action if they are aware that their supervisee's practice is not in accordance with the BAC Codes of Ethics and Practice for Counsellors'. This statement puts supervision firmly in an ethical context, it implies that the supervisor makes an assessment of the supervisee's practice with reference to the Codes and that he or she should intervene when the supervisee is practising 'not in accordance' with the Codes. Ethical supervision practice is defined both in terms of responsibility to the supervisee and to the profession.

The concerns of person-centred supervisors usually centre around the issues of *judgement* and *taking action*, both of which are seen as incompatible with non-judgemental acceptance and unconditionality. Within a person-centred framework, when there are concerns about a supervisee's practice, the challenge to the supervisor is to offer a consistent, accepting relationship through which the supervisee can achieve a greater degree of congruence in relation to the client. In doing so, the supervisor acts ethically: her response facilitates the therapist's ability to meet the needs of the client more fully, that is to *practise ethically*. This is a definition of ethical practice within the framework of person-centred therapy and is consistent with the core philosophy of the approach as expressed in the therapeutic relationship.

Therapeutic practice can be viewed from two perspectives, from *inside* the therapeutic approach of the therapist and from *outside* the approach. The *inside perspective* gives the above described view from the frame of reference of the approach – practice is 'assessed' through reflection on such issues as the core conditions, the therapeutic relationship and the therapeutic process as conceptualised in person-centred theory. The *outside* perspective is the view from the frame of reference of the profession and of the society and culture in which the profession operates. This view does not represent a particular counselling approach – it represents a moral and legal view of the activity of therapy and defines ethics in terms of moral and legal standards.

Ethical practice needs to be defined *both* in terms of the relationship with the client as conceptualised within a particular approach *and* in relation to the society in which the practice takes place – it is not a matter of choosing between these perspectives. The person-centred supervisor aims to offer a context where both frameworks are present – where the supervisee can evaluate her practice from both the perspective of person-centred theory and that of professional ethics, indeed a context where person-centred practice and ethical awareness can be integrated. An example of this integration would be the exploration of the ethical concept of 'boundaries' in the language of person-centred therapy. This might involve reflection on the *context of the therapeutic work,* on the *client's experience of the relationship,* on the *therapist's competence to meet the client at depth* and on the therapist's *over-involvement* or *under-involvement.* The supervisor who is able to see from both perspectives, who can function confidently within both frameworks and who offers the supervisee her congruent acceptance, creates in the supervision relationship an excellent basis for support, challenge and for open, respectful exploration and dialogue about both therapeutic and ethical issues.

Tina's session

> [*Picking up where we left Tina and her supervisor*]
>
> *Supervisor:* I agree that we need to think about P and about what would be the most appropriate way forward with him, and I also want to talk more with you about what has been going on in your work with P. And, what was that about writing him a note?
>
> *Tina:* I am worried that he will complain to the manager of the Centre. He is forever complaining, writing letters . . . and the manager does not have much time for person-centred counselling.
>
> *Supervisor:* You seem so anxious at the moment Tina . . . anxious about what your client might do, anxious about the manager's response . . . anxious about my judgement . . .
>
> *Tina:* I know, I guess I am panicking. I wouldn't know how to explain to the manager what happened, he does not understand person-centred therapy, he does not know what congruence is . . . and I don't want to break confidentiality either . . . what a mess!
>
> *Supervisor:* I really would like to understand what happened – more important, I would like to hear how *you* understand it and, yes, we will need to think about the ethical issues too.

Tina: I don't understand what happened . . . working with P has been difficult all along, I don't think he likes women. I can't tune in with him, I have tried, but I feel uncomfortable with him. I suppose I should have brought it to supervision earlier. I feel I have let him down . . . I suppose I'll have to face it, rather than run away from it.

Supervisor: Sounds like you've started . . .

The supervisor remains consistent in her acceptance of Tina. She acknowledges her fear and her need to find a solution, she responds with empathy but she remains focused on the context: Tina and her work. Tina feels vulnerable, but the supervisor does not reassure her nor does she judge her. She does not panic about the ethical aspects, while acknowledging that they are there. Though Tina appears somewhat defensive (talking about the manager's and the client's hostility), the supervisor continues to remain open to all of Tina's feelings and to trust her willingness to take responsibility, both for her work with her client and for her exploration in supervision. Challenge comes from the supervisor's congruent, consistent acceptance rather than from her authority or her judgement.

11 Future challenges: dangers and opportunities

Capitulation or radical rebellion

Carl Rogers once observed that life is a risky business and one of the underlying themes of this book is that the kind of risk-taking which comes from a full engagement with life is becoming increasingly difficult in the world of counselling and psychotherapy. Professionalisation with its creeping tendency towards institutionalisation has created a prevailing climate where many practitioners are fearful rather than courageous. It is not easy for a therapist to be life-affirming or fully present to a client when there is the nagging suspicion that it would be wiser to watch one's own back.

In such a situation person-centred therapists may be tempted to take one of two courses of action. By far the most insidious is to capitulate to the seemingly dominant zeitgeist and move towards a cautious, carefully circumscribed form of therapy where the key criteria are the achievement of prescribed goals, proven cost-effectiveness and predictable therapist behaviour as laid down in manuals of practice and detailed ethical codes. Within such a straitjacket it is perhaps possible to go through the motions of something that may look like person-centred therapy, but it will be lacking heart and the relational depth which demand the therapist's investment as a person who is both resourceful and vulnerable. It will be, in Buber's terms, an I-it relationship masquerading as an I-Thou encounter. It may keep the therapist in business but it will be without vitality and inspiration. It will be without risks but it will not enliven. The second course of action is altogether more radical and it is the kind of strategy which could be incited by such books, as Richard Mowbray's *The Case Against Psychotherapy Registration* (Mowbray, 1995) and the anthology *Implausible Professions* edited by Richard House and Nick Totton

(House and Totton, 1997). So powerful are the arguments deployed in such books against much of the currently received wisdom – whether this concerns registration, training or research, that person-centred therapists may be tempted to say 'a plague on all your houses' and remove themselves from the current counselling and psychotherapy scene altogether to set up an independent empire free of the shackles and constraints which anxiety-driven professionalisation seems inevitably to bring in its wake. Richard Mowbray in his book even coins the term 'humanologist' as a way, supposedly, of avoiding incarceration for those who will not ethically be able to subscribe to the requirements imposed by the statutory registration of counsellors and psychotherapists when it comes. The basic assumption in such writings seems to be that such registration will inevitably arrive, sooner or later, despite the fact that at a rational level it has little if anything to commend it. The shift of nomenclature from counsellor/psychotherapist to humanologist is reminiscent of Rogers' move from psychotherapist to counsellor at a time when he was threatened with legal action by the medical establishment for offering treatment (psychotherapy) which at that time only medical practitioners were licensed to provide.

This second way forward, which we might term radical rebellion, receives much posthumous support from the life and example of Rogers himself. Not only was there the famous shift from psychotherapist to counsellor, but there was also the moment in 1963 when he finally decided to leave the academic world and resigned from the University of Wisconsin where he had failed to integrate the departments of psychology and psychiatry as he had hoped to do when he went to the university in 1957 as the holder of Chairs in both disciplines. In 1963 Rogers was tired and frustrated. The academic world had become restrictive and alienating and he longed for a new kind of freedom. He knew he was at a professional crossroads and he opted for the Western Behavioral Sciences Institute, a non-profit making independent institute, and began life in California where he stayed until his death in 1987 (Thorne, 1992: 17–18). The significance of this move can be endlessly debated. For Rogers himself, there can be little doubt that his life was transformed and the subsequent creation of the Center for Studies of the Person, in La Jolla, gave him a base from which he was to make major contributions to the emerging encounter group culture and, later, to the study and facilitation of large groups, cross-cultural communication and the pursuit of world peace. It can justifiably be argued, however, that what was for Rogers a personally liberating decision which led to increasing self-fulfilment and global influence, was for the development of person-centred therapy an unmitigated disaster. His act of radical rebellion resulted in many other person-centred practitioners leaving the university world and hence the mainstream of the therapeutic profession. Gradually and, at first, imperceptibly, the influence of the person-centred approach began to wane, research activity all but ceased and what had been a leading school of psychotherapy and counselling was soon no longer centre-stage. It is not altogether fanciful to suggest that Rogers' radically rebellious decision to leave the university world was the determining moment in the eventual decline of client-centred/person-centred therapy in the United States of America.

A different path

For us, as we experience the British scene at the beginning of a new millennium, neither the path of capitulation to the prevailing zeitgeist, nor the path of radical rebellion, would seem to serve the best interests of the approach to therapy to which we have committed the best part of our lives. To be sure, the temptation to take one or other route is often well-nigh overwhelming. We are not infrequently scared and wonder when some litigious client or trainee is going to register a complaint that will be upheld because there is little understanding of, or sympathy for, the person-centred approach in many quarters of the increasingly regulated and 'manualised' therapeutic community. There are other times, too, when a great weariness of the soul sets in, usually after a particularly contentious committee meeting, and there comes a yearning for a freedom from nit-picking constraints and the desire to work in an altogether more sustaining environment. Person-centred practitioners, more than others, know the central importance of being prized and understood as well as the capacity to be open to experience. To be deprived of these sustaining ingredients is to risk falling into the very trap in which so many of our clients find themselves. To capitulate or to rebel can both become seductive possibilities on an almost daily basis and both may be leading us down a false path.

In Chapter 9 we explored what is, for us, the exciting theory that the actualising tendency is accompanied by a corrective 'nongrowth' dynamic, which, if we can but attend to it, will enable us to listen with the deepest respect to the totality of our beings and to find a way forward through dialogue rather than impulsive submission to the currently most strident configuration of our complex and subtly crafted Self. This 'both-and' rather than 'either-or' attitude towards ourselves need not lead to paralysis. On the contrary, the ability to attend to all parts of ourselves, lovingly and patiently, can bring us to a state of coherence and integration where we are able to make choices and embrace ways of being and doing which do not leave us feeling fragmented or discourteous or punitive to treasured parts of ourselves. We would suggest that this is the process – and it sometimes requires much discipline – which can lead to a deep sense of positive self-regard rather than to the uneasy feeling of there being a fifth column in the camp which will deal a lethal blow to our self-esteem just at the point when we need to be maximally self-affirming.

A lack of corporate self-regard

The desirability of positive self-regard is a cornerstone of person-centred belief and in the light of this it is perturbing to note how lacking person-centred therapists as a corporate body seem to be in this desirable attribute. We wonder if it is precisely because of our inability to listen attentively to the varying parts of our corporate experience that we often seem so uncertain or ambivalent about our corporate validity. Almost invariably, when person-centred therapists come together, there begins a lament about the lack of esteem we receive in the therapeutic world; about the facile misunderstandings of the major tenets of our approach; about the inhuman and interpretive treatment of clients by colleagues from other orientations; about the absurd rigidity of the detailed sub-clauses of ethical codes; about training requirements which seem to have no bearing on the effective functioning of a person-centred therapist; about views of the person held by others which are infantilising, pathologising or even demonising. In the midst of such lamentation – which can often be angry or despairing – it is often not difficult to detect an almost complete lack of corporate positive self-regard. It is as if there is a tendency, even among experienced person-centred therapists when they come together, to adopt a stance of inferiority and to feel helpless or hopeless in the face of the apparently confident, self-assured statements and practices of other orientations. Yet, at the same time, these same people, when challenged, usually have a profound trust in the efficacy of the approach to which they are committed, recount astonishing stories of client process and display an utter dedication to the way of working and being which in many cases has fundamentally changed the direction and the quality of their own lives. Why is it, then, that such personal conviction and experience does not, it seems, lead to a sense of corporate strength and affirmation?

The problem of power

The answer to this apparent riddle lies, we believe, in the deep ambivalence at the heart of the approach about the use and abuse of power. Again, it is possible to lay some of the responsibility for this at Carl Rogers' own door. We well remember an evening 20 or so years ago when in the midst of an impassioned discussion about the future of person-centred therapy, Carl quietly undressed and went to bed telling us that the future was in our hands and he was not much bothered about it. Maria Bowen in her moving tribute to Carl after his death recounts a somewhat similar episode:

> . . . I began to prepare myself for his death. One of the ways I did this was by becoming obsessed about what was going to happen to the person-centered approach after he was no longer with us. My fear was that it would become an orthodox system, so different from the unorthodox man he was. I became quite passionate and wrote several papers on the subject last year. In the midst of my passion I got quite irritated at his seemingly total indifference to the whole theory. I asked him: 'Don't you care about the future of your ideas?' He answered, 'No, I don't and I wish you would also stop caring so much. I know I can't control it, and you can't either. It will take the direction that the group wants, so why don't you just relax?' (Villas-Bowen, 1987: 4)

Rogers always professed that he was not interested in power but that he certainly wanted to be influential. We believe that there was an element of self-deception in this assertion. Both in his books, and in his commitment to the application of his ideas in the world arena, it is clear that he wished to be powerfully influential and it is difficult to distinguish this from the desire to be powerful. The confusion around this issue is further intensified by the theory and practice of person-centred therapy itself. As person-centred therapists, we are only too aware of the ways in which power is abused to the detriment of human development and human relationships. As therapists we are concerned at all costs not to add to this destructiveness. We wish to empower and not to disempower through the imposition of our own perceptions and prejudices. For us it is the very cornerstone of our practice that we cherish and respect the uniqueness and the resourcefulness of our clients and seek to facilitate a process whereby they come to recognise and to own their personal power and not to be forever the slaves of the expectations, needs and demands of others. We are, as it were, experts in empowering others and in not abusing our own power – and here, we suspect, lies the source of our corporate malaise. In our wholly legitimate and admirable desire not to *abuse* our power, we have somehow lost the ability to *exercise* our power. Carl Rogers did not help in this respect because he exercised influence – and did so massively and successfully – and apparently persuaded himself and others that he was not interested in exercising power.

Overcoming ambivalence to the exercise of power

It is our growing belief that once we can accept that we are powerful people, the challenges facing person-centred therapy in the years ahead can be met with relish and enthusiasm. The chief danger lies in our continuing to entertain a corporate self-concept which tells us that we are not up to the hurly-burly of the therapeutic marketplace and that our goods will not be valued by those who follow traditions which encourage the superiority conferred by recondite knowledge or the acquisition of a whole armamentarium of therapeutic techniques and strategies. Our experience often points in the contrary direction. Among our colleagues from other traditions, we often discover a longing to be freed from theoretical or clinical structures which seem to impede rather than enhance relationship. It is not uncommon for person-centred training courses, for example, to receive applications from those who have become professionally disenchanted with a more prescriptive or invasive approach in which they have originally been trained. While there is undoubtedly a defensive arrogance among many therapists (person-centred practitioners not excepted) there is, too, much evidence of a genuine humility among practitioners of almost all persuasions and a willingness to engage with the insight and the experience of traditions other than one's own. It would be a tragedy, in our view, if person-centred therapists lost heart at this stage when, precisely because of some of the unfortunate moves towards a sterile professionalism which we have explored in this book, there is perhaps a greater thirst than ever among both therapists and would-be clients for an engagement with what is truly human.

Once person-centred therapists can overcome their ambivalence about the exercise of power, they will be able to attend fully to the self configuration which tells them, with conviction, that their approach works and that it is based on an understanding of human development and human relationships of which the world stands badly in need at this juncture. At a period when the pace of life seems to accelerate daily, and when men and women find their private time and space reduced to a minimum, person-centred therapy proclaims the primacy of relationship. What is more, it points to the healing efficacy of a kind of relationship which seems increasingly rare in our culture. With its emphasis on unconditional positive regard, empathy and congruence, person-centred therapy reveals by implication, the poverty and the potential destructiveness of relationships characterised by surveillance, appraisal, rigidity of role, and the imposition of performance targets whether in work or social contexts. There is a challenge to person-centred therapists to extrapolate from their clinical experience the experiential data which can form the basis of a critique of the dysfunctional relationships which characterise much of our working and social lives. This in turn points to the need for person-centred therapists to become skilled and committed practitioner-researchers. We are ideally equipped to undertake such work for the qualitative research paradigm calls for precisely the interpersonal skills and the self-reflectiveness which are inherent in our approach to therapy (Mearns and McLeod, 1984). Person-centred therapists, we believe, have much privileged information about the cultivation of intimacy and the establishing of mutuality. They also have the skill to research these mysterious and life-enhancing aspects of living in relational depth. These are matters which are not only central to the conduct of therapy but also to the well-being of a culture. They also point indirectly to the damaging effects of under-involvement in relationship whether in the social or therapeutic context. One of our secret hopes, incidentally, is that such research will lead to the validation of our long-held hypothesis that under-involvement with a client on the part of a therapist is potentially much more dangerous than over-involvement which often seems to be a favourite stick with which to beat dedicated person-centred therapists.

A clarion call

We wish to end this book with a clarion call of encouragement and hope to our fellow practitioners. The opportunities ahead are, we believe, abundant. The danger is that we shall fail to extend to ourselves the core conditions which we willingly offer to our clients and, as a result, will lack the nerve to offer in the market-place the fruits of our knowledge and experience. In a world and in a profession where the creeping forces of institutionalisation and regulatory dogmatism are insidiously advancing, this would be a tragedy and, to use an old-fashioned but perennial concept, a gross dereliction of duty. We must be diligent, however, not to be carried away on an impulsive flight of innocent naivete in the mistaken belief that we are aligning ourselves with the actualising tendency. As we have suggested, this single motivating force in the human organism is more subtle and complex in its operation than we might initially imagine. We need to listen attentively to the many configurations of the Self before we know the sense of integration which comes from accessing the actualising tendency in its unique and socially mediated complexity. We will then be in a position where we can exercise our power without fear of abusing or damaging others. That is not to say that they will all like what we have to offer, but we may be sure that some will. It is our conviction that person-centred therapy is poised to make major contributions in almost all areas of the therapeutic enterprise. We have much on which to build: it will be fear or loss of nerve that prevent us from having the trust in ourselves and in our resourcefulness which we so gladly and appropriately place in our clients.

References

Allen, L. (1989) 'A client's experience of failure', in D. Mearns and W. Dryden (eds), *Experiences of Counselling in Action*. London: Sage. pp 20–7.

American Psychological Association (1995) Task Force on Promotion and Dissemination of Psychological Procedures, Division of Clinical Psychology. Training and dissemination of empirically validated psychological treatments; Report and recommendations, *The Clinical Psychologist*, 48, 3–23.

Angyal, A. (1941) *Foundations For a Science of Personality*. New York: Commonwealth Fund.

Austin, K.M., Moline, M.E. and Williams, G.T. (1990) *Confronting Malpractice: Legal and Ethical Dilemmas in Psychotherapy*. Newbury Park, CA: Sage.

Auw, A. (1991) *Gentle Roads to Survival*. Lower Lake, CA: Aslan Publishing.

BAC (1988) *The Recognition of Counsellor Training Courses*. Rugby: British Association for Counselling.

BAC (1991) *The Recognition of Counsellor Training Courses*. Second Edition. Rugby: British Association for Counselling.

BAC (1996a) *The Recognition of Counsellor Training Courses*. Third Edition. Rugby: British Association for Counselling.

BAC (1996b) *Code of Ethics and Practice for Supervisors of Counsellors*. Rugby: British Association for Counselling.

BAC (1997) *Code of Ethics and Practice for Counsellors*. Rugby: British Association for Counselling.

BAC (1998a) *Supervision: Issues and Ambiguities*. Report of the BAC Working Group on Supervision. Rugby: British Association for Counselling.

BAC (1998b) *How Much Supervision Should I Have?* Information Sheet. Rugby: British Association for Counselling.

BAC (1999) *Counselling Workloads*. Rugby: British Association for Counselling.

Baljon, M. (1999) 'Focussen in clientgerichte psychotherapie supervisie: het aanleren van congruentie', *Tijdschrift Voor Clientgerichte Psychotherapie*, 37 (1): 21–31.

Bandyopadhyay, B. (1997) 'Young and anxious', in S. Dunant and R. Porter (eds), *The Age of Anxiety*. London: Virago. pp 189–99.

Barrett-Lennard, G.T. (1998) *Carl Rogers' Helping System: Journey and Substance*. London: Sage.

Bearhrs, J. (1982) *Unity and Multiplicity*. New York: Brunner/Mazel.

Berne, E. (1961) *Transactional Analysis in Psychotherapy*. New York: Grove Press.

Binder, U. (1998) 'Empathy and empathy development with psychotic clients', in B. Thorne and E. Lambers (eds), *Person-Centred Therapy: a European Perspective*. London: Sage. pp 216–30.

Bohart, A. (1995) 'The person-centered psychotherapies', in A. Gurman and S. Messer (eds), *Essential Psychotherapies: Theory and Practice*. New York: Guilford. pp 85–127.

Bond, T. (1993) *Standards and Ethics for Counselling in Action*. London: Sage.

Bond, T. (2000) *Standards and Ethics for Counselling in Action*. Second Edition. London: Sage.

Boszormenyi-Nagy, I., Grunebaum, J. and Ulrich, D. (1991) 'Contextual therapy', in A. Gurman and D. Kniskern (eds), *Handbook of Family Therapy*. Vol. II. New York: Brunner-Mazel.

Boy, A.V. and Pine, G.P. (1999) *A Person-Centered Foundation for Counseling and Psychotherapy*. Second Edition. Springfield, IL: Charles C. Thomas.

Bozarth, J. (1998a) *Person-centered Therapy: a Revolutionary Paradigm*. Ross-on-Wye: PCCS Books.

Bozarth, J. (1998b) 'Playing the probabilities in psychotherapy', *Person-Centred Practice*, 6 (1): 9–21.

Brodley, B.T. (1998) 'Congruence and its relation to communication in client-centered therapy', *The Person-Centered Journal*, 5 (2): 83–106.

Brodley, B.T. (1999) 'The actualizing tendency concept in client-centered theory', *The Person-Centered Journal*, 6 (2): 108–20.

Brown, D. (1995) 'Pseudomemories: the standard of science and the standard of care in treatment', *The American Journal of Clinical Hypnosis*, 37 (3): 1–24.

Brown, M. (1979) *The Art of Guiding: The Psychosynthesis Approach to Individual Counseling and Psychology*. Redlands, CA: Johnston College, University of Redlands.

Buber, M. (1937) *I and Thou*. Trans. W. Kaufmann, 1970. New York: Charles Scribner's Sons.

Buber, M. and Rogers, C.R. (1960) 'Dialogue between Martin Buber and Carl Rogers', *Psychologia*, 3: 208–21.

Cain, D.J. (1989) 'The paradox of non-directiveness in the person-centered approach', *Person-Centered Review*, 4 (2): 123–31.

Cain, D.J. (1990) 'Further thoughts about non-directiveness and client-centered therapy', *Person-Centered Review*, 5 (1): 89–99.

Carroll, M. (1996) *Counselling Supervision: Theory, Skills and Practice*. London: Cassell.

Coe, M.T., Dalenberg, K.M. and Reto, C.S. (1995) 'Adult attachment style, reported childhood violence history and types of dissociative experiences', *Dissociation*, 8 (3): 142–54.

Colledge, E. and Walsh, J. (eds) (1978) *Julian of Norwich: Showings*. New York: Paulist Press.

Conradi, P. (1996) 'Person-Centred Therapy', in M. Jacobs (ed.), *In Search of Supervision*. Buckingham: Open University Press. pp 53–74.

Cooper, M. (1999) 'If you can't be Jekyll be Hyde: an existential–phenomenological exploration of lived-plurality', in J. Rowan and M. Cooper (eds), *The Plural Self*. London: Sage. pp 51–70.

Coulson, W. (1987) 'Reclaiming client-centered counseling from the person-centered movement'. Copyright: Center for Enterprising Families, P.O. Box 134, Comptche, CA 95427, USA.

Dryden, W. (1998) *Are you Sitting Uncomfortably? Windy Dryden, Live and Uncut*. Ross-on-Wye: PCCS Books.

Dryden, W., Horton, I. and Mearns, D. (1995) *Issues in Professional Counselling Training*. London: Cassell.

Dupont, H. (1994) *Emotional Development, Theory and Applications: a Neo-Piagetian Perspective*. Westport, CT: Praeger.

Egeland, B., Carlson, E. and Sroufe, L.A. (1993) 'Resilience as process', *Development and Psychopathology*, 5: 517–28.

Ellingham, I. (1999) 'Carl Rogers' "congruence" as a Freudian concept'. Unpublished manuscript.

Fairbairn, W.R.D. (1952) *Psychoanalytic Studies of the Personality*. London: Routledge.

Farber, B.A., Brink, D.C. and Raskin, P.M. (1996) *The Psychotherapy of Carl Rogers*. New York: Guilford Press.

Feltham, C. and Dryden, W. (1994) *Developing Counsellor Supervision*. London: Sage.

Festinger, L. (1957) *A Theory of Cognitive Dissonance*. Evanston, IL: Row, Peterson.

Fogel, A. (1982) 'Affect dynamics in early infancy: affective tolerance', in T. Field and A. Fogel (eds), *Emotion and Early Interaction*. Hillsdale, NJ: Lawrence Erlbaum Associates. pp 25–56.

Ford, J.G. (1991) 'Rogerian self-actualization: a clarification of meaning', *Journal of Humanistic Psychology*, 31 (2): 101–11.

Ford, J.G. and Maas, S. (1989) 'On actualizing person-centered theory: a critique of textbook treatments of Rogers' motivational constructs', *Teaching of Psychology*, 16 (1): 30–1.

Gaylin, N.L (1996) 'Reflections on the self of the therapist', in R. Hutterer, G. Pawlowsky, P.F. Schmid and R. Stipsits (eds), *Client-Centered and Experiential Psychotherapy: a Paradigm in Motion*. Frankfurt-am-Main: Peter Lang. pp 383–94.

Geller, L. (1982) 'The failure of self-actualization theory: a critique of Carl Rogers and Abraham Maslow', *Journal of Humanistic Psychology*, 22 (2): 56–73.

Gendlin, E.T. (1964) 'A theory of personality change', in P. Worchel and D. Byrne (eds), *Personality Change*. New York: John Wiley & Sons, Inc. pp 100–48.

Gendlin, E.T. (1968) 'The experiential response', in E. Hammer (ed.), *The Use of Interpretation in Treatment*. New York: Grune & Stratton. pp 208–27.

Gendlin, E.T. (1974) 'Client-centered and experiential psychotherapy', in D. Wexler and L. N. Rice (eds), *Innovations in Client-Centered Therapy*. New York: John Wiley & Sons. pp 211–46.

Gendlin, E.T. (1981) *Focusing*. New York: Bantam Books.

Gendlin, E.T. (1984) 'The client's client: the edge of awareness', in R.F. Levant and J.M. Shlien (eds), *Client-Centered Therapy and the Person-Centered Approach*. New York: Praeger. pp 76–107.

Gendlin, E.T. (1996) *Focusing-Oriented Psychotherapy*. New York: Guilford.

Gergen, K.J. (1972) 'Multiple identity: the healthy, happy human being wears many masks', *Psychology Today*, 5: 31–5, 64–6.

Gergen, K.J. (1988) 'Narrative and self as relationship', in L. Berkowitz (ed.), *Advances in Experimental Social Psychology*. Vol. 21. New York: Academic Press. pp 17–56.

Gergen, K.J. (1991) *The Saturated Self*. New York: Basic Books.

Girard, R. (1996) *The Girard Reader* (ed. J.G. Williams). New York: The Crossroad Publishing Company.

Gladstone, G. (1997) 'The making of a therapist and the corruption of the training market', in R. House and N. Totton (eds), *Implausible Professions*. Ross-on-Wye: PCCS Books. pp 171–85.

Glasgow City Council (1998) *Glasgow Children's Services Plan 1998–2001*. Glasgow, Scotland: Glasgow City Council.

Goss, S. and Mearns, D. (1997a) 'A call for a pluralist epistemological understanding in the assessment and evaluation of counselling', *British Journal of Guidance and Counselling*, 25 (2): 189–98.

Goss, S. and Mearns, D. (1997b) 'Applied pluralism in the evaluation of employee counselling', *British Journal of Guidance and Counselling*, 25 (3): 327–44.

Grant, B. (1990) 'Principles and instrumental non-directiveness in person-centered and client-centered therapy', *Person-Centered Review*, 5 (1): 77–88.

Greenberg, L.S., Rice, L.N. and Elliott, R. (1993) *Facilitating Emotional Change*. New York: Guilford Press.

Hackney, H. and Goodyear, R.K. (1984) 'Carl Rogers' Client-Centered approach to supervision', in R.F. Levant and J.M. Shlien (eds), *Client-Centered Therapy and the Person-Centered Approach*. New York: Praeger. pp 278–96.

Heider, F. (1958) *The Psychology of Interpersonal Relations*. New York: Wiley.

Hemmings, A. (2000) *A Systematic Review of Brief Psychological Therapies in Primary Health Care*. Staines, Middlesex: The Counselling in Primary Care Trust and The Association of Counsellors and Psychotherapists in Primary Care.

Hermans, H. (1996) 'Voicing the self: from information processing to dialogical interchange', *Psychological Bulletin*, 119: 31–50.

Hermans, H., Kempen, J. and Loon, R. van (1992) 'The dialogical self', *American Psychologist*, 47 (1): 23–33.

Hermans, H., Rijks, T. and Kempen, H. (1993) 'Imaginal dialogues in the self: theory and method', *Journal of Personality*, 61: 207–36.

Heron, J. (1997) 'The politics of transference', in R. House and N. Totton (eds), *Implausible Professions*. Ross-on-Wye: PCCS Books. pp 11–18.

Hofer, M.A. (1990) 'Early symbiotic processes: hard evidence from a soft place', in R.A. Glick and S. Bone (eds), *Pleasure Beyond the Pleasure Principle*. New Haven, CT: Yale University Press. pp 55–78.

Holdstock, T.L. (1993) 'Can we afford not to revision the person-centred concept of self?', in D. Brazier (ed.), *Beyond Carl Rogers*. London: Constable. pp 29–52.

Holdstock, T.L. (1996a) 'Anger and congruence considered from the perspective of an interdependent orientation to the self', in R. Hutterer, G. Pawlowsky, P.F. Schmid and R. Stipsits (eds), *Client-Centered and Experiential Psychotherapy: a Paradigm in Motion*. Frankfurt am Main: Peter Lang. pp 47–52.

Holdstock, T.L. (1996b) 'Discrepancy between person-centered theories of self and therapy', in R. Hutterer, G. Pawlowsky, P. Schmid and R. Stipsits (eds), *Client-Centered and Experiential Psychotherapy: a Paradigm in Motion*. Frankfurt am Main: Peter Lang. pp 395–403.

Honos-Webb, L. and Stiles, W. (1998) 'Reformulation of assimilation analysis in terms of voices', *Psychotherapy*, 35 (1): 23–33.

House, R. (1996) 'The professionalization of counselling: a coherent "case against"?', *Counselling Psychology Quarterly*, 9 (4): 343–58.

House, R. and Totton, N. (eds) (1997) *Implausible Professions*. Ross-on-Wye: PCCS Books.

Jamieson, A. (1998) Personal communication.

Jamieson, A. (1999) Personal communication.

Jung, C.J. (1960) 'A review of the complex theory'. *Collected Works*. Vol. 8. London: Routledge. pp 92–104.

Jung, C.J. (1970) *Practice of Psychotherapy*. London: Routledge.

Kahn, E. (1985) 'Heinz Kohut and Carl Rogers: a timely comparison', *American Psychologist*, 40: 893–904.

Kahn, E. (1996) 'The intersubjective perspective and the client-centered approach: are they one at their core?', *Psychotherapy*, 33 (1): 30–42.

Kahn, E. (forthcoming) 'Carl Rogers and Heinz Kohut: a historical perspective', *Psychoanalytic Psychology*.

Keil, S. (1996) 'The self as a systemic process of interactions of "inner persons" ', in R. Hutterer, G. Pawlowsky, P. Schmid and R. Stipsits (eds), *Client-Centered and Experiential Psychotherapy: a Paradigm in Motion*. Frankfurt am Main: Peter Lang. pp 53–66.

Kernberg, O. (1976) *Object Relations Theory and Clinical Psychoanalysis*. New York: Aronson.

Kilborn, M. (1999) 'Challenge and person-centred supervision – are they compatible?', *Person-Centred Practice*, 7 (2): 83–91.

Kluft, R.P. (1985) *Childhood Antecedents of Multiple Personality*. Washington, DC: American Psychiatric Press.

Kohut, H. (1971) *The Analysis of the Self*. New York: International Universities Press.

Kohut, H. (1977) *The Restoration of the Self*. New York: International Universities Press.

Kohut, H. (1982) 'Introspection, empathy and the semi-circle of mental health', *International Journal of Psychoanalysis*, 63: 395–407.

Kohut, H. (1984) *How Does Analysis Cure?* Chicago, IL: University of Chicago Press.

Kohut, H. (1985) *Self Psychology and the Humanities: Reflections on a New Psychoanalytic Approach*. New York: Norton.

Kraemer, G.W. (1992) 'A psychobiological theory of attachment', *Behavioral and Brain Sciences*, 15: 493–541.

Laing, R.D. (1965) *The Divided Self*. Harmondsworth: Penguin.

Lambers, E. (1993) 'Counselling can be non-directive', *Counselling News*, vol. 9.

Lambers, E. (1994) 'Person-centred psychotherapy: personality disorder', in D. Mearns, *Developing Person-Centred Counselling*. London: Sage. pp 116–20.

Lambers, E. (1999) Personal communication.

Laungani, P. (1999) 'Client centred or culture centred counselling?', in S. Palmer and P. Laungani (eds), *Counselling in a Multicultural Society*. London: Sage. pp 133–52.

Lewin, K. (1939) 'Experiments in social space', *Harvard Educational Review*, 9: 21–2.

Lewin, K. (1946) 'Behavior and development as a function of the total situation', in L. Carmichael (ed.), *Manual of Child Psychology*. New York: John Wiley & Sons.

Lietaer, G. (1998) 'From non-directive to experiential: a paradigm unfolding', in B. Thorne and E. Lambers (eds), *Person-Centred Therapy: A European Perspective*. London: Sage. pp 62–73.

Lynch, G. (1998) 'The dislocation of representation and reality', *British Journal of Guidance and Counselling*, 26 (4): 525–31.

Main, M. (1991) 'Metacognitive knowledge, metacognitive monitoring, and singular (coherent) vs multiple (incoherent) models of attachment', in C.M. Parkes,

J.S. Hinde and D. Marris (eds), *Attachment Across the Life Cycle*. London: Tavistock/Routledge. pp 127–59.

May, R. (1982) 'The problem of evil: an open letter to Carl Rogers', *Journal of Humanistic Psychology*, 22 (3): 10–21.

Mearns, D. (1991) 'On being a supervisor', in W. Dryden and B. Thorne (eds), *Training and Supervision for Counselling in Action*. London: Sage. pp 116–28.

Mearns, D. (1992) 'On the self-concept striking back', in W. Dryden (ed.), *Hard-Earned Lessons from Counselling in Action*. London: Sage. pp 72–4.

Mearns, D. (1994) *Developing Person-Centred Counselling*. London: Sage.

Mearns, D. (1995) 'Supervision: a tale of the missing client', *British Journal of Guidance and Counselling*, 23 (3): 421–7.

Mearns, D. (1996) 'Working at relational depth with clients in person-centred therapy', *Counselling*, 7 (4): 306–11.

Mearns, D. (1997a) *Person-Centred Counselling Training*. London: Sage.

Mearns, D. (1997b) 'Central dynamics in client-centered therapy training', *The Person-Centered Journal*, 4 (1): 31–43.

Mearns, D. (1997c) 'Achieving the personal development dimension in professional counsellor training', *Counselling*, 8 (2): 113–20.

Mearns, D. (1997d) *The Future of Individual Counselling*. Occasional Paper 12, School of Education, University of Durham. (The 1997 Ben Hartop Memorial Lecture.)

Mearns, D. (1999) 'Professionalisation and institutionalisation', *Counselling*, 28 (5): 344–5.

Mearns, D. and McLeod, J. (1984) 'A person-centered approach to research', in R.F. Levant and J.M. Shlien (eds), *Client-Centered Therapy and the Person-Centered Approach*. New York: Praeger. pp 370–89.

Mearns, D. and Thorne, B. (1988) *Person-Centred Counselling in Action*. London: Sage.

Mearns, D. and Thorne, B. (1999) *Person-Centred Counselling in Action*. Second Edition. London: Sage.

Merry, T. (1995) *Invitation to Person-Centred Psychology*. London: Whurr.

Merry, T. (1999) *Learning and Being in Person-Centred Counselling*. Ross-on-Wye: PCCS Books.

Moore, S. (1982) *The Inner Loneliness*. London: Darton, Longman and Todd Ltd.

Moustakas, C. (1994) *Phenomenological Research Methods*. Thousand Oaks, CA: Sage.

Mowbray, R. (1995) *The Case Against Psychotherapy Registration*. London: Trans Marginal Press.

Mowbray, R. (1997) 'Too vulnerable to choose?', in R. House and N. Totton (eds), *Implausible Professions*. Ross-on-Wye: PCCS Books. pp 33–44.

Mulgan, G. (1997) 'High tech and high angst', in S. Dunant and R. Porter (eds), *The Age of Anxiety*. London: Virago. pp 1–19.

O'Hara, M. (1995) 'Why is this man laughing?', *AHP Perspective*, 19: 30–1.

O'Leary, C. (1997) Personal communication.

O'Leary, C. (1999) *Couple and Family Counselling: A Person-Centred Approach*. London: Sage.

Page, S. and Wosket, V. (1994) *Supervising the Counsellor: a Cyclical Model*. London: Routledge.

Patterson, C.H. (1964) 'Supervising students in the counseling practicum', *Journal of Counseling Psychology*, 11 (1): 47–53.

Patterson, C.H. (1983) 'A client-centered approach to supervision', *The Counseling Psychologist*, 11 (1): 22–5.

Proctor, B. (1988) 'Supervision: a cooperative exercise in accountability', in M. Marken and M. Payne (eds), *Enabling and Ensuring*. Leicester: National Youth Bureau and Council for Education and Training in Youth and Community Work.

Prouty, G. (1994) *Theoretical Evolutions in Person-Centered/Experiential Therapy: applications to schizophrenic and retarded psychoses*. Westport, CN: Praeger.

Purton, C. (1998) 'Unconditional positive regard and its spiritual implications', in B. Thorne and E. Lambers (eds), *Person-Centred Therapy: a European Perspective*. London: Sage Publications. pp 23–37.

Putnam, F.W. (1989) *Diagnosis and Treatment of Multiple Personality Disorder*. New York: The Guilford Press.

Rappoport, L., Baumgardner, S. and Boone, G. (1999) 'Postmodern culture and the plural self', in J. Rowan and M. Cooper (eds), *The Plural Self*. London: Sage. pp 93–106.

Rennie, D. L. (1998) *Person-Centred Counselling: An Experiential Approach*. London: Sage.

Rice, L.N. (1974) 'The evocative function of the therapist', in D.A. Wexler and L.N. Rice (eds), *Innovations in Client-Centered Therapy*. New York: John Wiley & Sons. pp 289–311.

Rice, L.N. (1980) 'A client centered approach to the supervision of psychotherapy', in A.K. Hess (ed.), *Psychotherapy Supervision: Theory, Research and Practice*. New York: John Wiley and Sons. pp 136–47.

Rogers, C.R. (1939) *The Clinical Treatment of the Problem Child*. Boston: Houghton Mifflin.

Rogers, C.R. (1942) *Counseling and Psychotherapy*. Boston: Houghton Mifflin.

Rogers, C.R. (1951) *Client-Centered Therapy*. Boston: Houghton Mifflin.

Rogers, C.R. (1956) 'Reinhold Niebuhr's "The Self and the Dramas of History" ', *Chicago Theological Seminary Register*, 46: 13–14.

Rogers, C.R. (1957a) 'The necessary and sufficient conditions of therapeutic personality change', *Journal of Consulting Psychology*, 21 (2): 95–103.

Rogers, C.R. (1957b) 'Training individuals to engage in the therapeutic process', in C.R. Strother (ed.), *Psychology and Mental Health*. Washington, DC: American Psychological Association. pp 76–92.

Rogers, C.R. (1959) 'A theory of therapy, personality and interpersonal relationships as developed in the client-centred framework', in S. Koch (ed.), *Psychology: A Study of Science*, Volume 3. *Formulations of the Person and the Social Contract*. New York: McGraw-Hill. pp 184–256.

Rogers, C.R. (1963) 'The actualizing tendency in relation to "motives" and to consciousness', in M. Jones (ed.), *Nebraska Symposium on Motivation*. Lincoln, NE: University of Nebraska Press. pp 1–24.

Rogers, C.R. (1977) *The Right to be Desperate*. Video produced by the American Association for Counseling and Development, Washington, DC.

Rogers, C.R. (1978) 'Do we need a reality?', *Dawnpoint*, 1 (2): 6–9.

Rogers, C.R. (1980) *A Way of Being*. Boston: Houghton Mifflin.

Rogers, C.R. (1982) 'Reply to Rollo May's letter', *Journal of Humanistic Psychology*, 22 (4): 85–9.

Rogers, C.R. (1985) Personal communication with Maria Bowen.

Rogers, C.R. (1986) 'A client-centered/person-centered approach to therapy', in I. Kutash and A. Wolf (eds), *Psychotherapist's Casebook*. San Francisco, CA: Jossey-Bass. pp 197–208.

Rogers, C.R., Gendlin, E.T., Kiesler, D.J. and Truax, C.B. (eds) (1967) *The Therapeutic Relationship and its Impact: A Study of Psychotherapy with Schizophrenics*. Madison, WI: University of Wisconsin Press.

Ross, C.A. (1989) *Multiple Personality Disorder*. New York: John Wiley & Sons.

Ross, C.A. (1999) 'Subpersonalities and multiple personalities: a dissociative continuum?', in J. Rowan and M. Cooper (eds), *The Plural Self*. London: Sage. pp 183–97.

Rowan, J. (1990) *Subpersonalities*. London: Routledge.

Rowan, J. and Cooper, M. (eds) (1999) *The Plural Self*. London: Sage.

Schmid, P. (1996) 'Probably the most potent social invention of the century: person-centered therapy is fundamentally group therapy', in R. Hutterer, G. Pawlowsky, P. Schmid and R. Stipsits (eds), *Client-Centered and Experiential Psychotherapy: a Paradigm in Motion*. Frankfurt am Main: Peter Lang. pp 611–25.

Schmid, P. (1998) 'Face to face – the art of encounter', in B. Thorne and E. Lambers (eds), *Person-Centred Therapy: a European Perspective*. London: Sage. pp 74–90.

Schore, A.N. (1994) *Affect Development and the Origin of the Self*. Hillsdale, NJ: Lawrence Erlbaum Associates.

Schwartz, R. (1987) 'Our multiple selves', *The Family Therapy Networker*, March/April: 25–31 and 80–3.

Schwartz, R. (1997) *Internal Family Systems Therapy*. New York: Guilford.

Schwartz, R. and Goulding, R. (1995) *The Mosaic Mind*. New York: Norton Press.

Seligman, M.E.P. (1995) 'The effectiveness of psychotherapy: the Consumer Reports Study', *American Psychologist*, 50: 965–74.

Sennett, R. (1998) *The Corrosion of Character: the personal consequences of work in the new capitalism*. New York: W.W. Norton.

Smail, D. (1997) 'Psychotherapy and tragedy', in R. House and N. Totton (eds), *Implausible Professions*. Ross-on-Wye: PCCS Books. pp 159–71.

Sroufe, L.A. (1996) *Emotional Development: The Organization of Emotional Life in the Early Years*. New York: Cambridge University Press.

Stern, D.N. (1985) *The Interpersonal World of the Infant*. New York: Basic Books.

Stern, D.N., Sander, L.W., Nahum, J.P., Harrison, A.M., Lyons-Ruth, K., Morgan, A.C., Bruschweiler-Stern, N. and Tronick, E.Z. (1998) 'Non-interpretative mechanisms in psychoanalytic therapy', *International Journal of Psychoanalysis*, 79: 903–21.

Stillwell, W. (1998) *Questing Voices*. La Jolla, CA: Center for Studies of the Person.

Stolorow, R.D. and Atwood, G.E. (1992) *Contexts of Being: The Intersubjective Foundations of Psychological Life*. Hillsdale, NJ: Analytic.

Stolorow, R.D., Atwood, G.E. and Brandchaft, B. (1992) 'Three realms of the unconscious and their therapeutic transformation', *Psychoanalytic Review*, 79: 25–30.

Stolorow, R.D., Atwood, G.E. and Brandchaft, B. (eds) (1994) *The Intersubjective Perspective*. Northvale, NJ: Jason Aronson.

Swildens, H. (1980) 'De hulpverwachting in de therapeutisch relatie binnen de gesprekstherapie volgens Rogers', *Psychotherapie*, 2: 67–74.

Taft, J. (1933) *The Dynamics of Therapy*. New York: Macmillan.

Thorne, B. (1991) *Person-Centred Counselling: Therapeutic and Spiritual Dimensions*. London: Whurr Publishers.

Thorne, B. (1992) *Carl Rogers*. London: Sage.

Thorne, B. (1994) 'Brief companionship', in D. Mearns, *Developing Person-Centred Counselling*. London: Sage. pp 60–4.

Thorne, B. (1997) 'Counselling and psychotherapy: the sickness and the prognosis', in S. Palmer and V. Varma (eds), *The Future of Counselling and Psychotherapy*. London: Sage. pp 153–66.

Thorne, B. (1998a) *Person-Centred Counselling and Christian Spirituality*. London: Whurr Publishers.

Thorne, B. (1998b) 'Standards, stress and spiritual danger: reflections on contemporary education', *Education Today*, 48 (4): 26–30.

Thorne, B. (1999) 'The move towards brief therapy', *Counselling*, 10 (1): 7–11.

Thorne, B. and Lambers, E. (eds) (1998) *Person-Centred Therapy: A European Perspective*. London: Sage.

Tobin, S.A. (1991) 'A comparison of psychoanalytic self psychology and Carl Rogers' person-centered therapy', *Journal of Humanistic Psychology*, 30: 9–33.

Tudor, K. and Worrall, M. (1999) 'Necessary and sufficient: person-centred therapy as integrative therapy'. Unpublished manuscript.

Van der Kolk, B.A., Hostetler, A., Herron, N. and Fisler, R.E. (1994) 'Trauma and the development of borderline personality disorder', *Psychiatric Clinics of North America*, 17 (4).

Van Kalmthout, M. (1998) 'Personality change and the concept of the self', in B. Thorne and E. Lambers (eds), *Person-Centred Therapy: A European Perspective*. London: Sage. pp 53–61.

Van Werde, D. (1998) ' "Anchorage" as a core concept in working with psychotic people', in B. Thorne and E. Lambers (eds), *Person-Centred Therapy: a European Perspective*. London: Sage. pp 195–205.

Vanaerschot, G. (1993) 'Empathy as releasing several microprocesses in the client', in D. Brazier (ed.), *Beyond Carl Rogers*. London: Constable.

Villas-Bowen, M. (1986) 'Personality differences and person-centered supervision', *Person-Centered Review*, 1 (3): 291–309.

Villas-Bowen, M. (1987) *In Memory of Carl Rogers*. La Jolla, CA: Unpublished manuscript.

Warner, M.S. (1991) 'Fragile process', in L. Fusek (ed.), *New Directions in Client-Centered Therapy: Practice with Difficult Client Populations (Monograph Series 1)*. Chicago, IL: Chicago Counseling and Psychotherapy Center. pp 41–58.

Warner, M.S. (1997) 'Does empathy cure? A theoretical consideration of empathy, processing and personal narrative', in A.C. Bohart and L.S. Greenberg (eds), *Empathy Reconsidered: New Directions in Psychotherapy*. Washington, DC: American Psychological Association. pp 125–40.

Warner, M.S. (1998) 'A client-centered approach to therapeutic work with dissociated and fragile process', in L. Greenberg, J. Watson and G. Lietaer (eds), *Handbook of Experiential Psychotherapy*. New York: The Guilford Press. pp 368–87.

Warner, M.S. and Mearns, D. (2000) 'Normal and dissociated process'. Joint paper presented to the Fifth International Conference in Client-Centered and Experiential Psychotherapy. Chicago, June, 2000.

Watson, N. (1984) 'The empirical status of Rogers' hypothesis of the necessary and sufficient conditions for effective psychotherapy', in R.F. Levant and J.M. Shlien (eds), *Client-Centered Therapy and the Person-Centered Approach*. New York: Praeger. pp 17–40.

Wexler, D.A. (1974) 'A cognitive theory of experiencing, self-actualization and therapeutic process,' in D. A. Wexler and L. N. Rice (eds), *Innovations in Client-Centered Therapy*. New York: Wiley. pp 49–115.

Wilkins, P. (2000) 'Unconditional positive regard reconsidered', *British Journal of Guidance and Counselling*, 28 (1): 23–36.

Wood, J.K. (1997) 'Carl Rogers and transpersonal psychology'. Invited presentation for the VI International Holistic and Transpersonal Congress, Aguas de Lindoia, Brazil.

Wyatt, G. (1998) 'The multi-faceted nature of congruence within the therapeutic relationship'. Paper presented to the Person-Centred Forum, Johannesburg, South Africa.

Zeldin, T. (1998) *Conversation*. London: The Harvill Press.

Index